Loving Amy

A Mother's Story

Janis Winehouse

Thomas Dunne Books
St. Martin's Press ❦ New York

THOMAS DUNNE BOOKS.
An imprint of St. Martin's Press.

LOVING AMY. Copyright © 2014 by Janis Winehouse.
All rights reserved. Printed in the United States of America. For information,
address St. Martin's Press, 175 Fifth Avenue, New York, N.Y. 10010.

www.thomasdunnebooks.com
www.stmartins.com

Extract from the lyrics of "Fly Me To The Moon" by Bart Howard on
p. 177 © Palm Valley Music, LLC, USA, assigned to TRO Essex Music Ltd.
All rights reserved. Used by permission. International copyright secured.

Library of Congress Cataloging-in-Publication Data

Names: Winehouse, Janis, author.
Title: Loving Amy : a mother's story / Janis Winehouse.
Description: First U.S. edition. | New York : Thomas Dunne Books, 2016.
Identifiers: LCCN 2015037440 | ISBN 9781250078490 (hardcover) | ISBN
    9781466890688 (e-book)
Subjects: LCSH: Winehouse, Amy, 1983–2011. | Singers—England—
    Biography. | Drug addicts—England—Biography.
Classification: LCC ML420.W57 W54 2016 | DDC 782.42164092—dc23
LC record available at http://lccn.loc.gov/2015037440

Our books may be purchased in bulk for promotional, educational,
or business use. Please contact your local bookseller or the Macmillan
Corporate and Premium Sales Department at (800) 221-7945, extension
5442, or by e-mail at MacmillanSpecialMarkets@macmillan.com.

First published in Great Britain by Bantam Press, an imprint
of Transworld Publishers, a Random House Group company

First U.S. Edition: January 2016

10 9 8 7 6 5 4 3 2 1

In memory of Amy, Cynthia and Eddie

Contents

Prologue

There are times when Amy catches me unawares. She's right in front of me and in a second I am overwhelmed. This feeling comes with no warning. There is no route map for grief. There *are* no rules. I can't predict what might trigger this: her face flashed up on the big screen at the BRIT Awards; a song of hers playing in the airport lounge en route to New York; the Japanese tea set she bought me from a Camden junk shop that I stumble across while sorting through a cupboard at home; the mention of her name. Whether these moments are intensely public or intensely private, they stop me in my tracks, and I am paralysed with emotion. Yet I find them strangely comforting. They are a reminder that I can still feel, that I am not numb.

I worry about a day when that might change. I worry about the day when Amy stops being alive in my head and in my heart. I don't want that day ever to come. I don't think it ever will. I loved her. I will always love her, and I miss everything about her. Amy, bless her, was larger than life.

I find myself saying 'bless her' in the same breath as Amy's name a lot of the time. It's my way of acknowledging that she was not a straightforward girl. Amy was one of those rare people who made an impact. Right from the very beginning, when she was a toddler, she was loud and boisterous and scared and sensitive. She was a bundle of emotions, at times adorable and at times unbearable. All this is consistent with the struggle she went through to overcome the addictions that eventually robbed her of her life. Amy's passing did not follow a clear line. It was jumbled, and her life was unfinished – not life's natural order at all. She left no answers, only questions, and in the years since her death I've found myself trying to make sense of the frayed ends of her extraordinary existence.

I lost Amy twice: once to drugs and alcohol, and finally on Saturday, 23 July 2011, when her short life ended. I don't believe any of the endless speculation that Amy wanted to die. There was no doubt that she battled with who she was and what she had become, but she dreamed that one day she'd have children and there was a large part of Amy that had a zest for life and people. But she was a girl who kicked against authority, a person who always took things that bit further than everyone else around her. She used to say to me, 'Mum, I hate mediocrity. I never want to be mediocre.' Whatever else Amy was, she was anything but mediocre. She had a phenomenal talent and she pushed it to its limits; she pushed her life to its limits; she pushed her body beyond its limits. In her mind she was invincible, yet she was as vulnerable as any of us are. I have a recurring vision of her, wherever she is, saying to me through that mischievous smile of hers, 'Oops, Mum, I really didn't mean to do that. I went too far this time, didn't I?'

I did not expect to lose Amy when I did. Since the first night I held her in my arms she had always been a constant and close part of my life. But during the worst years of Amy's drugs dependency there were moments when I truly thought that every time I saw her it would be the last. Amy had become a slave to her drugs and parts of the daughter I'd raised were slowly being wiped away. In the past she'd have gone out of her way to get to me, wherever I was, but as her addictions took hold she became less reliable, less able to organize herself without an army of people clearing a path for her and clearing up after her. She became wildly sentimental and wildly ill-natured. She'd sit in front of me, her short skirt riding up her legs and her sharp bones protruding from her knees. I could see it happening. I could see her tiny body disintegrating, but there was nothing I could do. As her mother, I was completely helpless. I could ring her and I could visit her, but I couldn't save her. I knew that if I tried to I would lose myself too.

For some time, Amy had tried to protect me from the reality of her life. She wanted to keep me as a 'mummy' figure, untainted by everything she was experiencing. Amy had looked out for me from a young age, in particular after the breakdown of my marriage to her father Mitchell, and I suspect she didn't want to upset me. But mothers have a sixth sense and I was busy filling in the blanks. As Amy's troubles escalated there were certain things that became more and more difficult for her to hide.

The ups and downs of those years took their toll on Amy and everyone around her. Loving Amy became a relentless cycle of thinking I would lose her, but not losing her, thinking I would lose her, but not losing her. It was a bit like holding your breath under-water and gasping for air every time you reached the surface, then treading water while wondering what the next dive down might involve.

Also, by 2006 – the time when Amy's addictions began to consume her – I had not long been officially diagnosed with multiple sclerosis. I have suffered with the symptoms for more than thirty years, from just after I gave birth to Amy's older brother Alex, and it is why I now walk with the aid of a stick. Amy's unpredictability meant I lived constantly on tenterhooks, and my own health had reached crisis point too. I often caught myself thinking, 'Are all these things really happening to my family?' But then my own survival instinct kicked in.

I have always been a pragmatist, but thinking pragmatically about your own daughter's addiction is one of the hardest things a mother can do. I worked as a pharmacist until my MS forced me to take early retirement, so my medical background helped me to see Amy's problems more clearly as an illness. Even armed with that knowledge, however, I desperately struggled to keep myself together. I relied on counselling to make sense of everything that was disintegrating around me. I needed to talk things through with someone who wasn't emotionally wrapped up in the drama of our lives. Step by step I began to refocus my own life. I took time for myself, and although there were moments when I felt guilty about doing so, I stopped telling myself it was wrong. A new relationship with my now husband Richard, whom I've known since I was twelve years old, began to blossom. I am convinced that all those things, combined with my inner resolve, have given me an enormous amount of insight and strength both during Amy's life and after her passing.

Right up until that summer of 2011 I believed she had turned a corner – we all did. She had been clean of drugs for almost three years and we could see glimpses of a future again, even though her life was still punctuated with bouts of heavy drinking. Nevertheless, our expectations had shifted and I felt optimistic about what lay in store for her. Instead of questioning if or when Amy was going to die, I had begun to imagine a time when she would be better. Sadly, that day never came, and I will always feel tortured by a sense of what could have been, even though I have had to accept the reality.

Amy came into my life like a whirlwind and changed it for ever. Although I lived through it with her, sometimes her story does not feel real. I am a proud mother who watched her daughter achieve the success and recognition she desperately wanted. But soon that private and intense bond between us became public property. Amy's entire life became public property and I guess, as a family, we were always in tow. Everybody who took an interest in Amy believed they knew her, and everyone wanted a piece of her, in ways we were completely unprepared for. She, herself, walked an endlessly unsteady tightrope between withdrawing from the limelight and needing to be noticed.

In that way, Amy and I were different. Throughout her life and even now, the limelight was and is a place in which I feel uneasy. Unlike Mitchell, I struggle with being in the public eye. I have never felt comfortable walking on the red carpet, even though my husband Richard tells me I look as cool as a cucumber. Whether accepting awards on Amy's behalf or raising money for Amy's foundation – the charity Mitchell and I set up in the months after her passing – I've graced more stages than I ever thought possible. I do everything now with Amy in my heart. And if anything extraordinary happens – and since Amy's death lots of extraordinary things have happened – I think, 'Janis, it's all part of the story.' I'm just not sure yet whether it's *my* story or whether I'm watching the events of my life as if they were someone else's feature film. So much of what has happened to me and my family has been almost impossible to process. I find myself filing things in a 'surreal box' in my mind, to deal with later, just so I can carry on.

Telling the story of my life with Amy was first mooted back in 2007 when I was approached by a literary agent and asked whether I would consider writing a book. I wasn't entirely comfortable with the idea, but I came away from the meeting thinking I might like to, but only when Amy was well again. I called her and asked her what she thought of the proposal. 'Don't do it, Mum,' she told me in no uncertain terms. 'I don't want people to know who I am.' Enough said. Amy was happy to let the beehive and the eyeliner and the car-crash lifestyle become the only side of her the public saw, even though we knew she was a much more complex person than that.

Back then, I never considered going against her wishes. Now life has changed. I thought long and hard before finally agreeing to tell our story, but once I made the decision I found that the trepidation I felt at the beginning slowly disappeared. Recalling happy times as well as confronting some uncomfortable truths has helped me in my own journey. It has helped me understand how our ordinary life grew in so many fantastic ways, and self-destructed in so many others. I rediscovered parts of Amy's life too, the sort of precious memories that fade in the maelstrom of a working mother's life and get buried by the avalanche of fame and addiction. Over time, memories get eroded, and MS makes that process worse – that loss of sharpness is, regrettably, part of this degenerative condition – so I wanted to put mine on record before they are lost for ever. I have read and heard so many false truths about Amy over the years there was also a strong desire to set the record straight.

My family and friends, photos and Amy's own notebooks have all helped me piece our lives back together again. In sorting through the fragments it has struck me how, at various points, Amy's life closely mirrored aspects of my own in the years before she was born. Physically, Amy has my features. Our school reports are almost identical. We both loved adventure and, in our own ways, we both pushed the boundaries without necessarily thinking of the consequences. I quietly rebelled against a life of domesticity in 1970s and 1980s suburbia. Amy achieved superstardom by rebelling against the manufactured world of pop music. In the end, she rebelled against everything else too, and turned it inwards on herself.

Despite the obvious heartbreak, I am uplifted when I am reminded of what Amy achieved – what we achieved. I graduated with two degrees while bringing up Alex and Amy and I wanted to motivate both my children to imagine what it was possible to achieve. Amy grabbed opportunities with both hands and realized her potential early in life. My only hope is that she would approve of this book as a frank account of her life, although I can picture her shrugging her shoulders and saying, 'Mum, there's nothing to say about me, honest.'

Today, I wear Amy's necklace. It's a gold Star of David that she was given as a baby. I never take it off. I wear her ring too. On some days I even wear her clothes – her T-shirts – and I feel closer to her. As I said, there are no rules for grief. There are days when I feel at peace with Amy and there are nights when I wake up crying. But I try not to dwell on the negative parts of her life, nor on how her death devastated my family. I keep going, as I have always done, busying myself with anything I can. It seems to be the only way I can get through each day.

I celebrate Amy's talent and appreciate the great gift she gave to the world. It will live on well after I and my family have gone. The Amy Winehouse Foundation, too, has already begun to make a difference to the lives of other children who, for whatever reason, are set on a wayward and downward path in life. It means so much to me that all my proceeds from this book will be donated to Amy's charity. We want to work with many more children in the future and help them realize their potential, and I know Amy is with us every step of the way.

I choose not to mourn Amy. I have her albums and a live concert she performed in São Paulo on my iPod. Hers is the only voice that spurs me upstairs and on to my exercise bike to go through the workouts I do to alleviate the discomfort of my MS. I'm not sure I'd get there otherwise. There are moments, though, when I hear the nakedness of her voice and I wonder how much the world understood of Amy's vulnerability.

She was a singer, a superstar, an addict and a young woman who hurtled towards an untimely death. To me, though, she is simply Amy. She was my daughter and my friend, and she will be with me for ever.

1

Hurricane Amy

Now that I look back I should have realized life with Amy was going to be anything but plain-sailing. I was twenty-seven when I gave birth to her at Chase Farm Hospital, near Enfield, north London, on 14 September 1983, and from the very start she did things her way. I'd been admitted briefly the day before with contractions, but they turned out to be a false alarm and I was sent home. Late the following afternoon, Amy decided she was ready for the world and, for the second time in two days, her father Mitchell did the fifteen-minute drive to the maternity ward. At 10.25 p.m. Amy made her debut, but by then she was already four days late.

I don't remember much about those hazy few hours but I do remember holding Amy in my arms, looking down at her face and thinking, 'I've had the same baby twice!' My son Alex had been born almost four years earlier and, at birth, the pair bore an uncanny resemblance to each other – soft brown hair and almond-shaped eyes, and both of them the most beautiful babies I'd ever seen. I know every mother says that, but Alex and Amy were really cute.

With my second baby, I'd taken pregnancy a bit more in my stride and shed all the anxiety of being a first-time mum. I remember the apprehension when Alex cried or the split second of panic when he made a new sound I didn't yet understand. I'd live on adrenalin, ever alert but bone-tired. I felt calmer and more confident with Amy and I was blessed that the pregnancy had happened effortlessly for me. Aside from the odd bout of morning sickness, I can honestly say that those nine months were unremarkable – just a warm feeling of excitement bubbling away that I was expecting again – although with a three-year-old running around there wasn't too much time to think.

Before I had children I'd never seen myself as the maternal type. I'd been a bit of a free spirit as a teenager and I'd always wondered how I'd manage with a little person to look after. In those days there was a certain amount of pressure to settle down and have a family. All of my friends were doing so. Mitchell and I were both from Jewish families: it was the unwritten rule that if you got married, you'd give your parents a grandson or granddaughter. I didn't see myself fitting neatly into that traditional role, but the experience of having children did change me profoundly, as only bringing a new life into the world can. When I fell pregnant with Alex, *a* baby stopped being someone else's child when I felt his first kick against my belly: then he became *my* baby, and I loved him unconditionally. When Amy was born I thought of them both as simply 'my babies'.

Mitchell and I had planned for another child, partly because we wanted Alex to have a brother or sister and partly because Mitchell's grandparents were still alive. We wanted Ben and his wife Fanny, who by now were in their eighties, to see our family complete. Ben ran a barber's shop on Commercial Street near Whitechapel and we would often travel to the East End to visit them, climbing the treacherous staircase to reach their flat above the shop. I knew that whoever came along would just have to go with the flow, but for some reason – I have no idea why – I was convinced I was having another boy.

Life had been getting cramped in the two-bedroom flat in Winchmore Hill, north London, Mitchell and I had bought when we got married. Now that Amy was on the way we moved to a three-bedroom house on Osidge Lane, a suburban street in nearby

18

Southgate, where Mitchell had spent much of his life, in Bramford Court just off the high street. In our new house I'd play classical music on the stereo and walk around the living room talking to Amy, the bump who was growing day by day. 'You're definitely a boy,' I would say, rubbing my hand across my belly. Alex would also tell me as I tucked him into bed, 'Mummy, I can't wait to have a baby brother.' We wouldn't really have cared what we had just so long as it was healthy and happy. Secretly, though, I wished for a baby girl. Amy was worth all those months of waiting and hoping.

In the month leading up to her birth I had started taking raspberry leaf tablets. Maybe it's an old wives' tale but I'd heard that a daily dose would bring on the baby and ease labour pains. I'd almost convinced myself that giving birth this time round would be more like passing wind. Talk about wishful thinking. Having said that, I spent much of my four-hour labour standing around the ward clock-watching as my contractions grew stronger and more frequent. In the end I'd left it far too late for an epidural and once I'd reached the delivery suite I relied entirely on gas and air.

I'll never forget the midwife congratulating me on being so calm and quiet during the final stages. I couldn't stop giggling because she'd clearly been oblivious to the screams I'd let out into the gas mask every time I held it to my mouth as I pushed down. 'It's a girl!' I heard her announce as all 7lb 1oz of Amy finally popped out. I sat bolt upright. 'Oh shit!' I shouted, which probably sounded completely inappropriate, but my brain had to quickly readjust. A girl? Really? Wow.

Sometimes now I think Amy's life was written in the stars, that it was her destiny to be with me for only a short time. But at that moment, nothing could have been further from my mind. She was so perfect, and I had this overwhelming urge to hold and protect her. Nowadays babies are given to mothers to hold on their chest in the moments immediately after birth, but Amy was taken from me straight away and arrived back at my bedside cleaned and clothed and in a cot. The pang of that temporary separation completely unnerved me. I was desperate to see her face and touch her tiny fingers, and on the first night of her life I sat up quietly watching her. She was beautiful. I found it impossible to take my eyes off her.

For me, giving birth to a girl became a unique experience. Any mother knows the anxiety that comes with having children. We all worry about getting it wrong, but with a girl I'd convinced myself that I had a head start. Amy, bless her, was her own person from the off, but I could intuitively understand her, and when she was young I always felt that the connection between us was deeply emotional and complete. I looked forward to all those little rituals that come naturally when girls are together: dressing Amy, brushing her hair, talking with her, cuddling her. With a boy, the love is just as intense, but boys detach themselves more easily somehow.

Out went the name Ames that Mitchell and I had already chosen for another boy and in came Amy. It is Jewish tradition to name a child with the first letter of a loved relative who has passed away. My grandmother Hannah was also known as Annie, so Amy was named in her memory, and her middle name Jade was after Mitchell's stepfather's father Jack.

Alex had been born in University College Hospital, in the busy centre of London. In those days, new mothers were kept in hospital much longer, and I had four days of adapting to feeding and bathing him before I was discharged. From my window I could see the Post Office Tower dominating the city skyline and, when our families weren't crowded into the ward delighting in the new arrival, I would look out at the view and daydream. With Amy, I was back at Osidge Lane after two days. But at my bedside at Chase Farm I had enjoyed just as many well-wishers.

Mitchell and I came from large families who'd settled in London's East End from as early as the 1920s, so no matter what the occasion – births or Bar Mitzvahs – they would descend en masse. My dad Eddie, my brother Brian and sister Debra all trooped in alongside Mitchell's grandparents, his mum Cynthia and stepdad Larry. Our uncles, aunties, cousins, nieces, nephews and friends were all there too – even my present husband Richard, who was married to Stephanie, my best friend at the time. Wherever our family was, there was life, and waves of laughter. I remember Mitchell showing Amy off to anyone whose attention he could attract. He would lift her up and twirl her in the air.

Mitchell adored babies, and both Alex and Amy remain the apples of his eye, but from very early on he found the practicalities of parenthood difficult. I had noticed when we had Alex that the day-to-day childcare was left largely to me; when Amy arrived, that didn't change. Back then my days were filled with an endless cycle of washing dirty nappies and messy mealtimes and the nights were always disrupted, but I got on with things regardless.

I am an instinctively placid person. I have an inner determination that seems to run through my side of the family, but anyone who knows me will tell you I'm impossible to have an argument with. Perhaps, to my detriment, I accepted things as they were when the children were young, often keeping schtum to avoid any upsets and arguments. It was, and still is, my greatest vulnerability. But back then, conflict was never more than a step away.

The day after Amy was born, Mitchell came into the maternity ward in his customary sharp suit looking rather distracted. With his head in his hands he announced, 'Janis, there's something I've got to tell you.' I raised my eyebrows. I knew immediately that with an opener like that anything that followed was not going to end well. He admitted to me that he'd lost his job a few days before. It wasn't exactly the news I'd wanted to hear. We'd just moved house. We had a bigger mortgage to manage and I was cradling our new baby. But I'd known Mitchell since I was fourteen and I'd learned the hard way that as far as he was concerned, nothing would surprise me.

Mitchell was exciting – a risk-taker. Being with him was always an adventure, and in the early days of our marriage we had good fun. In the maternity ward that day there was a part of me that knew he'd be back on his feet soon enough; still, this was neither the time nor the place for such news. I was relieved when Mitchell's mother came to the hospital and took Amy and me back to the relative quiet of Osidge Lane where I felt safe and comfortable. Even now, our old house evokes the fondest memories of family for me.

There, in the first few months of her life, Amy grew into a bright and curious baby. She would often be wide awake and crying at night just when I thought I'd rocked her off to sleep. We had her nursery decorated in sunshine yellow wallpaper with white clouds and I spent many hours nursing her on a chair with a matching pattern. The colours reflected her personality – very loud and loads of fun – and it wasn't long before Amy was tottering around (I remember the elation I felt watching my baby's first steps). It was commonplace to find her practising her forward rolls, or bent over with her curly mop of hair on the carpet and her bottom facing skywards in an attempt to stand on her head. Both Alex and Amy loved playing peek-a-boo in the Ali Baba laundry basket we kept in our bedroom. I was so captivated with their heads bobbing over the wicker rim that I photographed them, and each framed picture sat on a shelf as a bookend, Alex at one end and Amy at the other.

Mitchell had brought Alex to see Amy in hospital soon after she was born. He'd sat on the chair by my bed and smiled nervously as Mitchell handed him his sister. My heart almost melted as I watched their first introduction. Dressed in a little white baby-gro and wrapped in a blanket, Amy looked unwieldy against his childish frame. He cupped her in his arms and looked terrified that her head would roll back or that she would drop. She stank, he said – she had that milky newborn smell. He frowned at her because, all of a sudden, he had been usurped by a red-cheeked impostor who was doing her damnedest to break the sound barrier. And to top it all, she was a girl!

But once Amy was home and Alex had got over his disappointment at having a sister rather than a brother, things changed. I would find him hugging Amy tightly and refusing to let go, having climbed into her cot. Soon the pair were inseparable, although after a few years Alex discovered that having a younger sibling could be annoying too – 'She's a pain in the bum,' he often complained. If he went to dance classes, Amy wanted to go to dance classes. If Alex had a friend, Amy wanted the same friend. The first proper word Amy uttered was 'Alex'. She wanted to be like him and she followed him around like a shadow, but she was also pretty competitive and never let him have the limelight for too long.

I remember, years later, when Alex was studying for his Bar Mitzvah, I recorded him rehearsing the passages from the Jewish bible, the Torah, that he had to read aloud on his big day. Unsurprisingly, on the same cassette is an eight-year-old Amy practising her own imaginary speech. If making a speech was required of Alex, you could bet Amy wasn't far behind, even though she had no ceremony to prepare for. I still have that tape. Aside from the videos of Amy's birthday parties, it's the only recording I have of her child's voice.

Even then, Amy rarely stayed quiet for long. You'd usually hear her before you saw her. She didn't arrive at someone's house, she bowled in. I'd often take her to Richard's to see his son Michael, who was born four months after Amy, and it was there that she earned her first nickname – Hurricane Amy. As soon as the door opened there she was, like a twister, whirling around and whooshing from room to room, always busy, busy, busy, full of energy and impossible to ignore.

I myself had lots of energy in those days. I worked right up until both Alex and Amy's births. I enjoyed working and earning my own money – I'd done so since leaving school at the age of sixteen – but I loved being a mum too. I was often mesmerized by the high spirits of my little girl, and I enjoyed helping both my children navigate their way through their young lives. On reflection, though, I had set myself the impossible task of being a perfect mother, having had no real relationship with my own – and if there's one thing I wanted to change when I had children, it was that.

My own grandmother, Deborah, who was an Eastern European Jewish immigrant, left her husband and had come to London from

Newcastle penniless and with three daughters. My mother, Esther Richman, was her youngest girl, and although I was born in Brooklyn, New York, we returned to Hackney in London's East End when I was eighteen months old. As the years passed we made the usual Jewish trek from the council estates of the East End to Stoke Newington before Mitchell and I married and settled in Southgate. We weren't a wealthy family by any means. Across the generations, all the women had exactly the same features – the joke was that we were so poor we could only afford one face. But I don't ever remember a time when there wasn't food on the table.

My dad Eddie, who worked as a ladies' garment tailor, was the most stable influence in my life. Despite growing up with his two brothers in the Norwood Jewish orphanage after the death of his father, he was a calm, gentle and kind man. Everybody adored Eddie. He'd had a tough life, though. Not only had he spent his adolescence in care, he'd been subjected to the most terrible anti-Jewish taunts while doing his military service. So, before he had us, he ditched the family surname 'Steinberg' and changed it to 'Seaton'. Seaton, it turned out, is a small seaside town on the east Devon coast – a place Eddie had visited as a youngster, and which held happy memories for him.

Despite those hardships he seemed to put his head down and get on with things. When he passed away six months after Amy, my cousin Martin reminded me how we used to call him Auntie Eddie because he seemed able to combine the caring role of both an uncle and aunt. In his later years he put himself at the centre of the family. I'll never forget the wall in his house which he called his 'hall of fame'. There were pictures of his parents and his brothers, his children and grandchildren, and every time there was a new addition to the family he'd find a space to hang a new photo. 'I don't have any favourites,' he used to say affectionately. 'I hate you all equally.'

So it was my father who was the figure of stability in our lives. My mother Esther, on the other hand, could never settle. She was a restless and petulant woman, always chasing what she thought was the next best thing. That's what had brought my parents to New York for eight years. She'd heard of an extended family there and dreamed it was the place where our fortune could be made; but she was to be greatly disappointed. My father ended up taking a lower-paid job than my mother had anticipated and we were back in London soon enough.

Esther's own father had died suddenly when she was thirteen years old, and I think that trauma greatly affected her. Even by the time she had her own children she'd never really grown up herself, and my older brother Brian and I were left to bring up our sister Debra, who was seven years younger than me.

My mother walked out on my dad for somebody else the day before my wedding. I was twenty-one and fresh-faced, carrying my bouquet and wearing a beautiful white lace gown I'd hired from Losners' bridal shop, but she was not there under the chuppah (bridal canopy) to help give me away. At the time I felt relieved: if she wasn't there she couldn't upset my big day. My mother had a nasty habit of making herself the centre of attention. But, deep down, I wished I'd had a mother with whom I'd had a warm relationship. I watched that day as my dad toughed it out, and that broke my heart more than anything. In many ways, when I had children I made a conscious effort to be everything my mother hadn't been, and I put a lot of energy into loving Alex and Amy by spending time with them as best I could and encouraging their development.

While I was trying to bring structure to the family home, it would be fair to say that Mitchell's family let Amy get away with murder. Unlike my family, the Winehouses were much freer than I was used to, far more raucous and certainly never dull. I was thrown into their family life but I liked them immediately: their openness appealed to my rebellious streak. Alex and Amy were the first and last of the babies in Mitchell's family too, and, as the youngest, Amy attracted oodles of attention from his mum Cynthia and her twin sister Lorna, to the extent that her brash behaviour was tolerated, encouraged even, and some of her naughtiness kindly overlooked.

With Cynthia, once you were family, you stayed family. But it took her a while to get used to me. Mitchell and I had been introduced as teenagers through my cousin Martin but we didn't start dating until 1974, when we bumped into each other again at a party. Through the crowd, Mitchell strode towards me and asked me to dance. It's funny: I knew then that if I danced with him we'd be together, and if I didn't, our relationship would never happen. I said yes, and from that moment on we were a couple. We were an odd couple, admittedly. I was nineteen and he was four years older. My hippy Biba dresses and blue beanie hat looked ill-matched alongside Mitchell's immaculate suits. But we were a couple none the less. I don't remember telling many friends, though. Mitch was known as a bit rowdy and I was sure they'd say, 'Are you mad?' So I kept it quiet to start with.

At first, Cynthia used to welcome me with 'Hello, Sharon' – the name of a previous girlfriend of Mitch's. 'Mum, it's Janis,' he would correct her through gritted teeth. 'Sorry, love,' she'd say. But it wasn't long before Cynthia and I grew close, and we remained so. I fondly called her Cynthie, and despite being the head of a wilder, more disorderly family than the Seatons, she would become a rock who provided me with practical and emotional support in years to come. In fact, she was a second mother to me.

Cynthia was strong and striking by nature, and often dressed in flamboyant bright red prints with blue and green eye-shadows and painted nails. She had once dated jazz legend Ronnie Scott before she married Mitchell's father Alec. She loved music and entertaining and she was drawn to spiritualism and the occult. From a young age Amy wanted to be like her grandmother, who must have always seemed glamorous and exciting to her.

If there was one person Amy was terrified of, though, it was Cynthia. She was not a woman to be crossed. If she wanted something done, it got done. If she didn't approve of something, you knew about it. Alex recalls the broyguss (grudge) she had against him for forgetting to say hello to her as he walked through her front door when he was eight. It would not have been intentional, just an oversight, but Cynthia took it to heart. Even as I write, I'm sure she's ticking Amy off. 'See, Amy, I told you this would happen!' I can hear her voice bellowing.

I will always maintain that when Mitchell and I divorced, my marriage ended but I kept his family. I truly loved Cynthia, and in the painful months before her death from lung cancer in 2006 I visited her every day to talk with her or hold her hand. I'm still close to Mitchell's sister Melody. The Winehouses are a loving and generous family, and once I became part of it I knew that whatever happened, that would always be the case.

From a young age Amy was accident-prone, and as a toddler there wasn't much that she didn't try to swallow. I had a picture hand-drawn of her when she was two years old by an artist who captured Amy in typical fashion – with her fingers in her mouth. It never stopped at fingers, though. There was one time when she was sat in her buggy playing with a toy from which she'd pulled the cellophane wrapper. As soon as my back was turned, into her mouth it went and within seconds she was thrashing around in convulsions. My heart somersaulted and I thrust my fingers down her throat to retrieve the cellophane, which thankfully I managed to pull out in time. Crisis averted – but not for long.

Amy and Alex had friends called Lauren and Adam Harrod who lived nearby. During Amy's first year at primary school, they'd always be in and out of each other's houses playing. One day I went to pick Amy up and was chatting in the living room when suddenly she burst through the Harrods' back door holding the palm of her hand up to her mouth. 'Mum, Mum!' she was shouting. 'I thought I'd eaten a mushroom, but Lauren says it's a toadstool!' I was frantic, and began ringing round anyone who could advise me on what to do. In the end I bundled Amy into the car and rushed her to Chase Farm Hospital, where I feverishly explained that my daughter had swallowed a toadstool she'd picked from a neighbour's garden. On that occasion she had her stomach pumped and was given an anti-emetic to quell any feelings of nausea. The doctors were satisfied she'd be OK but she was kept in overnight for monitoring just in case. For me it was a nail-biting twenty-four hours.

You'd think Amy would have learned her lesson, but she never did. My family had another nickname for her – 'Nudge', a Yiddish word that means she was always pushing the boundaries. If you told Amy to stop doing something that was exactly the green light she needed to carry on.

As if the toadstool incident wasn't bad enough, my family has never forgotten – and will never let me forget – the time I lost Amy in nearby Broomfield Park. I had been chatting with a friend and when I looked up, she was nowhere in sight. I began walking around shouting her name, but instead of her childish voice calling back 'I'm here, Mummy' I was hit by an empty, stony silence. I froze on the spot. Broomfield Park has three large ponds. 'Oh God, oh God, please don't let her be at the bottom of one,' I kept repeating to myself. Realizing I needed help, I alerted the park-keeper and a full-scale search began.

Alex was playing nearby with his friends in the park when I collected him and I remember barely being able to utter the words 'Amy's gone'. I retraced our steps. We grabbed every passer-by. 'Have you seen a little girl? Seven years old, brown hair, dark eyes?' Please, please say yes, I was praying. At one point I was even on my hands and knees rummaging around in the shrubbery to see if she was hiding or had been caught up in something. Panic came over me in waves and I felt a sickening sense of guilt. I'd failed her. I hadn't looked after her properly.

The moment the police were called, what had started as an ordinary afternoon at the park started to take on a more sinister turn. Alex, who was distraught by this point, jumped into the police van with me and we were driven around looking for Amy, who had simply vanished. When dusk started to fall we were advised to go home and wait because there was nothing more we could do. Home was the last place I wanted to be. I wanted to be out looking for my baby girl and would do so all night if necessary. For a start, I had no idea how I was going to explain this. I could hear the questions already. How the hell had I lost Amy? Had I looked everywhere? Was I absolutely sure she was missing?

I had all but given up hope when Mitchell's sister Melody appeared at the park gates, hand in hand with my smiling daughter. Along with confusion, I was overcome by a feeling of sheer relief. I rushed over to hug her, whispering, 'Thank you, thank you.'

Apparently a friend of Melody's had been in the park with her children and seen Amy on her own. She'd invited Amy back to her house to play and Amy had instantly agreed. The friend had phoned Melody, who lived nearby, to tell her Amy was there, and Melody had picked her up and returned her. It took me a long while to forgive that friend. And so far as Amy was concerned, when I'd calmed down my relief turned to anger. I kept thinking, 'I don't know what goes on in that girl's head!' She hadn't thought for a second I'd be agonizing about her disappearance. She didn't care about the consequences. It was as if she had no stop button.

Any parent knows that in situations like this the imagination can run wild. But I can honestly say that the scenarios playing out in my head hardly ever centred on some awful person having taken Amy. Instead they were about her wriggling free from my hand and running into traffic, or her hiding and me not being able to find her. I can barely believe now that when Amy was a toddler I had to wait until she was asleep to have her fitted for new shoes because the moment she was awake and out of her buggy she'd run off. Yes, my biggest fear was definitely Amy herself, because she appeared to have no fear whatsoever.

Amy's escapades were legendary, but there was also a different, less confident side to her. She was often clinging on to me and she was never happy if my attention was divided when we were around other children. Shortly after Amy finished nursery at Yavneh, which was attached to Southgate Synagogue, she began pre-school at

Hampden Way Nursery. I had returned to work part-time after Alex was born but in the intervening years I had also trained as a pre-school playgroup leader, and Amy was often in my group. I remember one day helping a child called Niraj. We were building blocks together, but Amy kept appearing by my side and pulling at my arm, saying, 'Mum, Mum, what about me, Mum? What about me?'

Sharing me was a problem for Amy. In her first year at primary school she drew a picture of me in her school jotter with the words 'I can hide behind my mummy' written below. It's funny how children can say or write something quite innocently that is loaded with so much meaning. Amy didn't stop hiding behind me as she got older. There are pictures of us together on holiday in Disney World, Florida, around seven years later where Amy looks as if she's clinging on to me for dear life.

She never wanted to be a party girl either, even though she thrived on getting attention. Once, she had a joint birthday party with her friend Zara. Zara's grandmother had noticed Amy sitting on the side and when she tried to cajole Amy into joining in with the other children, Amy simply looked up and said, 'No, I'm bored.' It was her birthday, but she wasn't comfortable. Quite often she would fold her arms and sulk when she didn't feel in control. Amy spoke volumes even when she was silent, but if she did respond, she could be pretty blunt. If she didn't want to play games, she wouldn't. You'd gently try and coax her. 'Do you want to do this, Amy?' But she would fold her arms and say, 'No.' She liked her own space, and she also liked to be a leader, which we always put down to her being something of an individual.

Looking back, I think Alex and Amy had to cope with a lot when they were growing up because although they were part of a loving family, it was also an unusual one. Aside from the whirlwind that surrounded Mitchell, shortly after Alex was born I had not been well. I was experiencing a very odd tingling feeling in my body. It was like having pins and needles all over and it would sometimes last for hours. I was only twenty-four years old so the last thing I expected was anything to be seriously wrong with me.

My doctor suggested I was suffering from a bout of post-natal depression and prescribed an anti-depressant called Amitriptyline. In a way, I'm glad he did so. What I didn't know then was that my symptoms were the very early stages of MS. Had that label been placed on me at that young age, I fear I might have seen myself as an ill person and maybe even retreated from life. My doctor had referred me to a neurologist for a spinal tap (an uncomfortable procedure where they take a sample of the fluid that flows around the brain and spine to analyse for abnormalities) but the results had come back inconclusive. I simply carried on regardless.

All this happened before I fell pregnant with Amy. During one appointment I remember being advised to think twice before trying for another child. Admittedly I was bloody-minded about ignoring that advice but only because I genuinely felt optimistic that every-thing was going to be OK, that this feeling, whatever it was, would pass. As it happened, the feeling did pass, but I noticed that I became tired more easily than other people and my moods were sometimes low and sluggish. With two children in the mix, I often felt sapped of energy, but I kept going.

I have to say that when the diagnosis was eventually made it didn't really change that sense of determination. I've always wanted to be a person who is defined by what I can do, not by what I can't. Nevertheless, I was working part-time and having to be both Mum and Dad at home. I can say now that Mitchell can be the sweetest guy imaginable, and we are in the fortunate position of having an amicable and affectionate relationship. When the children were young, though, Mitchell was always working, earning the money. The Winehouses were good at making money and this was the 1980s, when entrepreneurial ambition was aggressive. We must have been the only family in Osidge Lane to have a Jaguar and a Rolls-Royce Silver Shadow parked out front. I remember Alex coming home from primary school complaining that none of his friends believed his dad owned a Rolls-Royce. 'But it's true, Mum. He really does, doesn't he?' he would ask, to which the reply was always, 'Yes, Alex, he *really* does.'

When Alex was born, Mitchell was working for a double glazing company. By the time Amy came along he was still in the double glazing industry, and working long hours. Mitchell, bless him, can be a bit flash, a bit of a show-off; as fast as he would make money he'd pour it into clothes and shoes and cars and be overly generous with his friends. When he did come home, he'd shower Alex and Amy with presents and the house would be filled with an explosion of love. 'Daddy, Daddy!' both children would shout as they heard the key turn in the lock. They'd be so excited to see him. They'd run up and give him a tremendous hug and cover him in kisses.

Amy talked about 'Daddy Mitchell' and 'Mitch Winehouse' as if they were two separate people. Mitch Winehouse was the fantastic raconteur who would sit her on his knee and beguile her with 'Mitchellisms' – family stories of the old East End, the gangsters and the spivs. Then there was Daddy Mitchell who, no sooner had he arrived, would be itching to be off again. Even now, Mitchell finds it hard to be in one place for too long. He's got to be up and doing something else all the time. It's just the way he is.

Our children didn't want for anything. They loved him and he loved them, but I was the constant, the go-to for their practical and emotional needs. I can't pretend I didn't resent Mitchell for that because at times I did feel frustrated and tired, but I also embraced the role because Mitchell was working such long hours. 'Janis, this is the hand you've been dealt and you're going to have to get on with it,' I thought. Still, sometimes, just sometimes, I longed for someone else to take the reins.

Looking back, I do wish we could have had more time with just us as a family.

2

Child Of Mine

I loved being a mum to Alex and Amy, but since my teens I'd always felt the need to challenge myself. When I had a family, that voice took a back seat, but it never really went away. So, when Amy was three, I began studying for an Open University degree.

Originally I'd opted to do a humanities degree but, being a more popular subject, there were no spaces left, and I was forced to switch to general science. By coincidence, my friend Stephanie had also applied to do the same so we ended up studying together. We both had young children and distance learning meant we could study mainly from home. The course was flexible enough so that I could take or pick up the children from school, work part-time if I wanted to and fit in my study in the evenings.

Neither of us was thinking of pursuing further education to become torchbearers for women's lib. Stephanie and I were teenagers in the late sixties but we were by no means bra-burners. We were just two mums in search of something more than children and suburbia. For me it was about proving to myself that I wasn't stupid, that I could get a formal qualification. Other than my pharmacy technician training, I hadn't had the opportunity to carry on with my education after school so my degree became a personal rite of passage. What I hadn't anticipated was how empowering those years would turn out to be. I look back on them now with a combination of pride and amazement at how driven I was to fit it all in.

Every evening took on a familiar routine. I'd feed and bath Alex and Amy and we'd read together upstairs. When Amy was very young she loved the story of *Goldilocks and the Three Bears* which would always leave her wide-eyed and giggling. *Cat in the Hat* by Dr Seuss was another of her favourites, and we got through *Postman Pat* and the *Thomas the Tank Engine* series too. We would sit up in Amy's room, which was at the front of the house, and, dressed in her pyjamas, she would tuck herself under my arm. Alex often snuggled in on the other side, and we'd open a book.

Stephanie told me that one time when she picked Amy up from reception class, Amy was carrying a note addressed to home. It was probably about a school trip or something, but Amy effortlessly read it aloud while skipping out of the classroom door. Another parent who'd been looking on commented how remarkable it was that Amy could read so fluently at such a young age. From early on I realized she was bright and perceptive and I encouraged her learning because she seemed to absorb any information that was put in front of her very quickly.

I was also thrilled that she'd inherited my love for the cartoon character Snoopy. When I was growing up, my brother Brian had a cuddly toy Snoopy that was very dear to him. When I sneaked his *Peanuts* comic books into my room to see what all the fuss was about it didn't take long for me to become hooked on the introverted Charlie Brown and his completely flawed but loveable sidekick dog. So I'd read comics with Alex and Amy before lights out too.

Once the children were tucked up I'd make myself a cup of tea, open my books and work late into the night on the downstairs sofa. As youngsters, Alex and Amy got used to me studying, and I wanted them to see me with my head in a book. I especially wanted Amy to see that I was more than 'Mummy', to learn that if she too grabbed opportunities, the world could be her oyster in whatever path she chose. Looking back on it, I was being pragmatic, and perhaps even subconsciously showing Amy the way to have some command of her future. Our home was undoubtedly more chaotic than others, but I always thought that if the children could learn by example that would be more helpful than being strict about rules.

I could write an epic about how much fun Stephanie and I had at the OU summer school one year. Cynthia and her sister Lorna looked after Alex and Amy while we decamped to Nottingham for the week. For those five days we threw off the shackles of being somebody's mum or somebody's wife. It was hilarious: Stephanie and I suddenly transformed into two über-gossips as we discovered how and why our fellow students came to be there and observed who was paired up with whom by the end of the week. Boy, did we enjoy that feeling of freedom. It reminded me of being a giddy teenager, which was the time when I'd truly discovered that life was there for the taking.

Back when I was nineteen and I'd just finished my apprenticeship to become a pharmacy technician I got it into my head that I wanted to go to Miami to work. It's definitely a Seaton trait, and one that Amy inherited too: when I get something into my head no obstacle is ever too great to get in the way of me achieving my goal. Half of the time I'm not even sure I see an obstacle, or if I do I work out a way to get over, under or around it in record time. Plucky or stupid? I've never been able to decide which. A few of my family were already living in Miami so I knew I'd have an instant contact out there, and, having been born in the States, I was also armed with an American passport. I saved up the money for the air fare, hopped on a plane, turned up at an aunt's house on Collins Avenue and announced to her that I was going to search for a job.

Landing in this vast, sprawling city filled with skyscrapers was in itself an intoxicating experience. The climate was hot and humid – a million miles away from cold, rainy London – and downtown pulsated with a myriad of people, languages, cultures and food. I fell for Miami's tropical paradise instantly, and I've always loved the Americans' can-do attitude. I hadn't the faintest idea in what direction I was going, but the very next day I was on a bus bound for North Miami General Hospital. I was surprisingly unselfconscious back then, and having marched through the glass-fronted entrance I asked for the pharmacy manager and told him, 'Hello, I'm Janis Seaton. I'm a pharmacy technician from London and I'm looking for work.'

By a complete miracle, the department needed a pharmacy assistant, and in the end I stayed in Miami for almost a year. I also worked at the Baptist Hospital in South Miami. I spotted an advert in a local newspaper for an apartment-share and within a month I'd moved in with a complete stranger called Devonda and her scrap of a dog. My family thought I was crazy, and when one of the pharmacists I worked alongside learned where I was from, her face was an absolute picture. She threw her hands up in the air and shouted in her thick Miami drawl, '*London?* You come from *London?* What the *hell* are you doing here?'

Of course, I had no answer other than 'because I can', but I honestly relished every minute of my stay in the country. Nowadays girls think nothing of taking a gap year or travelling the world, as Amy did, but back then, few of my friends had ever embarked on that kind of adventure. Many considered my get-up-and-go outlook as 'Janis being bonkers' rather than 'Janis being a trailblazer' but I never thought for one moment that my plan would fail – and it didn't. The Sunshine State has always held a special place in my heart, and when I returned home I stayed in touch with my aunts and many cousins there.

Once I was married and I had Alex and Amy there were things I wouldn't have been able to do without Cynthia's help, and completing my Open University course was one of them. OK, I admit, there were a few re-sits along the way, and it took me five years to get my degree in the end, but I still have the framed certificate on the wall upstairs. Happily, both children came to my graduation at Wembley Arena, and because my course covered modules in lots of different subjects, I was always able to help them with their homework. I could sit with Amy and work through a maths problem with her, even though maths had been one of my worst subjects at school. I felt very pleased with myself and, now, I even had letters after my name. Who'd have thought it?

Disappointingly, despite my best efforts Amy didn't appear cut out to take an academic route. She had a real sparkle in her eyes but she lacked concentration in the subjects she wasn't interested in. At primary school, Amy's teachers always commented on how easily she could grasp what was being taught, but she needed constant stimulation, which was near impossible within a structured class setting.

She loved singing, though, and would pick up lyrics and tunes instantaneously and belt them out with her own unique twist. I don't recall Amy ever being the clichéd kid who shut herself in her bedroom and sang into a hairbrush in front of the mirror. She sang wherever she was. As a toddler, *Mary Poppins* was one of her favourite musicals and she would jump around the living room singing 'A Spoonful Of Sugar' or 'Jolly Holiday' at the top of her voice. We also sang Jewish hymns together. A common expression in our house would be 'OK, Amy, enough', but that would go in one ear and out the other and she'd carry on regardless. Richard's mum Doreen always said of Amy, 'She's got a pisk on her, that girl.' 'Pisk' is another Yiddish word, meaning 'a loud mouth'. She wasn't wrong.

At Cynthia's, Amy was surrounded by jazz music, anyone from Frank Sinatra and Ella Fitzgerald to Sarah Vaughan. I was a big fan of Carole King and James Taylor, both great American songwriters, and I'd have their music playing at home or in the car. As a teenager I'd spent many Sunday afternoons listening to live music at the Roundhouse in Camden: it feels comforting, and a little surreal, that so many years down the line Amy's name has now become synonymous with the venue. I'd go to the Roundhouse with my friend Anna to see the Who, and I remember seeing Elton John there before he went to the States and became famous. The States must have changed something in Elton John because he was the dullest performer I'd ever seen. But then, the mainstream didn't always interest me. On one occasion I went there and in the foyer the promoters were giving out free records. I picked up Jimi Hendrix's *Are You Experienced?* and my brother Brian and I played it on the turntable in his room at home – now *that's* what I called music! I'd go with Brian on Friday nights to the Playhouse Theatre, too, to queue for tickets for the weekly live recording of Radio 4's *I'm Sorry I'll Read That Again* with John Cleese and Tim Brooke-Taylor.

Perhaps it was because I had an older brother that my musical and cultural tastes didn't always follow those of my friends. I was experimental, the kind of person who became switched on by a piece of work because it seemed interesting in itself and might lead to another new discovery rather than because it was popular. This meant that Amy was exposed to lots of different music, entertainment and art as a child, on both sides of the family. My Uncle Leon was a horn player and his son Mark ended up drumming in one of the incarnations of the Joe Loss Orchestra. Performance played a large part in the life of the Winehouse family, too. When we visited them, Cynthia and Larry, Mitchell's stepfather, would always say, 'Go on, Amy, show us how you can sing,' or to Alex, 'Go on, do "Oklahoma" for us.'

Because I didn't possess any talent for singing, let alone performing, I have to admit I used to wince when the children were made to get up and 'do a turn'. Amy seemed much more confident than Alex. She could affect an all-singing all-dancing Shirley Temple, but even so there were occasions when she showed some reluctance to get up in front of others. She reminded me of my sister Debra, who now sings in her own jazz ensemble in her spare time. Debra has a lovely voice and as a kid she was always asked by my parents to sing for us, especially if we had family visiting from America. But as the notes flowed out effortlessly from her mouth, Debra's fingers were always nervously clutching at the material of her dress – in the exact same way Amy did years later when she performed.

Amy adored Michael Jackson, and in 1988, when she was five, I took her to see his film *Moonwalker*. 'It was brill,' she wrote in her notebook afterwards. 'Michael Jackson is handsome. I love him. He is nice and I went to see him. I love Michael's songs. All the kids love Michael. I do too.'

And when Amy loved something, she *really* loved something. Whether it was Michael Jackson or her Cabbage Patch dolls Fe and Melina whom she seemed almost superglued to, there were no half measures. Amy and sweets were a disastrous combination. We didn't keep a lot of sweets in the house because both Mitchell and I have a sweet tooth and it was better to put temptation out of our way, and I used to regularly tick Amy off because she would try to steal the sweets from the synagogue on festive Shabbat days. 'Why not, Mummy?' she'd grin. The answer 'because it's naughty' never washed with Amy. She was always making notes of items she wanted, or things she was going to buy with her pocket money. In them, the word SWEETS always appeared in big, bold capital letters as if the size of her writing related to how many of them she wanted to cram into her mouth.

Amy's quiet time at home was always spent drawing or reading or writing stories about nothing in particular – observations that now, when I read them, seem quite mundane. She'd put together little rhymes, and one Mother's Day, when she was still at primary school, she made me a handmade card which read:

> Mum, you are the best,
> A mechanical genius too,
> You fix people's bikes and I love you.
> You saved my life,
> Oh thanks so much,
> You'll always have that special touch.

I bet that dad is lucky to
Have someone as special as you.

I'm so pleased that I kept all the cards Amy sent me, but I now look at them through a completely different lens. Amy was my clever, funny, naughty little girl. Who would ever have thought then that I'd now be talking about her in the past tense?

In the summer of 1990, Mitchell and I sat in a crowded hall listening to the murmur of conversation and the last-minute whispers from behind the stage curtain as we nervously anticipated the performance. Other than at family gatherings, this was the first time we'd be seeing or hearing Amy sing in public.

Amy had started attending a theatre class called Stagecoach held in a church hall near Southgate where children of all ages could enrol. Each week she would sing, dance and act for three hours, and she always came home brimming with ideas. We'd turned up at the group's end-of-year showcase – a cabaret of sketches and songs – because Amy was to sing a solo number. Whether they were good or bad, I never missed Amy's shows. It was the one thing, other than writing stories, that she seemed to have a genuine passion for and I wanted her to know that my support was unconditional. She seemed up front and fearless on that first occasion; I don't remember her telling me she was scared. In fact it was me who had terrible butterflies in my stomach, knowing she would be facing the audience alone.

As she walked on stage, the music started. There was a moment's pause that felt like an eternity before Amy opened her mouth and sang. Mitchell and I glanced at each other, then stared back at Amy, and we knew we were both thinking the same thing: 'This girl can *really* sing!'

It's funny: I have no recollection of the song she sang. What I do know is that whatever apprehension I'd had beforehand disappeared. Within seconds I'd become mesmerized by my six-year-old girl putting her heart and soul into the show. She looked to be in her element, concentrating so hard on getting every note perfect. This was a very different Amy to the one I was already being confronted with by her teachers at school.

I used to dread parents' evenings when Amy attended Osidge Primary School, which was five minutes from our home. Her teachers were always very encouraging of Amy's abilities, but every comment was followed by a 'but'. 'Mrs Winehouse,' they would say, followed by a roll of the eyes or an apologetic grimace, 'Amy is a very capable girl, *but* she doesn't sit still' . . . '*but* she doesn't concentrate' . . . '*but* she misbehaves in class'. She was one of those girls who could do most things she turned her hand to *but* only if and when she wanted to.

There were a few troublemakers in her year. Amy had a partner in crime at Osidge, her long-term friend Juliette Ashby. No sooner had they met than they were joined at the hip. They'd pretend to be Wham's backing singers Pepsi and Shirlie and act out songs, and Juliette told me after Amy's passing that the pair would often be found under a tree in the school grounds, giggling and inventing lyrics, when they should have been in class. Or they'd deliberately talk so loudly they'd be thrown out of the lesson. Once Amy and Juliette reached secondary school, there were certainly occasions when I asked for them to be separated because they were constantly up to something.

If you looked at some of Amy's official school photos from Osidge Primary you'd think butter wouldn't melt in her mouth, but the reality was quite different. She was a don't-mess-with-me girl who said, 'I am what I am, and if you don't like it, tough.' Amy built a wall around herself from early on and she seemed to let few people in. The more up front and brassy she could be, the less people would be inclined to get to know her and her insecurities. Believe it or not, she was sensitive to life hurting her, even though she outwardly communicated the opposite. At home, I became her security blanket. If we were out shopping in nearby Brent Cross she would often hold my hand. Amy held my hand in public right up until the time she left home at eighteen. It didn't bother me at all because I accepted it as her way of showing affection. She seemed to need to check that I was there for her.

I soon began to realize that Amy was never going to feel fulfilled at school. For one thing, her experiences were far richer outside the classroom. She was an adventurer. She needed to see, feel, touch and smell life rather than learn about it from a textbook. And the reason I knew this was because I had been exactly the same at that age.

I had passed my eleven-plus exam and initially gone to grammar school in Dalston in east London, but within a year I was pleading with my mother to be transferred to the nearby comprehensive, Woodberry Down, probably because I sensed I was a whisker away from being expelled. There I developed a real interest in science and knuckled down and passed a handful of exams, but I had been so unhappy at grammar school and consequently very unruly, always talking and messing around and making the teachers' lives hell. Although I was bright, I felt out of place. We'd been left by my mother to find our own way so I'm not sure I felt comfortable with other children who came from more stable backgrounds. Perhaps, too, I didn't deal well with the expectations placed on me. 'Janis, can you do this?' the teachers would say, to which my reply was usually, 'No, I'm not doing that.' So it's no surprise that Amy displayed the same indignant behaviour.

While sorting through some boxes recently, I discovered my school reports, which I hadn't seen for forty-odd years. I'm ashamed to say the similarity between Amy's behaviour and mine around that age is startling. The overall assessment for the summer term of 1967, for example, states that I 'found concentration very difficult'. In French, the criticism was scathing: 'Janis made little effort and the work she has done has been produced with the utmost reluctance'. My music report was slapped with a zero grade and had the accompanying note: 'Janis has done no work this term'. Fast-forward almost thirty years and Amy's music lesson appraisal could have been lifted from my old discoloured papers: 'If Amy put a quarter of the effort she puts into disrupting the lesson into learning her flute she could be a good player.'

Like me, Amy could never focus on one thing. She'd start something, then all of a sudden her interest would turn to something else and she'd follow that path for a while. Formal education proved too structured for her. Instead, she devoured what was around her. Whether it was books or films or poetry or music or the hustle and bustle of growing up in a big city, she soaked life up and it spilled out of her in the most creative ways. One year, when she was going through a French phase, my birthday card read 'Chére Maman! Bonne Fête Maman! Je suis mechante quelque fois, mais tu es trés patiente! Je te donne un dîner delicieux! Je t'embrasse, grosses bises, Amy x' (Dear Mum! Happy Birthday Mum! I am very naughty sometimes, but you are very patient! I give you a delicious dinner! I hug you, many kisses, Amy x). On the front of the card, designed by Amy, is a picture of me in a lab coat complete with pens sticking out of my top right-hand pocket. On another card she'd cheekily written, 'I love you mummy because you are beautiful. This is not the whole reason I love you, but it helps.'

If there was one thing Amy was, it was brutally honest. She saw herself in a similarly blunt way – a girl, yes, but certainly not delicate or feminine. When she was eight she brought home a self-portrait from art class. It showed her dressed in her favourite sweatshirt with a large heart emblazoned across the chest, and she had outlined it with thick black acrylic paint. The picture was very simply drawn, and her angular face appeared very striking, but I was taken aback at how crudely, yet accurately, it captured her.

Where Amy went, drama was never far behind. Her wild and crazy ways were harmless enough, but I was never short of a story to tell if anyone asked about her. There was one afternoon at home when I heard a loud thud upstairs; for a moment, the floor shuddered. In her bedroom Amy had a loft bed with a wardrobe and a study desk underneath, so I rushed up to see what had happened and found Amy trundling down the stairs sobbing and holding her wrist. 'I fell out of bed, Mum,' she wailed, 'and I'm really hurt.' So we had yet another emergency outing to Chase Farm Hospital. After an X-ray, her injury was downgraded from a fracture to a sprained wrist which she had bandaged up for a time.

A few months later Amy again got herself caught up in her quilt cover, plunged out of bed, and landed on the other wrist. This time it was a clean break and she was howling with pain. I wondered how long it would be before we were on first-name terms with the hospital's accident and emergency staff.

Amy's antics were often wilfully anarchic and I have to admit that even I was hard pushed to keep a straight face at times. I found myself sighing, 'Oh Amy,' because no one else could even have thought up some of the things her imagination conjured.

She and my now husband Richard's son Michael used to play outside in the street on their bikes after school. They would have been around eight at the time, and if you watched the two of them together they were like a real-life Topsy and Tim. Ever the extrovert, Amy insisted that they race down the pathway near Richard and Stephanie's house to see who got to the bottom of the hill first. After an exhilarating first run, Amy changed the rules: the next time they raced they didn't only have to cycle down the hill, they had to do it with their trousers and pants around their knees and their bums in the air. Michael, being a more reserved child than Amy, was less certain this was a good idea but he was soon persuaded by her that riding a bike bare-bottomed down a suburban street was perfectly normal. The power Amy had to persuade anyone to do anything was breathtaking at times. So they perched their feet on the pedals, raised their white cheeks off the saddles and sped down the pathway. They hadn't a clue that waiting for them at the end was an elderly man open-mouthed at the sight fast approaching him. 'Get back home and put some clothes on!' he shouted, to which Amy gave a two-fingered V sign and carried right on. Michael, being

Michael, thought they probably should go home and get dressed but Amy couldn't have cared less. It was just Amy being Amy. It would have been impossible not to love her even if you tried.

To ask if Amy's behaviour was challenging would be like asking if the Pope were Catholic. My life was spent constantly developing new strategies to get her to do the simplest things, from brushing her teeth before bed to getting her uniform on for school in the morning.

Everybody has their own parenting style. I always felt that instead of disciplining Amy, which never seemed to work anyway, it was better to sit her down and reason with her about what was right and what was wrong and why certain things needed to be done this way or that. The only problem was, Amy could never sit still for long. If she did she'd grow bored with what was being said. 'OK Mummy, I'm sorry Mummy,' she would say, but they always turned out to be empty words because the next minute she'd be back doing whatever she'd been asked not to do. My friend Penny, who used to bring Amy down to the gate at Osidge Primary to meet me after school, often willed me to 'put my foot down' with her a bit more, but Amy was so headstrong that we would have spent every waking hour at each other's throats.

My own parents had not been strong disciplinarians, but I do recall on the few occasions when my father lost his temper, which was very uncharacteristic of Eddie, he put the fear of God into us. Somewhere along the line I vowed that if ever I had children I would never punish them like that and never, ever hit them. Mitchell did not believe in smacking the children either.

Neither of us were people who lived our lives by many rules, and with Mitchell working so hard it was impossible to stick to them because they would constantly be broken. I wanted to do my best as a parent but it wasn't in my nature to play the role of 'bad cop' all the time. If there's one thing I wish the children had had growing up, it's greater consistency. There was no rigid way of doing things in our family.

In the end it was usually Cynthia who stepped in as the voice of authority. She sensed that I didn't cope well with conflict so, if the situation demanded it, she would roll up her sleeves and give Amy a good verbal dressing down. To a certain degree, it worked. When we went to Cynthia's for Friday night dinners Amy was always ready on time, which was a miracle, because in the same way Amy arrived into the world so she continued – late for everything. Both she and Alex became mindful of how smartly dressed they were or if they had a hair out of place, because if they looked in any way scruffy Cynthia would almost certainly pick them up on it.

We spent most Friday nights with Cynthia and her family. The flat she had moved to on Southgate High Street was round the corner from us, and because Friday was the start of Shabbat in the Jewish week there would always be a spread of chicken soup or roast chicken and potatoes followed by tinned fruit and ice cream. It was impossible not to come away from Cynthia's feeling stuffed.

Mitchell's family weren't practising Jews, but Friday night dinner was the one custom the Winehouses always adhered to. Amy loved being around the family. As soon as we arrived she would insist on helping Cynthia in the kitchen, preparing the food or setting the table. She never wanted to be a guest. 'Mum, sit there,' she would say. 'I'll serve you.' After we'd eaten, Amy would always get up and offer to clear the plates and take them to the kitchen, saying to her nan, 'Let me do this for you.' She was exactly the same when we went to see my dad, whom she called Pop Eddie, and whom she adored. So Amy wasn't always naughty. In fact she was often eager to please, and she never really lost her love for being around family occasions – even though, years later, it became much harder to see.

At around this time, in 1991 when Amy was seven going on eight, Cynthia saw an advert for the Susi Earnshaw Theatre School and suggested that it could be something Amy might like to attend. The school, in Barnet, is still going strong today. The Saturday mornings at Stagecoach had really occupied Amy, and the arrangement at Susi Earnshaw was similar: three hours a week of singing, acting and dancing classes, which she took to immediately.

Amy wasn't the sort of girl who came home and told you in exhaustive detail about everything she'd done. She was almost businesslike about it, and the classes became part and parcel of her weekly routine. Cynthia or I would take her or pick her up. I think Cynthia saw early on in Amy a raw talent that she herself had had to a lesser degree when she was a young woman. Back in the sixties, Cynthia and her sister Lorna had been involved in a singing group, and there was perhaps a time when both of them could have pursued a career in the performing arts, but either the demands of having a family took over or Cynthia simply wasn't driven enough. Whatever the reason, it never happened. Instead, Cynthia became Amy's biggest fan. And, at times, her worst critic.

I'll never forget the time when Cynthia took Amy to an audition for the title part in *Annie* which Susi Earnshaw sent several girls to. Amy struggled because the song she was asked to sing in front of the directors was in too high a key, and she did not get the part. I don't think Amy was too upset by it, but Cynthia would not let it lie.

'You should have got it, Amy,' she shouted, and wagged her finger. 'You were much better than the others. It should have been you.'

We laughed it off as Cynthia being overly pushy, and although her manner was never short of in-your-face, I knew at heart she really rooted for her granddaughter. I noticed, too, that while Amy was at Susi Earnshaw I did not have to cope with any of the issues over her behaviour that I had been forced to deal with elsewhere, and the sessions seemed to engage her in a way primary school never had.

Towards the end of that same year I also made the decision to plough myself into something I enjoyed: I took out a student loan and prepared to embark on a second degree. Funnily enough, it was

Mitchell who'd suggested I return to studying, this time to become a fully qualified pharmacist.

Mitchell was always very proud of what I'd achieved at university and he encouraged my efforts. The problem was the usual one: he offered little practical support at home to ease the burden of juggling work, study and childcare, so whenever I wanted to spread my wings that bit further it was a decision I knew would involve one more test of stamina.

Apart from my brief stint as a playgroup leader, and later as a lab technician at Alex and Amy's secondary school, I had always been either a part-time or full-time pharmacy technician. A second degree would allow me to make the jump to pharmacist in four years – a three-year course plus a year's on-the-job postgraduate training. I enrolled at the University of London School of Pharmacy in the autumn of 1992 and began work towards becoming a Bachelor of Pharmacy.

Unlike at school, I felt very alive during both my degree courses. I became a born-again student with a newfound enthusiasm for knowledge. There was the science to get through, of course. Much of my time was spent in the lab looking at the chemical structures of drugs and what their effects are on the human body. Other modules required me to become a mini-expert in pharmacy law; I learned all about the rules and regulations surrounding drug licensing and drug use. What a terrible irony that a few years down the line I would be confronted with drugs in such a personal way. Sadly, the leap between understanding the theory of clinical drug use and being faced with your own addicted daughter is an emotional light-year wide.

Nevertheless, being a full-time mature student felt a lot stranger because, unlike during my OU degree, I was surrounded by people a good ten or twenty years younger. It would have taken more than that to put me off, though, and perhaps there was a part of me that needed to regain control over my life in ways I wasn't able to at home. One of my tutors pulled me aside one day and whispered to me, 'Janis, this is your Road to Damascus.' He was right, although I didn't fully appreciate at the time how right. Further education had already been a turning point for me both personally and professionally, and as 1992 drew to a close my life was rapidly shifting direction again, but my marriage to Mitchell was reaching its final stop.

3

Dad's Gone – Can We Get a Hamster?

Alex and Amy were growing up fast and expanding their horizons, but my relationship with Mitchell had been waning for some time. Despite being married with children, I felt as if I were a single mother.

Most marriages aren't perfect. Ours had been a marriage built on love, but like most couples we had our ups and downs. We had a wide social circle and family nearby and in the eighteen years we spent together we enjoyed life, but it was the lack of close time together that perhaps set us apart from other couples we knew.

When Amy was around eight we moved to a larger house ten minutes from Osidge Lane and Mitchell would always say to me, 'Janis, don't worry, everything is being taken care of.' Yet there was a niggling feeling in the back of my mind that the picture Mitchell was painting was too rosy. He was involved in a new business venture so I suppose I chose the easy way out by not asking him too much about his work. Our relationship had always been like that. But it was when Mitchell's business failed that our marriage seriously began to unravel.

Both children knew that something was afoot. Privately, the spark and intimacy that had once defined our marriage had gone, but I didn't yet understand the reason why. Separation, let alone divorce, had never been in my plans. Nobody goes into a marriage willing it to fail, but I guess you learn more about each other on the journey and adapt around each other's imperfections. I always joke that I knew the worst of Mitchell before I ever knew the best of him, and in some ways Amy's passing has brought our families closer together. It goes without saying that there's been an awful lot of water under the bridge since our separation more than twenty years ago.

I am not a fly-by-night person by nature. I stick at things, and back then I wanted Mitchell and me to work for us, for Alex and Amy, and also for our families. Whatever else was going on behind closed doors, I felt a great loyalty to the Winehouses – especially Cynthia – because we all looked after one another. As the months went on, however, all the clues pointed towards the reality that Mitchell was having an affair. He'd be up and off most weekends telling me he had to go to Bolton, where the company had offices. 'Bolton' almost reached mythical status among our friends and apparently became a bit of a standing joke.

The experience of marriage breakdown was so different to how I would have imagined it. I suspect most women, if asked, will say infidelity is the last thing they would tolerate, but the bottom line is that's often easier said than done, especially when there are children involved. I certainly went through a process of denial. Sadness, anger and confusion were the feelings I oscillated between. Early on, I almost convinced myself it wasn't happening simply because it hurt too much to face the truth.

Subconsciously, the life I had been building away from Mitchell had given me some confidence to tackle the situation – that tutor wasn't wrong when he said my degree was my 'Road to Damascus'. I thought that if we could work at mending the gulf that had emerged between us it was still worth giving it a chance. So one day I suggested we attend marriage counselling and, to my surprise, Mitchell agreed.

There are moments in my life that are indelibly marked on my brain, and this first meeting is one of them. There'd been all this stuff clunking around in my head at home and suddenly I was sat within four walls wondering how the hell I was going to say it all. I told myself just to talk openly and honestly about everything, and if we both did that things could be resolved between us. Unfortunately that didn't happen.

Whatever was occurring in our marriage we were determined to shield Alex and Amy from it. We rarely argued in front of the children – in fact we didn't really argue at all – but in my own mind I questioned the impact our unusual home life might have on Alex and Amy.

Every Saturday I sorted the paperwork at Mitchell's company and took various job bookings. That day I was working on Mitchell's computer and opened up a letter from him to his friend Phil. Mitchell had known Phil since attending Jewish club together as youngsters. They were close friends, and although Phil had moved to New York some years before, Mitchell often visited him and he became Mitchell's confidant. We'd all eventually become friends. Endearingly, Amy used to write little letters to Phil, and he enjoyed reading about her latest adventures.

When this particular letter appeared on the screen I was careful not to miss a single word. It confirmed everything I had suspected. Mitchell had been living a lie for a long time, it told me. While everybody thought he was happily married to Janis, he was in love with someone called Jane.

I sat stunned, staring at the words, and slowly tear after tear began to roll down my cheeks. I only had to read that letter once. It was agonizing to see what had become of my life presented so starkly in front of me. This was the betrayal I had been anticipating. It was a relief, almost, to know that the game was finally up, but inside I felt a searing, inconsolable pain.

I picked up the phone to my friend Stephanie. 'You'd better come down with a packet of cigarettes,' I told her.

After weeks of deliberation, I confronted Mitchell and we agreed that enough was enough. To this day it still hurts.

Mitchell's duplicity, I believe, was partly because Mitchell was a law unto himself but also, I suspect, he didn't want to hurt anyone or risk losing the children. As for me, my overwhelming feeling was that I'd failed, even though I knew deep down that I had fought to keep my family together. But there was no going back now. I had to move on from a relationship that was destroying my self-confidence and my family.

Through the feelings of humiliation and grief, my path emerged clearer than ever. I would continue with my studies and bring up Alex and Amy as best I could. Two years later, when I turned forty and my decree absolute dropped through the letterbox, I was doing just that: ensconced in the School of Pharmacy I was surrounded by microscopes and gram-negative bacteria in petri dishes; at home, I was being Mum.

While our separation was inevitable, it was bitter and painful, and telling Alex and Amy was no easier. On the day we broke the news to them, Mitchell called them into the dining room. It was the hardest thing either of us could do, but Mitchell spoke calmly.

'We've got something to tell you,' he said. 'Mum and I are going to separate.'

The way Mitchell reasoned it was strange to me. He told the children that they were lucky. His dad had died of cancer when he was only sixteen so the fact that Alex and Amy would still be seeing him somehow put them in a better position. I suppose he was trying to soften the blow, and I remember the atmosphere being surprisingly casual. Alex was half swinging on a chair and eating a sandwich. When Mitchell finished speaking, Alex fell back on the seat and started choking on the bread. Disconcertingly, Amy, who had been standing very quietly, suddenly erupted into a fit of the giggles. She was nine and Alex was twelve and I'm not sure the reality of the situation really sank in. Later, Amy told me that they both felt confused because, although they knew there were problems, neither she nor Alex heard us argue that much.

I had confided in good friends in the months leading up to our split but I had not fallen apart. I'd persisted in telling myself, and those closest to me, that I was OK. 'I'm all right, I'll deal with it, I'm fine, don't worry about me' – this was my default mantra. Looking back, I was paddling frantically underneath, just managing to keep my head above water. Those words came back to haunt me years later when Amy became ill. She used exactly the same act – 'I'm fine, don't worry about me' – in the darkest days of her addiction and in the year before she passed away, and I identified with it immediately.

But, like all disasters in our family, humour helped us through. Thank God for laughter. In our more riotous moments, Stephanie and I had always fantasized that if either of us killed our husbands we'd provide alibis for each other. As events turned out, her services weren't required.

Mitchell moved out over a period of weeks and Amy's campaign to get a pet hamster, which had been running for some months, reached fever pitch. 'Please, Mum, can we get one?' she'd pester me every two minutes. We already had a cat called Katie, who'd turned up on our front doorstep and who'd stayed after we'd started feeding her. She was a mish-mash of black, white and ginger and had the most tolerant of natures, which was fortunate because when Amy hugged her there was no escape. Alex had christened her Katie Bush Winehouse and the children adored her.

Not satisfied with one pet she could squeeze, Amy didn't let up about a hamster, and one afternoon, when she was really trying my patience, I promised her, 'Amy, when Dad goes, we'll get a hamster.'

After that the hamster went clean out of my mind, but not Amy's, oh no. As soon as Mitchell had taken his final belongings from the house, Amy turned to me and said matter-of-factly, 'Dad's gone – can we get a hamster?' You could always rely on Amy to deliver a showstopper.

Despite the turmoil of those few weeks, I had to laugh. In lots of ways it was typical of Amy. Even at nine, she had unflinching focus when she'd set her sights on something she wanted. I'd like to think it was Amy's childlike way of saying 'The past is the past, Mum, it's time to move on,' but I suspect Amy plainly meant 'I want that hamster now, Mum!'

In the end Amy did get her hamster, whom she named Penfold: she loved the cartoon *Danger Mouse* and Penfold was his bespectacled hamster assistant. All in all, with three goldfish called Sylvia, Lennon and McCartney, our cat Katie Bush Winehouse, and now Penfold, we had a pretty full house.

Of course, Alex and Amy were part of Mitchell's life, and on the surface nothing much changed. They saw Mitchell as often as before. Amy appeared to carry on as normal but I did constantly worry about how both children were dealing with our separation. I learned over time that Amy buried her feelings. Even though she was a loud and forthright child, rightly or wrongly, and typically of children, she felt Mitch had left her and Alex too, and her behaviour was often about chasing Mitch's attention. I'm sure it's why she was never happy just making music – she needed to be the *best* at making music.

Both children were sensitive towards me and didn't talk about the break-up for fear of upsetting me or making the problem worse. I have since read interviews with Amy where she talked about our split and described how she would find me at home crying. I genuinely don't recall that happening and I suspect that was Amy being characteristically over-dramatic. Our separation was desperately sad, but once it happened I treated it as a clean break that allowed me to forge a new life. From then on the children had their separate time with Mitchell; for the remainder of the time the three of us had our life and our fun together.

Cynthia, bless her, didn't take the news at all well. After Mitchell left, she sat in my living room in tears. While I'd been worrying about whether the Winehouses would still be part of my family, she'd been worrying that I'd suddenly stop bringing the children round to see her and Larry, or that somehow we'd lose contact. I reassured her that that would never happen. Whatever the circumstances, Mitchell's family were part of my family and they always would be. I can only imagine how awful it must be for families who are irrevocably divided by divorce, where children lose touch with a parent or grandparents. For us, there was never any doubt about whether that bond would be maintained.

Friends asked me if I would change my name back to Seaton but I had no inclination to do that. I was a Winehouse and I remained so until I married Richard in 2011, when I became Janis Winehouse-Collins.

Just before Mitchell and I split, we'd moved to a three-bedroom new-build in a leafy cul-de-sac in Barnet called Greenside Close. There I would often find Amy with her bum perched out of the top left-hand window and her legs dangling down – it was a twenty-foot drop – singing and singing and singing. God knows what the neighbours must have thought, other than that she certainly put the hours in.

In the spring of 1994 all the practice paid off when Amy was chosen to play Rizzo in an adaptation of the musical *Grease* for her leavers' play at Osidge Primary. It would be an understatement to say she immersed herself in the role. Amy attended the after-school rehearsals religiously and sang the songs incessantly around the house. Handing her the part of Rizzo was an inspired move, as close to typecasting as you could get: in *Grease*, Rizzo is the unofficial leader of the girl gang the Pink Ladies who uses her chewing-gum one-liners and status to mask her insecurities. As school productions go, it was a huge success. The amazing thing was that Amy played the part as if she really was Rizzo. She sang a version of 'Look At Me, I'm Sandra Dee' and spoke a few lines, and even though she was only ten years old her American accent was flawless. Talk about ballsy! Her tough-girl attitude and dynamic voice shone out from the stage, her constant readjusting of her pink jacket and black dress the only giveaway of her nervousness.

When I look at that DVD now I realize how meticulously she

must have studied the film; she'd absorbed every nuance of that complex character. Secretly, though, she'd hankered after the lead part, Sandy. In her notebook, which sat in a box in my garage for years, she'd made a list of who was playing each part and had added her own commentary alongside. Next to the name of her classmate Laura Wallis, who ended up playing Sandy, she'd written 'seethe!' in brackets. Beside Danny, played by Toby Richmond – or 'Tobywoby' as she'd nicknamed him – she'd scribbled 'chosen well', and beside the part of Rizzo she'd circled the words 'me, Amy!'

Unfortunately it was also around this time that Amy's problems at school began to escalate. I've often wondered how much our separation contributed to her increasingly bad behaviour, but Amy had always been hell bent on pushing the boundaries and it may be that she would have followed a destructive path whatever the circumstances. All I know is that there was a time when I had a handle on Amy and however far she pushed her luck she knew when to stop – eventually. Now, at home as well, she was becoming more and more unmanageable. It was as if a lid had been lifted and Amy had started to boil over.

At school, most of the other children in her class wanted to learn and they felt annoyed with her. She was not only loud, she was intimidating too. She needed to be in control of her surroundings and that played out in all manner of ways in the classroom. Amy veered between playing the class clown to being spiteful and domineering and, if I'm honest, a bully. On the other hand, if you were Amy's friend she would protect you with every inch of her life. She kept a circle of old school friends even when she became famous.

Not for a moment did I think Amy was an angel, but there is a story about her which is very hard for me to tell because no mother wants to be faced with the reality that their child doesn't fit in. As the summer term drew to a close at Osidge Primary, Amy was asked to bring two T-shirts into school. As a last-day-of-term ritual, all the children would sign one another's shirts as a memento of their time there before they graduated to secondary school. From her shoes to her homework, Amy constantly lost her belongings, so it didn't surprise me when she returned home that evening without it. What I didn't know is that Amy's shirt had been signed with the most hateful insults. My friend Stephanie had picked Amy up that day. Having taken one look at what had been scrawled on the white material in indelible ink, she had thrown the shirt in the bin before I could see it.

Every parent knows how cruel children can be, and perhaps this was the only way Amy's classmates could 'get back at her' without ever having to physically stand up to her. Apparently Amy had worn the shirt as if she really didn't care – as if she was proud of it, even – but that would have been Amy, putting a wall up around herself again. Inside it would have hurt her, and she never confided in me about it.

Fellow mums and friends would always try to protect me from the full force of Amy out of kindness, and I'm grateful for that, but the bottom line is I was her mother and I knew in my heart that Amy was angel and devil rolled into one. It was obvious she stood out from other children. She took the lead in friendships and rivalries and in other situations she simply didn't want to fit in. Deep down she wanted to be liked, but she also worked hard at alienating herself. In Amy's mind, her vision of the world was the right vision; feeling misunderstood by her peers no doubt fuelled her misbehaviour.

Amy made lists obsessively. That summer, as she prepared to leave primary school, she listed all twenty-nine of her classmates, their telephone numbers and the names of the secondary schools each one was going to. She listed the shops she loved – the usual teenage chains like Miss Selfridge, Top Shop and River Island. She also listed all the activities she was going to do to keep fit which included 'borrowing Auntie Mel's step and video', 'dancing vigorously' and 'flirting'. The words she used to describe herself were listed as 'loud', 'bright', 'bold', 'melodramatic', 'wild', 'imaginative', 'spontaneous' and 'in-your-face'. Most of all she made lists about her room. According to Amy, her room was 'beautiful', 'innovative', 'imaginative', 'thoughtful', 'influential', 'inspiring', 'spiritual', 'cosy' and, finally, 'cool'. The one thing it was not was tidy. I often have dreams about Amy, and in them she is always a little girl. They are not scary or sad dreams but they almost always take place inside her room which was the untidiest I have ever seen.

Despite her messiness, she made extensive plans about how she was going to arrange everything in it. Amy's room became her retreat; it was a space she gave a great deal of attention to. If she wanted to be alone, her room was the one place she would go. It was private, and she felt safe there. It was just her and her stuff and her thoughts and her writing and her music; it became a sanctuary where she could express herself in ways she couldn't elsewhere. If she needed something bought for her room, she would often try the trick of playing two parents off against each other, asking me for one thing and then, if the answer was no, trying Mitchell. If that didn't work there was always Pop Eddie and Nan Cynthia to work on, with varying degrees of success.

One thing's for sure: her notebooks from that time show little sign of her being racked with the kind of mental illness she struggled with in the last few years of her life. I have tried hard not to let my later experiences with Amy and the reams of column inches speculating on every aspect of her life destroy my positive attitude, although it's hard to imagine that they haven't made me a more cynical person. Nevertheless, it's my instinct to remain trusting of human nature. Occasionally, though, just occasionally, I hear or read something that fundamentally disturbs my way of being.

Many books have appeared about Amy over the years but no author has ever spoken to us, Amy's family, in the lead-up to publication. A couple of years ago one particularly poorly researched book came out that claimed Amy had tried to take her own life at the age of ten. Apparently she had been with a friend (who un-surprisingly remains anonymous throughout the book) when she began clutching her stomach and foaming at the mouth and she told this 'friend' she'd overdosed on pills. Other than to sell copies, I'm not sure what kind of sick joke the author was trying to play, but any half-intelligent person would realize this story is complete fiction. A ten-year-old overdosing on pills and miraculously recovering does not happen without someone else knowing about it. Strangely, the 'friend' didn't call for help or run and tell an adult.

I'm angry at myself for even bringing this book up and giving it airtime, but I feel I have to set the record straight for Amy as she is not here to do so for herself. Amy was complicated, yes. She was troublesome, yes. And yes, she was set on a path which no one could have predicted would end as tragically as it did. But at ten, Amy was not suicidal.

In fact her notebooks demonstrate that she was in many ways an ordinary north London girl with an overactive imagination, mixed up in make-up and boys and trying to find her place in the world. Amy's love of poetry and stories and fun came through in her writing. Her spelling and grammar were superb, and I remember the months when she became preoccupied with writing haikus, a very short but complicated form of Japanese poetry. Her poems were all rather madcap but she'd spend ages up in her bedroom working on them, tinkering with the words. Here are two examples from 1995, 'Life' and 'Mad':

> Life as a punk
> Is going down the chippy
> 'Mellow out man,'
> Are the words of a hippy
> Life in love makes you feel great
> Life's crap if he likes you
> But he thinks you're just a mate.
> What are you on about,
> My friends all say.
> But they don't know tomorrow
> Like I did yesterday.

***

Some folks think they're strawberries
The apples disagree
To all sane people reading this
It's just insanity.
Tho' people gawp and people stare
At cats thinking they're dogs
The deranged folks just do not care
And the chickens think they're frogs.
Do you listen to a purple?
The answer is quite sad.
And to sum up the lives of these poor peeps
I use two words: quite mad.

It now brings me a lot of comfort to read these childhood poems. In the thick of raising her I became blind to Amy as a girl with creativity bursting out of her. Instead, all I saw was a naughty girl – a role Amy played up to because it was expected of her, a role that attracted her the most attention. When her career finally took off I watched helplessly as history repeated itself over and over. The more insecure Amy became, the more her behaviour turned destructive, and sadly it's that behaviour that the world had such an appetite for.

I don't recall Amy ever telling me that she wanted to be a star but my hairdresser in Barnet remembers Amy poking her head round the door if we were ever shopping there and announcing that she wanted to be famous. Seeing your name up in lights is a dream most kids have at some stage so I don't think anyone took Amy too seriously. In 1993 Amy and her friend Juliette had formed a rap act called Sweet 'n' Sour inspired by the American hip-hop duo Salt-N-Pepa. Amy still loved Michael Jackson, but she was also listening to a lot of US hip-hop, especially girl bands like TLC who were making their mark at the time. Sweet 'n' Sour gave no public performances and were short-lived but the pair practised their songs down to the very last detail. Amy was, of course, Sour, and for a period of time they insisted on everybody calling them by their newfound stage names. They even wrote notes to each other in character.

But if Amy didn't get attention through entertaining people, she was certainly starting to get it in other ways.

Just after her tenth birthday, I was in the lecture hall at university when I received a phone-call telling me that Amy had been arrested for shoplifting at the local Asda supermarket in Southgate. She was with a group of girls I wasn't keen on and I dare say they'd all egged each other on, but she'd been found in the make-up department stuffing lipsticks into her pocket and had been picked up by the store's security guards.

Amy should have been in school that afternoon, and when I arrived the police had been called. Amy was sitting in a dingy back room surrounded by TV monitors. Two uniformed officers were standing over her and her pockets had been turned out on the table in front of her. Believe me, I loved Amy with every bone in my body, but there were times when I could quite happily have throttled her.

As I was ushered into the room I took one look at her face. She was terrified. It was no longer me she had to answer to, it was a different kind of authority, and her cheeks were red and puffy from crying. She was given a stern talking to by one of the officers and received a formal warning, and it scared her in a way I hadn't seen before. I rarely called Mitchell if there was a problem with Amy because as far as I was concerned he was leading his own life, but I did call him on that occasion to step in and play the heavy. Cynthia went bananas too, and I hoped the whole incident would be a lesson to Amy. She'd been caught. Her actions suddenly had consequences way outside the family and it might, just might, calm her down.

If only Amy had been that straightforward.

4

We Three

As unhappy as Amy became at school, she persevered, and in her first year at secondary school at Ashmole Academy, 1994/95, her marks were surprisingly good: she gained As in English, Religious Studies and Drama, and Bs in Maths and Science. But I got the usual complaints about her, and if I ever discussed her behaviour with her she'd often say, 'Mum, I just want to sing.'

She'd continued with her Saturday mornings at Susi Earnshaw, and had been chosen to act in a play called *The Brutality of Fact* which ran for a season at the New End Theatre in Hampstead. As she was underage she couldn't appear for the whole performance so she was given the bit-part of Marlene, the daughter of a devout Jehovah's Witness. The play was set in Boston, and the role required Amy to mimic an American accent which she appeared to manage effortlessly, just like she had done for her primary school staging of *Grease*.

Amy also appeared at the London Coliseum in an English National Opera production of *Don Quixote* in the autumn and winter of 1994. Unfortunately I had to work on the Saturday of Amy's audition so I'd arranged for Richard to take her and drop her back. Having seen Amy perform, director Sir Jonathan Miller hired her immediately, and by sheer chance he ended up hiring Richard's son too, although he'd only come along as an onlooker. Given the show's Spanish theme Miller had needed children with a Mediterranean look and Amy and Michael were perfect candidates because of their dark hair and dark eyes. They were to run on stage in little yellow togas cheering and screaming, stand still on a ladder for the duration of one song, then run off. Although their appearance lasted no more than fifteen minutes it took days and days of rehearsal at the theatre in St Martin's Lane and Michael and Amy were given the best part of a term off school. Richard, Stephanie and I took it in turns to drop them each morning at Arnos Grove tube station where they were met by a chaperone and taken into central London.

Of course, Amy thought all her birthdays had come at once. Ashmole Academy needed a licence from the local council to take her out of lessons and that made her feel pretty special. She saw it as the first time her ability had been properly recognized by her teachers. Instead of her being the class problem, she was suddenly being paid £174 by a theatre company for her efforts – her first ever pay cheque.

I sat high up in the gods on the opening night and my heart swelled watching those two eleven-year-olds run on stage in front of well over two thousand people. Amy fidgeted, of course. In her head she wouldn't have been satisfied until she was out front taking the lead role, however improbable that was back then. But she was terrific, and I was slowly beginning to realize that the stage was where she truly felt at home.

I had exactly the same feeling when, at an end-of-term concert at Ashmole Academy the following year, she sang the Alanis Morissette song 'Ironic'. Mitchell had bought her the album *Jagged Little Pill* for Christmas and she must have learned it off by heart because that evening, as we sat in the assembly hall, the audience were completely taken aback. 'Whoa! *That* was really good!' I was thinking. Her powerful, guttural voice seemed to come from nowhere. I knew she could sing, but even I was unsure where or how that sound had been created. Amy, being Amy, barely reacted when friends and family, including Cynthia who was sitting with us, congratulated her on how brilliantly she'd performed that evening. 'Yeah, it was OK,' she shrugged nonchalantly.

I savour those moments now. They are pieces of happiness I hold on to because, although Amy was hard work at the best of times, I never stopped believing in her and I wanted more than anything for her to find a place in the world that made her feel fulfilled.

Amy's academic marks didn't get any better, unfortunately, and she spent hours of her secondary school career standing in corridors or sitting on a chair outside the headteacher's office. If Amy was ever in trouble, she'd sing. It calmed her in stressful moments and she used it as a coping mechanism, but I'm sure many of the teachers assumed she was being insolent. Looking at her notebooks, I'm not sure what work she actually got done. She had a proper schoolgirl crush on her long-haired guitar-playing science teacher. In fact, as I remember it, quite a few of her classmates' mums did too! It's probably just as well he didn't see the poems she wrote about him when she should have been concentrating on his lesson, like this one from 1996:

> I think my heart is just . . . there
> But it's doing things I cannot control.
> Ever since masterhead's leave
> The Monty Python rip off
> Took away my breath.
> It was a good sketch.
> All his idea. Probably.
> 'And I'm Billy Bones. You'll
> Find nowt girlie about me.'
> 'He's a real man,' I shouted.
> And he is.
> I go to sleep. He's in my mind.
> I wake up. He's still there.

It's something I've got to get over
Before I become (even more) obsessed.
Science is my favourite subject
But I have to sit at the back.
He's got angel eyes
And God's hair.
Maybe he is God.
I wouldn't be surprised.

As Amy's passion for performance continued to blossom, I graduated as a Bachelor of Pharmacy with third-class honours from the University of London. Amy was twelve when I began my one year of pre-registration training at a chemist's in Bush Hill Park near Enfield. My hours were long, and when I eventually completed the year I became a fully qualified locum pharmacist.

As a locum, my work dispensing drugs took me all around London but also to towns outside the M25 like Cheshunt and Potters Bar. One of my longest days was travelling north to Buntingford in Hertfordshire, which ended up being a good seventy-mile round trip. At first the job was daunting but, quietly and gradually, I began building a reputation for myself. It surprised me because suddenly I had a real sense of purpose at work.

Being self-employed, I could choose my own hours. My salary took a leap because I was now in a senior position, and working from pharmacy to pharmacy gave me both responsibility and independence. But there was always a part of me that felt torn between the time I spent at work and the time I spent at home. Regrettably it's a common feeling among working mothers. I felt guilty that I couldn't always be there when the children came back from school or that I wasn't always there throughout the holidays. I tried to create as much family time as possible – I have a memory of nights spent playing the word game Boggle with Amy, which she loved – but I'd often spend evenings in the kitchen cooking large pots of stew or sauces, dividing it into portions and putting them in the freezer so that the children could eat whenever they came home from school if I wouldn't be back in time to have their dinner ready.

We all had to be up and out of the house early, and getting Amy to school on weekday mornings continued to be a daily assault course. I'd stand in our downstairs hallway and shout, 'Amy! Amy! Come on, Amy, *get up*!' When that didn't work I'd climb the stairs and open the door of her room where she'd be lying in bed with the covers up to her neck and her eyes tight shut. 'Come on, lady, time for school,' I'd repeat. Sometimes I'd have to pull the covers off her and drag her out, and after much protesting about how she was too tired and that she didn't want to go she'd get up and reluctantly throw on her white shirt and navy-blue pullover. I'd be surprised if Amy ever made it to school on time. She could sleep for England. It's not unusual for teenagers to sleep for England, I know, but I believe Amy experienced depressions in her early teens. Unfortunately, she worked equally hard to conceal her low moods from the people closest to her, including me.

Once Amy was in the spotlight she talked openly about her history of depression and her habit of self-harming which was especially distressing for me. By then she was being photographed regularly with a lattice of scars on her arms – her private weaknesses, exposed to the world. She claimed in several interviews that she'd first cut herself when she was nine, as more of an experiment than anything else.

Self-harm is such a secret way of dealing with distress or negative emotion – one which sadly many young girls are drawn to – that it is impossible for me to know when it became an ingrained part of Amy's life. At home I didn't see any tell-tale signs, and I'd like to think I would have noticed. Realistically, though, that doesn't mean it didn't happen. What I did witness were the times when Amy's unhappiness gave way to anger and frustration, and it was then that she changed from an ordinary angst-ridden teenager into someone whose behaviour had an uncontrollable edge to it.

Richard has a clear memory of Amy at his son Michael's Bar Mitzvah. Amy was taller than most of the boys and girls who came that afternoon to the party and she was awkward-looking, dressed in a long black skirt and a chunky pair of Dr Marten boots. Beforehand we'd been guests at Michael's traditional ceremony and we'd followed on to the Apollo function room, near Cockfosters, where around fifty people packed into the hall. Bar Mitzvahs are a big deal, and the room was filled with round tables all set out with food. There was music and dancing and a chance for everyone to con-gratulate Michael on his coming of age.

Jewish parties are always boisterous family affairs, and while I had no qualms whatsoever about turning up to those kinds of events as a single mum, I was conscious of the fact that such occasions might heighten Amy's sense of her own family being fragmented. That day all the other children were accompanied by their mums and dads, and she had only me. As a thirteen-year-old trying to forge an identity, she struggled with that. My brother Brian came with his wife Jann and there were some family friends, but not people who had any influence over Amy, who was as usual hanging off my arm. For other parts of the evening she was noticeably alone, sulking in a corner with a face like thunder, just like she had always done at parties.

Bar Mitzvahs are definitely a 'boy thing' and I remember the boys huddling in a tight group dancing together arm in arm. Amy kept trying to muscle in on their fun and ended up making a complete nuisance of herself, which of course provoked a familiar reaction. Other children seemed to develop a pack mentality around Amy, probably because it was the easiest way to force her back. Unable to command the attention she wanted, she stormed out of the hall and smashed her boot through the outer glass doors of the venue. Few people actually saw it happen although there was a bit of a kerfuffle outside while the celebrations continued inside.

By the time I got to hear about what Amy had done, she was back in the hall and on my sister-in-law's lap, her head buried into Jann's chest, sobbing. Brian told me afterwards how he had watched Amy lift her head several times and scan the room to see who was watching, and when she realized no one was taking any notice she'd bury her head into Jann's chest again and sob even louder. Needless to say, Richard was presented with a hefty bill by the manager the next day for the damage done to the door.

Furious does not even come close to how I felt that evening. It was so unfair of her to hijack Michael's big moment and turn it into her show. But I also felt an overwhelming sense of powerlessness. Every time Amy stepped out of line I was unable to present the united front that two parents can, and there was no doubt she took advantage of that. 'Mum, you're not tough enough. I know that if I really want to do something I can do it,' I recall her saying to me one day, and – it gives me no pleasure to say it – she was right. The truth is, I was finding it a struggle to keep every ball I was trying to juggle in the air.

I don't know how much the onset of MS played a part. I can't say it was something I was aware of at the time because, other than feeling tired, no recognizable symptoms had surfaced in the years after Amy was born. Although she could run rings round most adults, she saw something in me that I couldn't necessarily see in myself. When I opened her diary after her passing I was surprised to find a diagram she'd drawn in July 1995 which she'd called the 'Mind Map of My Life'. Underneath the heading 'Family' she'd written 'My mum. Getting more tired recently. Working too hard.' She'd made the same observation about me in a series of drawings she'd called 'Places in my Heart', where she also admitted to missing her dad.

During term time I was fortunate to have a strong support network which included other mums, my auntie Mary, who also lived nearby, and Cynthia. Amy would occasionally go on school trips during the summer break and I also always tried to take the children away each year, either abroad or to my sister Debra's in Newcastle.

One year I accompanied Alex on an organized school skiing trip to Italy that parents could participate in. I could have taken Amy too but I decided against it for fear of her ricocheting across the slopes on the Dolomite Mountains and breaking more bones. Leaving her behind felt so cruel, and she wasn't best pleased, but she was such a liability that the idea of spending weeks in a foreign hospital filled me with horror. Instead, I took her to Paris when she was thirteen with my American cousin Bonnie and her son Jay. We walked for miles around the Eiffel Tower, along the River Seine to Notre Dame Cathedral and up the beautiful stone staircase to the Sacré-Coeur in Montmartre. I can picture her now bombing up the stairs to our hotel room, tearing open the sash window and leaning right out over the sill, bellowing down to a man selling baguettes on the street, 'I'd love one of those, they look great. Can you bring one up?'

In the last year she spent at Ashmole she went away on her own on an adventure holiday, which she also thoroughly enjoyed. It was a summer break I'd arranged with PGL holidays at a camp near Hathersage in the Peak District, and the letter she wrote home to me was in typical Amy fashion. (Incidentally, Katie the cat wasn't dead, but you can't fault Amy for her love of a good drama.)

28 July 1996

Dear Mummy,

I arrived safely and I'm missing you already. I am writing on my flip flop so it's a bit messy, but I'll try my best.

I've made a new friend. Her name is Catherine. She is 15. She likes my purple lipstick. She says hi!

I know that Katie is dead. You can tell and I sense it anyway. My love of the Beatles is keeping me sane, and I've worked out my favourite songs which are, It's Only Love, I've Seen A Face, and that one that goes 'For Tomorrow May Rain but I'll follow the Sun'. I like those songs they're really good.

How is Sylvia, Lennon and McCartney? Make sure the cat stays away. Has she been on my bed much?

Today we are doing pioneering and archery, 2 things I am quite experienced in. Annoy Ally poos [Alex] for me and hug the cat a lot for me. You can hug yourself from me too if you want.
Tomorrow we are doing horse-riding and shopping in the village.
    If Jules [Juliette] rings tell her I'm on holiday (she won't ring cos she's in Corfu).
    I miss you loads mummy,
    Amy x

Alex had turned sixteen, and like most teenage boys he didn't want to hang around with his younger sister. He had his own group of friends. Alex and Amy bickered, as most siblings do, but they remained close. He didn't take kindly to Amy entering his room, though. It was strictly forbidden, and she was most definitely banned from playing his red Stratocaster guitar which Mitchell had bought him as a present. If he was out, though, she used to sneak in and strum a few chords and keep her fingers crossed he wouldn't notice. Once Alex had gone to university Amy also dived into his CD collection, which he left behind. Alex was always more into rock music but she would pick out Thelonious Monk and Miles Davis from his collection and play them on his three-disc CD player.
    It was becoming increasingly obvious to me that Amy would never follow her brother to university. In fact her interest in school was all but non-existent – at this rate she'd be lucky if she passed a single GCSE. For months I had been scrabbling around, trying to find a solution, when a colleague at one of the pharmacies I was working at told me about an advert in *The Stage* magazine calling for entries for a scholarship at the Sylvia Young Theatre School in Marylebone. So I brought a copy home.
    I put it under Amy's nose to see what she thought. I wasn't pushy about it – I am not a pushy person. In fact Amy and I always had a bit of a joke together. I'd say, 'What do you call a mother who's not a pushy Jewish mother?' and she'd say, 'Mummy, that's you!' Instead I talked it through with her. If she got in it would be a big move for

her. Instead of walking the short distance to Ashmole each morning she'd have to travel thirteen miles into central London by bus. Perhaps she wouldn't see Juliette so much, or her other friends Lauren Gilbert and Lauren Franklin. None of this seemed to bother Amy and, happily, she jumped at the chance. It was a real relief for me because I could see that secondary school was never going to hold Amy's attention.

I helped her with the main application form, but she also needed to send off a written assessment to be completed in her own words which she worked on in her room by herself. Amy was certainly a girl who wore her heart on her sleeve:

> I would say that my school life and school reports are filled with 'could do betters' and 'doesn't work to her full potential'. This is because my present school is a horrible place to go to every day. But I guess all schools are. I want to go to somewhere where I am stretched right to my limits and beyond. To sing in lessons without being told to shut up (provided they <u>are</u> singing lessons). But mostly I have this dream to be very famous, to work on stage. It's a lifelong ambition. I want people to hear my voice and just forget their troubles for five minutes. I want to be remembered for being an actress, a singer for sell-out West-End and sell-out Broadway shows. For being . . . just me.

I've read those words a thousand times; they still make me smile and ache at the same time. To remember her as this kid with so many hopes and dreams is too bittersweet for me to dwell on for long.

I accompanied Amy to the audition where she sang 'On The Sunny Side Of The Street'. She needed no words and no music. Everything she did was from memory, and she delivered the song with such amazing feeling. Sylvia Young has since said publicly that when she saw Amy and heard her voice that day she imagined the next Judy Garland. I have to admit I was a bit more low-key. It wasn't that Amy was wrong for the scholarship, it's that by then she was so starry-eyed about succeeding I was worrying about how she might cope with a rejection. Lots of young girls want to sing. Lots of girls *can* sing and yearn to be famous, but less than a handful ever make it. I encouraged Amy in every way possible, but I also tried to keep her feet on the ground and be realistic about her chances. I knew I'd be the one who would have to pick up the pieces should that dream ever come crashing down.

Fortunately, that year scholarships were handed to four students and Amy received a part-scholarship which meant that half of her term fees were paid through a bursary and half by us. She left Ashmole in the summer of 1996 and began the new term at Sylvia Young's in September. At last, both she and I had a focus. Dropping her off or picking her up from auditions suddenly had more purpose. No longer was Amy banging around in a system that didn't accommodate her – and, God willing, I wouldn't ever have to be banging around again either, trying to find a place that engaged her. She was doing what she wanted to do. Soon after she started at Sylvia's she was placed one year ahead of her age group in her performance classes because, although the teachers could see that she was easily distracted, they also saw that she was a very bright and talented girl.

Amy always looked back on her time at Sylvia Young's as the happiest of her life. She made friends there, in particular Tyler James, who even then was a sweet and vulnerable kid about whom she talked incessantly when she came home. They seemed to understand each other straight away, and although Tyler was never one of Amy's boyfriends, they were what you'd call soul-mates. She loved the performance part of the course which included ballet and tap, acting and singing. She was signed to the Young 'Uns Agency (now the Sylvia Young Agency) as soon as she started and bagged a part as an extra in the BBC2 series *The Fast Show* where she played a fairy in a 'Competitive Dad' sketch. It was her TV debut and very exciting for us.

Unfortunately the academic side of things continued to bore her to tears, and it wasn't long before she started to lose her sense of direction. The smarter teachers realized what Amy was about and tried to work with her idiosyncrasies and her need to express herself, but she often turned up with her uniform all over the place. She'd chew gum in class. She'd wear her silver hooped earrings to school which was a big no-no; she'd take them out if she was told off, but she'd put them back in ten minutes later. She'd sit in class writing notes, or gossiping about boys, or scribbling lyrics. She even pierced her lip at the back of the class.

Disappointingly, by the spring term of 1998 her report was treading a familiar path: 'Amy should have a good performance career ahead of her, but her clear inability to concentrate and focus in vocational classes may result in her not benefiting from training.' Funnily enough, that same year she also won a certificate of merit for her creative writing.

Amy's acting-up at Sylvia Young's was about to reach crisis point. Katie, our cat, was quite old and ill then and had virtually got to the point of organ failure. One day I took time off work to drop Katie at the vet's, and I was left with the heartbreaking decision of whether or not I'd have to put her down. As I left the surgery fretting over that dilemma, Amy's teacher at Sylvia Young's, rang me and asked if I would come into school that afternoon to talk about Amy.

I rearranged my work schedule and drove in. It ended up being a short meeting and her teacher laid everything out quite plainly. Amy wasn't doing what she was supposed to be doing, he said. She was set to fail her GCSEs and I should consider sending her somewhere else. Although I should have known it was coming, I left his office in a complete panic, jumped into the car and headed straight back to the vet's. 'Should I have the cat put down or Amy put down?' I asked myself. I'd had about as much as I could take from her. Sylvia Young's had been her golden opportunity and she'd blown it. Having said that, I was also unimpressed with her teacher. I'd got the distinct feeling that he was only interested in his reputation and wanted Amy out because her predicted marks would reflect badly on him.

I spent the May and June of that year looking around for another school, and eventually settled on The Mount School, an independent for girls in Mill Hill. An all-girl environment would benefit Amy at this crucial stage in her education, I felt, and Mitchell agreed to put up the money to send her there. But no sooner had I secured her a place than Sylvia Young herself rang me.

'Janis, why are you taking Amy out of school?' she said. 'You don't have to take her out.' She then explained that she really hadn't wanted Amy to go.

I understand Amy's teacher left Sylvia Young's shortly afterwards. But, in my mind, the damage had been done. I didn't see a way back for Amy and I was growing more and more anxious she'd throw her education away. Sylvia always remained in touch, though, and to this day she talks very fondly of Amy and has described on many occasions the potential she saw in her early on. One year after Amy's passing the school joined with the Amy Winehouse Foundation to offer an annual scholarship to other children just like her.

That summer we were all desperate for a break, and it so happened that there was an opportunity to travel to the States. My cousin Joan lived in Boca Raton, an hour north of Miami, and we'd received an invitation to her twin boys' Bar Mitzvahs. My dad came with us and we arrived a few days early to spend time with the family and soak up the Miami sunshine.

I'd first taken Amy to Miami shortly after my separation from Mitchell. It was the place to which I always returned to find peace of mind and recharge my batteries. Alex had come along too on that occasion and Joan remembers Amy as a chubby, stubborn child with brown curly hair, stuck to my lap shouting 'Mummy, I love you!' at every opportunity. She took to Joan's pool like a fish: she'd swim for hours in the fifty-degree Florida winter. We spent a couple of long weekends at Disney World where she was happy and free, and no sooner had we returned from the Magic Kingdom than she and her cousins Eric and Ryan would jump into the heated pool and splash around late into the night.

On the 1998 trip, Joan met us at the airport and when we arrived at our hotel the bellboy wheeled Amy into the lobby: perched on a rolling luggage cart, she sat lost in her own world with a guitar on her lap. Amy spent much of that holiday either practising the chords of Alanis Morissette songs or jotting down her own compositions in her notebooks to the point where the constant noise started to annoy some of her older cousins.

Later that week, the twins' Bar Mitzvah was held on the beach at the Hillsboro Club, a private resort on the most beautiful peninsula overlooking the Atlantic Ocean. Our large party commandeered the stretch of soft white sand and I remember sitting back with my dad and watching the luxury yachts glide past on the horizon. There was the usual food and dancing, and as the tropical breeze began to drop in the late afternoon, all the children gathered round in a circle and played music together.

Amy's cousin Jay had brought with him his acoustic guitar, and whenever we looked over, Amy was sat in the middle of the circle holding court or quietly scribbling away. That evening, against the backdrop of the ocean and a pale pink sunset, she and Jay strummed and sang Jewish spiritual songs during a service to mark the close of the Sabbath. It was very moving, and we all sat in silence to listen. It took me right back to when Amy sang hymns to celebrate the festival of Hanukkah – the Jewish Festival of Lights which happens in November and December. There was one hymn called 'Ma'oz Tzur' that was one of Amy's favourites and she'd repeat it over and over until she got the words right. Now, though, she could sing with the guitar. She could play five chords, she told Alex in a postcard home.

One or two other surprises emerged from the trip to Miami that year – not that I knew about any of them at the time. One incident Joan kept close to her chest for many years was that she'd mistakenly picked up Amy's cosmetics bag and alongside the numerous eyeliners and lipsticks she'd started carrying around with her, several condoms fell out. Amy bolted over and begged Joan to keep this a secret. 'Please, please, do not under any circumstances let my mum know,' she pleaded, and Joan did keep her word. She never did tell me that story until we chatted in London in the days following Amy's funeral.

By the time Amy reached The Mount, so far as education was concerned she had switched off. With its mock Tudor frontage and leafy surroundings it was a far cry from the schools Amy had been used to. 'Stuck up', she called it. Her dark brown skirt and brown jumper uniform was abhorrent to her and she frequently commented that all the other girls 'looked like little shits' walking round in theirs. She felt utterly detached but, under pressure to find somewhere at short notice, I'd been left with little option but to send her. I just prayed she'd get through her GCSEs, then maybe we could think about the next hurdle to leap. And there was going to be another hurdle – that I was sure of.

More worryingly for me, all the enthusiasm she'd had for performing seemed to drain from her too, which was completely unlike Amy. However much she'd mucked up her time at Sylvia Young's her acting and singing classes were the one thing she'd hooked in to, but at The Mount she even turned her back on the school concert. In rehearsals, her music teacher had stopped the class to direct Amy on singing in the correct way.

'If you don't do it in the right key you won't be doing it,' he had told her.

'I'm not doing it then,' she shouted, and stormed off.

In the run-up to parents' evening that term she must have anticipated she'd be in trouble because each of her classmates had written a note home to me which Amy delivered in a handmade envelope.

Amy's mad but you have to love her. Katie.

Thanks for sending Amy to The Mount because she has made it a much more musical place. Hannah.

Amy's a fantastic singer and she's gonna take care of you in her old age. Try not to kill her after parents evening tonight. Romina.

I'm glad to say Amy has not fallen asleep in class or loud-mouthed the teacher. Be proud of her because she has the most beautiful voice-box. Serena.

The first message I took from the envelope was from Amy.

To mum, I love you so much. I don't have any work to do, so honestly I'm not wasting time. You're a good mum. Amy.

Of course, that meant Amy did have work to do and wasting time was exactly what she was doing. I was getting reports back that she'd started to play truant, too. I found myself in no-man's land with no clue where to turn next.

As a mum you never stop worrying about your kids, but I had spent years either saving Amy from disaster or diverting her with the hope that she'd grab an opportunity and run with it, but nothing had seemed to work. However much time and energy I ploughed into her, Amy wanted more; whatever I gave, it never seemed to be enough. Of course, my mother's instinct was to carry on rescuing Amy no matter what. Isn't that what love is? In years to come my notion of what love is would be tested way beyond that of most parents. In those days, though, I willed myself not to lose faith in her, nor in myself in the process, but I had to accept there was no rulebook made for Amy.

I know Amy played on Cynthia's mind too. Cynthia held regular séances in the living room of her flat in Southgate. It sounds peculiar now, but at the time it was popular with lots of people. Every Tuesday she'd invite a group of regulars round and she'd either get her Tarot cards out or attempt to communicate with the spirit world. I went every now and then, just for the hell of it I suppose. I'm a big believer in fate but I'm undecided about everything else, although I'm a very open-minded person and my curiosity always gets the better of me. Richard always teases me about being involved in that kind of mumbo-jumbo but Cynthia's séances fascinated me. Once everyone was gathered in a circle she'd dim the lights and we'd all talk until she received a message. She told me once she'd had a message back when Amy was around four or five years old. 'Someone always needs to look out for Amy,' the voice from the other side had told her. Over the years, she claimed to have had several messages about Amy and how she needed to be 'looked after'. The voices inside my head were a little more down-to-earth, but I had certainly realized that, just like the spirit world, Amy resonated at a different frequency.

5

Take The Box

In that autumn of 1998, when Amy moved to The Mount, another change in our lives was afoot. I had been dating other men and I'd made a firm decision that I wanted to be in a relationship again. My friend Phil's sister Hilary was also single and we often teamed up together to go out to Jewish singles nights. We had such a giggle at times and I can safely say there were definitely men there who needed warning signs attached to them, but there were also others I wanted to get to know better.

There was one get-together when I got talking to a man called Tony who I'd known from years back but hadn't seen for a while. Tragically, Tony's first wife had died of cancer and he was bringing up his son and daughter single-handedly. We ended up going out together for a few meals and we found that we actually got along. It's pretty nerve-racking when you're recently divorced with two children and about to take the plunge into a new relationship, but Tony had shown me that he was serious and I felt confident enough to consider us long-term.

It's clear to me now that I had chosen someone who was the opposite to Mitchell. Tony was calm and cautious, a quietly considerate man. The only problem was that he lived in Leigh-on-Sea in Essex, on the north bank of the Thames Estuary. It seemed like the back of beyond for a Londoner like me. We discussed the possibility of my family moving but, while Leigh-on-Sea is a very quaint and picturesque town, I was afraid I might die of boredom there. I couldn't imagine uprooting Amy either. Alex, too, had started at Canterbury University but hadn't settled in too well and was spending most weekends back at home.

Amy was not going anywhere, she said. End of story. She was discovering the city and could already find her way round the tube as if she were a commuter. With its open-air markets and thriving music scene she'd made a beeline for Camden while she was still at Sylvia Young's, and she was spending more and more time there, with or without me knowing. More importantly, the majority of her friends were in London.

Tony's son Robert was Alex's age and his daughter Caroline was the same age as Amy but they couldn't have been more different as teenagers. Caroline excelled at Jewish Girls Brigade; Amy had managed no more than a week or two as a senior before the girls there turned bitchy on her and she refused to go back. Caroline was conscientious at school; Amy couldn't give a damn. But Tony's kids wanted to be in London too so he sold up in Essex and we all moved in together.

Tony found a house in Guildown Avenue in North Finchley, a four-bedroom townhouse not far from where Amy and I had been living in Greenside Close. Alex and Robert took the upper two rooms while Caroline, Tony and I took the middle-floor rooms. Because there was no bedroom for Amy we had the garage converted. While Amy was happy about having her own space, it quickly became obvious that neither she nor Alex wanted to be there at all. They found the transition difficult because we just weren't the same family any more.

As a new couple Tony and I remained hopeful that things would settle down and work out, and we both put a lot of effort into the relationship, but somehow the arrangement never seemed to fit. As the months wore on we naturally drifted into two distinctly separate families living under one roof. The layout of the house didn't work that well either. The living room was on our floor, which meant that Amy was disconnected downstairs and tended to retreat to her room.

Tony and his family were more Orthodox than we were. They attended synagogue and cooked kosher food. I observed festive days and holidays and had taken the children to the synagogue when they were younger but we weren't strict religious people. Tony and his kids sat together at mealtimes, which we rarely did, and he always talked fondly of the family holidays they had been on when his wife was still alive. My experience of family life had been the polar opposite. Even during my marriage to Mitchell we hadn't done much as a family, and although the kids had Cynthia and others dropping in and out, there was little continuity to their lives, which only became more fragmented when we separated. To Amy, 'family' had become more of a romantic idea than something immediate or tangible. It was me, Alex and her now, and she was fiercely protective of that unit. But my feeling was that by then she'd lost faith in family life completely, if she ever really knew what it was. More and more of her time was spent out with friends, and when she was at home she was obstinate and hard work.

Amy and Tony never saw eye to eye. She found him boring and she overpowered him, and he realized early on he could never be a father figure to her. Instead, he purposely took a step back and left her to it, and I did the same with his children. Managing your way round a step-family can be like tiptoeing across a minefield at times, and when I think about it now, those two years spiralled into an unhappy time for Amy, who could barely find her place in the world, let alone at home.

While the rest of the house was neat and neutral, Amy painted her bedroom bright blue. Admittedly it was an improvement on the black she'd used on her walls in Greenside Close (she'd lost interest halfway through that redecoration job and it remained unfinished, with her bunk bed pulled in front to cover the mess). But she was always good at drawing and, like me, she loved Japanese art. On her bedroom wall in Guildown Avenue she recreated Katsushika Hokusai's *The Great Wave* from a book of paintings I had. It looked amazing, but completely incongruous with the rest of the house.

Strangely, Amy's room felt the most comfortable in that house. If ever I had a friend over and Amy wasn't there we'd often gravitate towards it and sit among her mess for a good gossip. 'Mummy, have you been in my room again?' she'd tick me off. But it was a fair swap, I thought, because normally it was me chasing Amy for the clothes she'd 'borrowed' from my wardrobe.

Around this time I noticed another change in Amy. She was wilder, but I couldn't always work out in what way. I wasn't thrilled about the crowd she was mixing with, and when we lived at Greenside Close I'd caught her smoking in the back garden on a couple of occasions. After some straight talking she'd hugged me and said, 'Sorry, Mummy, it won't happen again, Mummy,' but I knew Amy well enough to know she'd carry on if she wanted to.

We'd never had a lot of alcohol in the house, even when Mitchell and I were together. Mitchell hardly drinks at all, and while I'll say yes to a glass of wine now and again it's never been a habitual part of my life. I was realistic enough to know that Amy let her hair down with her friends – don't all kids? – and I never noticed any alcohol missing from the house or saw any evidence that she was holding parties while I was at work. And I never, ever saw her drunk. If she ever was, she did a good job of hiding it.

There were cans of lager going around at some of her friends' sleepovers, that I do know: she wrote in her diary at the age of twelve in one of her 'party reviews' that she 'drank loads but wasn't pissed'. I dare say there may have been some exotic cigarettes being passed around there too, but I could never be sure. I've since asked friends of Amy's what they think 'drinking loads' meant. Was Amy so adept at leading a double life that I was utterly clueless about what was going on under my nose? I still don't really know the answer to that question. In many ways Amy was ahead of the game, but according to her friends she was describing no more than a few cans of beer in a room of dishevelled-looking teenagers.

As a working single parent it was impossible to organize my time well enough to police Amy. Even if I had, the chances are she would have rebelled even more. But that didn't ever stop me worrying about her. Up to this point she'd coped with the upheavals in her life and I hoped and prayed that all this was a phase she'd eventually get through. But at Cynthia's husband Larry's fiftieth birthday party, when Amy would have been fifteen, the alarm bells started to ring.

On that occasion we all descended on a club called Charlie Brown's in Wood Green. There was the usual buffet and band and an unlimited supply of alcohol at the bar. Cynthia had asked Amy if she would sing that evening. One of Larry's favourite songs was 'A Song For You' which was written by Leon Russell but made famous by the likes of Andy Williams and Donny Hathaway; it was even recorded by Amy herself years later. That evening I watched as she was handed a drink, but I also noticed that her glass was never empty. She kept returning to the bar, having it refilled with Southern Comfort and lemonade, and knocking it back. Cynthia was beside me, standing on the periphery of the crowd, glaring at her all-knowingly. 'She's an alcoholic,' she said to me under her breath.

Cynthia was overdoing it a bit, I thought. Amy wasn't visibly drunk, but she did seem different. Even Alex, who was very protective of Amy, whispered in her ear a couple of times that she should stop, but she ignored him. Mindful of what Cynthia had said, I took Amy aside too.

'OK, Amy, that's enough,' I said to her.

'OK, Mummy,' she responded, brushing my hand away dismissively as if to say, 'You can say what you want but I'm doing it anyway.' As if alcohol was the only thing that could get her up to perform.

There was something unsteady about her, but I couldn't decide whether this was a headstrong young girl letting her hair down a bit too much at a family function, or a girl drinking with purpose. She sang brilliantly, but I came away with an uneasy feeling in the pit of my stomach.

In the summer of 1999, Amy's GCSE results came through. I was disappointed with them, but I can't say that I was surprised: she scraped five of them – a B in English, Cs in English Literature, Science and Maths and, irony of all ironies, a D in Music. By that stage she was so disillusioned with formal education that she wanted out completely. She was finished with The Mount, but also, like every place she'd been before, The Mount was finished with Amy. There was no question of her staying on for A levels. Knowing what I had been like at school I didn't try to force the issue, though of course I would have liked it if she'd got a proper education under her belt.

After much indecision over what to do next, she applied to the BRIT School in Croydon, south London, because a friend of hers, Tamsin, whom she'd kept in touch with since Sylvia Young days, had a place there. I'm not even sure Amy lasted a term. She was motivated enough to make the four-hour journey there and back each day but she'd enrolled in classes in musical theatre and she quickly realized that wasn't for her. Her eager childhood dream of being an actress in 'sell-out West-End and sell-out Broadway shows' had been lost somewhere along the line, usurped by a wild child who said 'up your jacksie' to all of it. In Amy's eyes, musical theatre was all about playing the game – about having a good voice, having a good performing arts background and getting up on stage and repeating the same show night after night. She saw no originality in it. For her it felt like a safe option, and in retrospect, Amy was too 'out there' even then to fit neatly into that box.

Amy had been working on and off in a tattoo and piercing parlour in Camden and at Rokit, a market stall that sold vintage shoes and clothes. After she finished at the BRIT School she combined that with trying to pursue her musical interests, but I desperately wanted her to stick at just one thing.

Amy was still on Sylvia Young's agency books in 2000 and, having kept in mind her talent rather than her behaviour, Sylvia recommended that Amy meet Bill Ashton, who was the founder of the National Youth Jazz Orchestra. The orchestra didn't hold auditions. Instead Amy was to turn up at rehearsals at the Cockpit Theatre near Sylvia Young's school and if she wanted to join in, she could. According to Bill, Amy's first words to him were, 'Hello, I'm Amy Winehouse – that's a Jewish name.' That story has always made me laugh. It could be me all those years ago pitching up in Miami and asking for work. It's frightening when you see yourself in your child and think, 'Hello Amy, I know exactly where that personality trait has come from!'

The NYJO singing coach Annabel Williams recalls Amy as an awkward sixteen-year-old sat in a corner chain-smoking for much of the first session. She didn't sing at all on that occasion but she kept turning up and observing the other musicians, and when eventually she did step forward to the microphone for one of the big band numbers, she nailed it in one.

A month later, Bill and the NYJO were due to perform at the Rayner's Hotel in west London when Bill's singer dropped out at the last minute. He rang the house early one Sunday morning and asked if Amy would step in. I've never seen her get out of bed and get dressed so quickly. She didn't know the songs. 'I'll learn them on the tube,' she told him, and she did. She sat with her Discman on the Northern Line from Woodside Park learning the repertoire and performed four songs without a leadsheet or words. Knocking around somewhere is a live recording of her with the NYJO from July 2000 that I'd love to hear.

Despite being bold and up front about everything else, Amy was in fact incredibly secretive about her music. She always had her notebooks around which she scribbled in but she would never say, 'Mum, do you want to hear this?' or 'Look what I've been doing.'

Even when she recorded her first album *Frank*, I had not heard a single recording until she handed me a sample tape in the months before its release. Music was Amy's passion but she also saw it as her work. Although to outsiders her attitude seemed devil-may-care, she was actually very driven to achieve what she wanted to achieve. She just wanted to do everything her way.

Amy started doing some gigs in local pubs with her friend Juliette and she'd kept in touch with Tyler James, who had recently signed to the management company Brilliant! I remembered seeing Tyler and Amy in a production at Sylvia Young's. Tyler's voice hadn't broken then and although he had a good sound he was only developing. Now he was starting to make his way in the industry.

Brilliant! soon became Brilliant 19 when it was taken over by 19 Management Ltd, a company founded by Simon Fuller who was responsible for the Spice Girls' success. Not that this meant much to Amy at all. She had her own spin on Girl Power which centred on her heroines like Sarah Vaughan and Dinah Washington, and she leaned more towards American hip-hop rather than British pop or the manufactured girl groups that were emerging at the time.

Brilliant 19 was headed by Nick Godwyn, who was also managing the artist Billie Piper, who had been in Amy's year at Sylvia Young's and later starred in *Dr Who*. Alongside him was fledgling A&R man Nick Shymansky who was just nineteen years old and seemed to gel with Amy immediately. Whereas Nick Godwyn was strictly about business, Nick Shymansky came across as a very sweet guy who, as well as recognizing her talent, genuinely liked Amy as a friend. We're still in touch; he's a real darling. Last year he helped us celebrate Amy's thirtieth birthday with an event at the Proud Galleries in Camden commemorating ten years since the release of *Frank*.

Amy's first meeting with Nick Shymansky was as off-beat as Amy herself. With Tyler already on the books, he was talent-spotting for Brilliant 19, set on lengthening his roster. Apparently he and Tyler had been sifting through old Motown records one evening when they had an idea to put together a duo – Tyler and a female voice. Tyler started raving about Amy whom he hadn't seen for a while, and she must have accompanied him to the studio after that because two weeks later Nick got a package through the post. Sealed in a bright yellow jiffy bag covered in smiley hearts and glittery stickers and with the word 'Amy' written all over it was a demo tape. Nick put it on in his car and immediately thought Tyler was playing a practical joke. Perhaps he'd put some authentic recordings from the fifties on a tape? No, it was Amy.

The next challenge was pinning her down. After a few abortive attempts at meeting, Amy eventually turned up at Turnham Green tube station in west London near where Nick was working at the time. He's described her since as 'nervous' – nervous about getting into something that wasn't right for her and nervous because, although she was a natural singer, she had no idea what the music industry was all about. None of us did. Apparently she spent much of the time they were together that day quoting Sigmund Freud and mocking Nick because he had no idea who Freud was. Surprisingly, she didn't let on that she wrote her own lyrics, preferring to wait until she trusted him.

A few weeks later she invited him to hear her sing at the NYJO Sunday morning rehearsals. When he walked in Amy was there, smoking Marlboro Reds – strong cigarettes – and she was this tiny figure in front of this huge orchestra. 'Amy's voice was by far the biggest instrument,' Nick has remarked since. She carried the room. If ever Bill Ashton rang me to get hold of Amy he'd always say, 'Mrs Winehouse, Amy has a fantastic voice.' Yes, I thought, but she smokes far too much!

Nick Shymansky passed Amy's tape to Nick Godwyn. On it she'd recorded a song, written by her, called 'Oestrogenus' – a six-minute poem with bad guitar playing but a voice that immediately gave him goosebumps. When they invited her along for a chat she waltzed in with her baby guitar, broke a string and then refused to play for them. Luckily they asked her back, and she did sing this time. But when they asked her what she wanted to do with her life, she replied, 'I don't know really – sing a bit. Be a roller-skating waitress?' Oh, Amy.

It wasn't until the early summer of 2001 that Brilliant 19 and Amy came together formally. Mitchell was becoming more involved in Amy's life, and he remembers Nick Godwyn taking myself and him out for a meal to discuss Amy's future. I have no recollection of that, but I do remember being invited to Brilliant 19's offices, which were next to Battersea Park on the south side of the River Thames. There we were introduced to both Nicks and they talked about the potential they saw in Amy and the prospect of signing her. Mitchell and I had no idea then what that really entailed. There was no record deal on the table, just the potential for a management deal.

Amy was underage, only seventeen, and if I'm truthful, my mind was full of questions. Where would this take her in her career? Did she really have a hope of making it in an industry that was notoriously hard to break into? And then there was Amy herself. The bottom line was that I still saw Amy as a little girl. *My* little girl. I knew she had the talent and the drive, but I also knew she lacked the emotional maturity to take such a big step. She was wise beyond her years in some ways, and that comes through in all of her lyrics, but she never seemed able to apply that wisdom to herself. Furthermore, I'd lived through the recklessness with which she'd approached her last years in education, and I was worried that if something was demanded of her that she wasn't happy with she'd react badly and throw it all away in a self-destructive fit of pique.

Brilliant 19 convinced us that they had her musical and business interests at heart, but I still had reservations about whether Amy would get the personal nurturing she needed. Afterwards, Mitchell and I discussed the proposal and both of us felt that Amy needed more education, more time to find her feet before she signed anything. It wasn't a case of us seeing Amy as a star and pushing her towards a deal – far from it. Mitchell and I were required as second signatories, but it was Amy who insisted that was the only path she wanted to follow. Amy couldn't have cared less about the business side of things or even selling records. She simply wanted to write songs and to sing and be recognized as a musician above everything else. This was what she saw as her ticket to success.

The following few months were spent negotiating Amy's contract, which was finally signed with Brilliant 19 in June 2001. The deal was to last four years during which time the company would look after all her activities in the entertainment industry including not only her music but any television, radio or personal appearances she might make, with Brilliant 19 taking a standard 20 per cent cut.

Over a period of four months from October 2001 she received £6,000 in advances which was paid out in four instalments and which I kept for her in an Abbey National savings account. The money was recoupable against her future earnings but it allowed her to give up the day job she had started at the World Entertainment News Network (WENN), an online news agency owned by the father of Amy's friend Juliette, Jonathan Ashby. She'd begun learning the ropes as a showbiz journalist after quitting the Camden stalls, but it soon became clear that she wasn't cut out for it. I don't remember her being paid very much and she didn't particularly enjoy it – Amy hated anything that had structure to it and that included getting up to go to work. But it was while she was with WENN that she met fellow journalist Chris Taylor. She made a play for him and the pair started going out with each other. It was her split from him that was to inform the lyrics of most of the songs on her first album *Frank*.

Up to that point, Amy hadn't seemed interested in relationships as such. I vaguely remember a timid boy called Matt who used to appear at our house in Greenside Close now and again, and I knew she had a group of friends older than her in Camden. Like a lot of teenage girls, it was a side to her life that she kept private. I would never have been able to get the full story out of her even if I'd tried.

Chris was seven years older than Amy and I did meet him a few times. I guess he was what you might call her first serious boyfriend.

Amy was obsessive about most things and I noticed she needed to be in control of her romantic affairs too. Chris was quiet and shy and a bit of a wallflower if I'm honest, and there was a large part of Amy that initially wanted to look after him. It was her way of dominating the relationship, but that also conflicted with her desire for a boyfriend who would protect her and 'be a man', and in the end Chris didn't match her idea of what a strong man should be and it frustrated her. It was he who finished with her and, on the surface at least, Amy didn't appear upset about it at all.

Everything must have come to a head the day they were downstairs talking in her room in Guildown Avenue. I hadn't heard the front door go but a while later Amy shouted to me, 'Mum, can you take me round to Chris's?' She was sat on the living-room floor piling some of his belongings and presents he'd given her into an old shoebox and she wanted to return them to him. Like most mums I was Amy's regular taxi service, which was hilarious because by then her father had done The Knowledge and was actually a cab driver.

I drove Amy to the block of flats in Holloway where Chris lived and watched her as she pressed the buzzer to the security door, which eventually clicked to let her in. She couldn't have been gone more than five minutes but she returned without the box. 'OK, Mum, let's go,' she said as she piled back into the front seat. And that was that.

In one of Amy's early radio interviews she told that story. It formed the lyrics of the song 'Take The Box', which she didn't write until she signed her publishing deal in 2002 and which was released as the second single from her debut album. She claimed then that she'd hailed a black cab and taken the box round to Chris's. What a fib that was! Clearly as a burgeoning pop diva it was far too shameful for her to admit that it was her mum who'd driven her there in a Nissan Cherry and waited for her on the roadside below with the handbrake on and the engine running.

Nick Godwyn and Nick Shymansky seemed to get the measure of Amy quite quickly. She was being paid to develop her talent as an artist, which meant time writing and recording in the studio. Except that Amy would never turn up to the studio on time, and when she did she'd muck around if left to her own devices. If ever she was expected to be somewhere and she hadn't turned up, her management would end up calling Cynthia. They'd sussed that she was the only person Amy would jump for. Cynthia pointed Amy in the right direction on many occasions.

In the end, though, they realized that if Amy couldn't come to the studio, the studio would have to come to her. One afternoon a van and a group of technicians turned up at Guildown Avenue and started lugging pieces of equipment into Amy's blue garage room. There were microphones, tape machines, various other bits of recording equipment and loads of boxes. It was an attempt to get her to work on some original material before she cut a demo recording that could be used to court record label interest. It was all set up in the corner of her room, but had she told me it was arriving? Of course not. 'Oh it's just some guys, Mum. They're moving some stuff into my room.'

Having all this equipment installed at home didn't make Amy apply herself any harder. She worked best spontaneously, not to deadlines or with a management company breathing down her neck. She and Juliette used to sit down there for hours, but on the whole Amy worked when it suited her, not because someone had told her to.

That summer of 2001, as Amy was getting focused on her music, Tony and I decided to take a holiday in Italy. In the run-up to going away I had been feeling tired and emotionally drained, but physically I was OK. A couple of years earlier I had started going to see a counsellor, Jacky Lewis, who'd been recommended to me by my friend Penny. Recognizing that I wasn't happy in my life had been a big leap for me to take. My relationship with Tony ticked over but there was definitely something that didn't work about it, even though we ended up staying together for another seven years. Coping with Amy while holding down a full-time job had taken its toll too and suddenly I'd felt overwhelmed with the task of figuring out what was important and what was not. I'm not a person who openly admits to emotional weaknesses but things had stacked up over the years and there had been times when I felt I'd lost my way as a parent and as a person.

Having good friends to talk to helped, as did going to yoga, which I still do on a Tuesday night. In fact I came to rely on that yoga class as my only sanctuary. For an hour each week it made me feel human again – calm and a bit more balanced – while Amy's problems raged around me. Back then, though, it was Jacky who worked with me and slowly helped me realize that I needed to take a step back and not assume responsibility for all of Amy's behaviour.

Once Amy signed to Brilliant 19 it seemed to stabilize her. It seemed she'd finally found a place where she felt comfortable, which allowed me to take my foot off the pedal a little. Bizarrely, that felt stranger than worrying about her all the time. This readjustment was of course easier said than done, and I had no idea then that within a matter of months my own survival would depend on learning to take a step back.

As soon as Tony and I boarded the plane in Luton, bound for Naples, I knew something wasn't right. There had been a stomach virus going around and I spent much of the three-hour flight hunched over the cramped aircraft toilet retching and being sick. When we landed I had to be helped down the steps of the aircraft because I was hit with waves of dizziness and could hardly stand. We debated turning back, but I wanted to stick it out. It was bound to be the bug. But the bug didn't leave me for the whole ten-day holiday.

On the day we were due to visit the Ancient Roman ruins of Pompeii I was too weak to eat, and although I spent the whole day willing myself to be OK, my body was a mess and nothing tasted right to me. It was a relief when we touched back down in the UK, but even then I had to be helped on to the runway to the awaiting bus. I'd developed a pulsating headache that simply wouldn't shift, and a few days later, when we were back in Guildown Avenue, I collapsed in the living room. All of a sudden my legs turned to jelly and I felt my limbs give way under the weight of my body. As I came crashing to the floor, my heart was pounding out of my chest. What the hell was wrong with me?

I booked an initial appointment with my doctor, and the follow-up was due on the morning of 11 September. There are days that replay in my head like scenes from a horror film and that day is one of them because it was the day the World Trade Center came under attack. Smoke was billowing from the Twin Towers when I switched on the news that morning. It seemed unbelievable that this major tragedy was unfolding in New York, the city I was born in and a place I held so dear. I drove to my appointment with the radio on, glued to the latest news. People in the street and in the surgery waiting room talked about nothing else. I clearly recall the fascination and fear that had gripped the city.

As I sat with my GP, it slowly dawned on me that another tragedy was unfolding. There was no terrorist attack this time; there weren't thousands of people dead; there was no global catastrophe. Instead it was a small and private tragedy, one that shook my life with an equal force.

The doctor suggested that I could be suffering with Ménières disease, a rare condition that affects a person's inner ear. It would explain my dizziness, vomiting and loss of balance. If that was the diagnosis, it could be managed, he told me, but he was also going to refer me for tests at Barnet General Hospital: the familiar pins and needles I'd felt throughout my body before I fell could be the signs of multiple sclerosis.

I quietly took in the news, but I was numb. My mind filled with the words my GP had said to me all those years ago after Alex was born. 'Don't worry, Janis, it's unlikely to be MS,' he'd said. 'You'd feel a lot worse and it's most likely you'd be in a wheelchair.' Had the symptoms been there all these years? Had I blindly ploughed on, feeling exhausted, thinking this was a normal part of a busy life? Or had I purposely put off confronting the possibility that this was something serious? I'm still not sure.

After twenty years I needed to know exactly what I was facing. I needed to prepare myself to fight whatever was wrong with me. Tests began within months, but it was another two years before my condition finally revealed itself.

6

Frank

In the spring of 2002, Amy started working with a west London producer called Major when Nick Godwyn at Brilliant 19 secured a publishing deal for her. She had no recording contract as yet but EMI Music Publishing Ltd wanted to represent her growing catalogue of songs, and she signed the deal in April. By then Amy, at the age of eighteen, had twenty-seven songs under her belt, but only three – 'Amy, Amy, Amy', 'You Sent Me Flying' and 'What Is It 'Bout Men' – made the final cut of her debut album.

She received her first advance from EMI on 21 May – a cheque for a whopping £73,437.50. Neither of us had ever seen a cheque that size and it was then I realized that the music industry paid out *big* money.

By then, Amy had employed an accountant, Margaret Cody, a young woman in her late twenties whom Amy had first visited in her office in the West End. Margaret's appointment had had little to do with her professional credentials. Amy had been given a list by Brilliant 19 of potential accountants to see but it was left up to her whom she chose. Although Mitchell and I were signatories to her management deal and, along with Margaret, we also ended up being counter-signatories to any cheques paid out from Amy's

Above left: True to form, Amy arrived into the world four days late.

Above right: Although I was convinced I'd be having another boy, I was so thrilled when my beautiful little girl came along.

Left: Alex was disappointed when his hoped-for little brother turned out to be a little sister! But soon they were inseparable.

Below: Who would have thought that this little girl would go on to achieve so much.

Above: Hurricane Amy!

Below: Both Alex and Amy loved playing peek-a-boo in our laundry basket.

Above: My mother and father, Esther and Eddie. My dad was the most stable influence in my life when I was growing up.

Above: Celebrating my and Mitchell's engagement – the collars were a lot larger back then!

Below: Me in Miami in 1972. I was only nineteen when I decided I wanted to find work over there. Just like Amy, once I got an idea into my head I didn't let anything stand in my way.

Left: Amy was always a bright and curious child.

Above: A relief to have Amy securely in a swing, rather than off on one of her legendary escapades.

Below: Amy in the garden at our Osidge Lane house. That home will always hold fond memories for me.

Above: Amy's nursery class at Yavneh, which was attached to Southgate Synagogue. She's easy to pick out!

Below left and right: Amy at Osidge Primary School. She might look like butter wouldn't melt, but the reality was a different story altogether.

Above: Amy and me at my graduation.

Above: Amy at our house in Greenside Close. It was here that she used to sit with her legs dangling out of one of the top bedroom windows, singing her heart out to passers-by.

I can hide behind my mummy

Middle: On holiday at Disney World. Although Amy appeared outwardly confident, she would often cling to me like this. Her note, **above**, from primary school also shows how she often sought my protection.

Right: Amy's self-portrait, painted when she was eight.

Above: Amy at Alex's Bar Mitzvah. I recorded Alex rehearsing his passages for his Bar Mitzvah. Of course, Amy just had to join in and I still have the tape of her speech as well as her brother's.

Left: Amy was a bright girl, but would only apply herself at school if she felt like it.

Below: A cheeky mother's-day card from Amy.

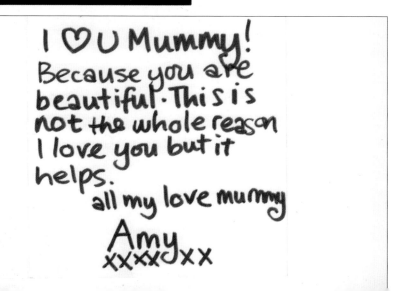

I ♡ U Mummy! Because you are beautiful. This is not the whole reason I love you but it helps.
all my love mummy
Amy
xxxxoxx

Right and middle: Amy's bedroom was her sanctuary, both when she was young and into her adult life. She was always making plans for her room, as you can see from these notes in her diary.

Bottom: Two drawings from July 1995. In one, she notes that I'm working too hard, and in the other, she admits that she misses her dad.

Things I need for my room

a pyramid candle - 758
a pyramid candle holder - 758
a scented candle holder - 758
black velvet curtains - IKEA? - Pop Eddie?
more black silk or chiffon material -
a new, low bed Pine - Mum - Pop Eddie
a taller, narrower bookcase that I can paint black (with white bits)
A black + white Keanu Posters Asda - mum
New dresser handles - mum (black)
An arched mirror - B+Q ?
A nicer, less tatty bin - IKEA or B+Q
2 pine shelves - B+Q

Try for:
Dresser Handles
Arched mirror
B+Q
Shelves, and
bookcase
B+Q
with Mum

Try for:
Pyramid candle
Pyramid holder
small candle holder
in 758.
one Saturday
with
Dad.

Try for:
curtains +
material at
Pop Eddie's,
with Mum.

Reference

scented candle holder from Pearsons.
gold candle holder from Ikea.
low bed from The Pine Bed Store.
pyramid candle holder from Fenwicks
black silk from Pop Eddie
bin from discount store in Finchley.
long cherry scented candles from 758
long candle holder from 758
Incense 'Virgo' from 758
incense holder 75p from 758
small candle holder from 758
small Sandalwood candle 75p from 758
string of bells(?) from 758
moon + sun bedspread from Fenwicks
Sun, Moon, Star candle holder
Silver candles 50p each from Whiteleys
letter mirror from America
2 black candles from Body + Soul
this notebook £7 from the Tate
Gallery gift shop.
rug from Evolution good Green
star candle - birthday present.

9.1.96.

Stuff I wanna acheive in 9T6

stop biting my nails
make my bureau into a homework area ✓
get a new TV ✓
CLEAN MY Room and put the drapes on ✓
new curtains ✓
Some Shelves ✓
finish painting my room ✓
Get rid of my bookcase or put it somewhere else
HAS new room layout:

COOL
MUM?

BED
rug
radiator

door
bookcase | drawers | bureau   ← = is the shelves

Bookcase may have gone one
downstairs with shelves instead.

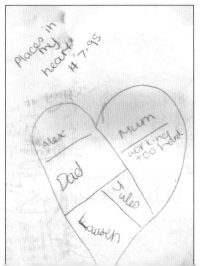

Places in my heart 14.7.95

Alex
Mum working too hard
Dad
Jules
Lauren

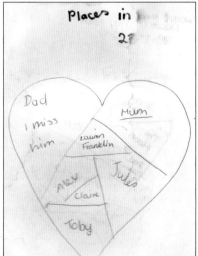

Places in
2?

Dad
I miss
him

Mum

Lauren
Franklin

Alex
Claire
Jules

Toby

account, we gave Amy respect from the beginning and entrusted her with deciding who she wanted to work with.

'I want Margaret,' she'd told me after their first meeting.

'Why Margaret?' I was interested to know.

'Mum, she had these great shoes on,' Amy laughed.

I recall thinking at the time that perhaps we should have been more hands-on! But she'd chosen well: Margaret stayed with Amy as her accountant throughout her career and now looks after the Foundation finances too.

Unbelievably, although Amy now had an accountant, she had no bank account: all her earnings had previously gone into the savings account I held for her. So one afternoon I took her to the Halifax branch in North Finchley and together we opened an account. She couldn't have been less interested, but needs must. The whole thing seems so amateur when I look back on it now, but at that time we had no idea whatsoever how big Amy would become.

It was also around this time that Amy left home. When she told me I wasn't exactly surprised but I was momentarily taken aback by the suddenness of it. 'You're *moving out*?' I questioned her. She hadn't prepared me for that bombshell at all. I'm not sure whether it was because Amy knew my health was suffering, but she stopped involving me in some of the decisions she made. Certainly the place she and Juliette moved to in Leopold Road in East Finchley was her choice. She now had financial independence and she put down a year's rent on the two-bedroom ground-floor flat. If there's one thing Amy was, it was generous to her friends, and Juliette lived there rent-free.

From the moment Amy left Guildown Avenue I noticed a change in our relationship. Regardless of what was going on, Amy had always been with me, and in my own way I'd tried to guide and protect her as best I could. Now she was going it alone, and I said goodbye to my daughter with mixed feelings. I missed her from day one. She was such a big personality around our house that suddenly there was a quiet emptiness in the rooms. Until Amy moved out I hadn't appreciated how demanding she'd been, but now I missed being wanted by her, even rescuing her – just being a mum, I suppose. And I worried that she wasn't ready for the world. Although I had work to fall back on, which was a real saviour for me, she was constantly on my mind. I tried desperately to maintain close contact with her. Admittedly she didn't always make that easy. There were times when I would call and call her mobile phone but I would never get an answer, and then she'd appear back at our house in Guildown Avenue as if by magic and act as though nothing had ever happened. One afternoon she turned up at the house with blood dripping down her legs wheeling a bike that wasn't hers. On the way over she'd collided with a car at a junction and gone over the handlebars. Amy the walking disaster – reassuringly, some things hadn't changed.

Although Amy barely uttered a word to me about leaving home, the significance of it must have been on her mind. Not long after, she wrote the song 'Brother' that eventually featured as an outro on *Frank*. Understandably Alex isn't too keen on that song because in it his little sister tells him off, but I've always read the lyrics differently. For me it was Amy's way of saying, 'I've got to leave now, please look after Mum.' It was written with sensitivity and care for me.

Whatever Amy could express in lyrics, though, she could never quite demonstrate in real life. At times it was as if everything I had hoped for as a mother was melting away. Teenagers are so wrapped up in their own world that I put some of Amy's disappearing acts down to that. Unbeknown to me, however, Amy was now smoking cannabis on a daily basis. Once I realized this it took me some time to admit to myself that that was what was happening. I always thought she'd be smart enough to know when to stop.

I was sure to get a phone-call from Amy if there was a problem or she needed something, and my instinct was always to help her out. That still included being Amy's taxi service. She would often ask me to take her here or there, or if I was over at her flat she'd say, 'Mum, I need to drop something off at a friend's house,' and we'd hop in the car and go. I knew some of Amy's friends – there was a nice crowd she played pool with regularly at the Bull and Butcher pub every Sunday night – and after about the fourth or fifth time of pulling up at different places and Amy running out of the car for five minutes while I waited, I started to wise up to what was going on. I didn't recognize any of the addresses – they all looked a bit seedy. These other people she was asking to visit weren't friends. She was buying cannabis right under my nose.

I kept Amy's actions and my part in them a secret from everybody, but it gnawed at me then and it still gnaws at me now. Was Amy seeking validation for her drug use by involving me? By helping her, did I enable her to continue, or would she have done so anyway? If I'm brutally honest, there was a part of me that didn't want to admit failure. I was Amy's mother. I didn't want to reveal to anyone, not even to myself, the reality that I couldn't control her. At the same time I wanted to protect her: Cynthia would have hit the roof if she'd been made aware of the full story. I also knew that however much I tried, I couldn't change Amy. She'd often said she confided in me because I didn't judge her, and I wanted that communication channel always to be open to her. But I was beginning to find myself trapped in Amy's deceit.

It might be natural for parents reading my story to have a strong opinion about the decisions I made, but I can guarantee I had no idea how I might act until I was placed in that awful position. I don't think any parent can know. What I couldn't do was ignore it, and some months after Amy moved out I broached the subject with her. As a pharmacist I was clued up on how powerful any kind of addiction could be. When you dispense drugs you see things over the counter that others don't. There were addicts to whom I handed over the heroin substitute methadone on a regular basis. Some of them looked down-and-out and clearly slept rough, but many were well dressed and well spoken and had managed to get to the point in their recovery where they could hold down a job. Some turned up periodically. Having got clean, any trigger might set their habit off again and they'd be back to drugs then back on methadone. Then there were the addicts who were illegally signed to several different GPs so that they could pick up prescriptions for methadone twice or three times over. Because I was a locum travelling from place to place it was part of my job to keep an eye out for this and report it. Such was the hold their habit had on them it led them to lie and cheat and exist in a world that excluded kindness or consequences. Yet somehow, even when a few years down the line it became obvious to me that Amy was using hard drugs, I refused for a long time to associate the behaviour I saw as a pharmacist with that of my own daughter.

Other than at work, drugs had never touched me personally. I had not recognized the signs that Amy could be prone to addiction, even though Cynthia had seen it in her that time at Larry's birthday party. I have had to accept, too, that there was a part of me that downplayed the gravity of what she was doing in order to protect myself.

Did any of those impulses make me a terrible mother? I convinced myself they did, but I've come to learn through our work with parents and children at the Foundation that mine was a surprisingly common reaction. More often than not parents of addicted children use denial as a coping mechanism before they are ready to face the truth; some never accept the problem, choosing to cover it up even after that person is dead. As a mother who has struggled with both scenarios, I empathize with any person going through a similar experience. It is a far more complex beast when you are living with it. The process of finding your way through the labyrinth of emotions that go hand in hand with coping with addiction is all-consuming.

On the day I tackled Amy about cannabis, I asked if it was the only drug she had ever taken. Inwardly I braced myself for her reply, but even I was not expecting the answer she gave.

'I've smoked heroin, Mum, but it was nothing,' she said, completely belittling the seriousness of it.

'*Heroin?*' I spluttered.

'Yeah, but I just tried it, Mum. It's not for me.'

She changed the subject immediately and refused to elaborate. To this day I do not know if that was the bravado of an eighteen-year-old rebel trying to be more streetwise than she actually was or whether she was telling the truth. There were certainly no signs then that heroin was a habitual part of Amy's life. She wouldn't tell me who she'd smoked heroin with, or where or when, but her words left me cold. I warned her clearly about the dangers of hard drugs.

In years to come Amy would publicly and privately claim that she'd not touched a Class A drug before meeting her husband-to-be Blake Fielder-Civil. She even had a saying: 'Class A drugs are for mugs'. Was this a case of conveniently forgetting what she'd told me? Was she going through her own process of denial? Sadly, I will never know the answer.

This is the first time I have ever revealed that conversation, and, my God, it hurts. What she said that day hit me like a ten-ton weight. I knew enough about addiction to realize that there might already be little I could do, but that didn't stop every single inch of me wanting to shake Amy with the little strength I had and scream at her, 'What the *hell* are you doing? You're going to break my heart!'

From then on I was forever suspicious of all of Amy's wild goose chases, but thankfully not all of them turned out to be as disturbing. For instance, Amy always rang me for medical help if any of her friends had a problem – though she never asked me for help with her own problems. From tapeworms to common colds, I doled out advice on every illness possible. She even phoned me with health updates on her pet canary. The things mothers do!

That canary was a particularly sorry incident, though it did inspire Amy to write the lyrics for 'October Song' which also appeared on *Frank*. She'd bought it not long after moving to Leopold Road, and kept it on her bedside table in an antique bird-cage she'd picked up from a Camden market stall. Now, there was one thing about Amy: she adored birds and animals but she was never that dedicated to looking after them. Penfold the hamster, which she had wanted so badly, had regularly taken nosedives down our stairs, desperately clinging on to the inside of its wheel as it bounced down each step; she almost killed her friend Michael's hamster doing the same. Amy *loved* that canary, which she'd named Ava after the glamorous 1940s movie star Ava Gardner, but it hadn't occurred to her that Ava would start chirping as soon as the sun rose. 'Chirping is what canaries do, Amy,' I kept telling her whenever she rang me, irritated with Ava's morning chorus.

She used to open the cage regularly and let Ava fly around the room, but, unfortunately, feeding her regularly didn't top Amy's list of priorities. 'Mum, I don't think Ava's very well,' she told me one day; and the next week I woke early to another phone-call: 'Mum . . . I think Ava's dead. Can you come over?' Ava was certainly dead: Amy had found her under the sofa as stiff as a board. That poor canary. She would have had no idea that when Amy set eyes on her she'd be popping her clogs within a matter of weeks.

By the time I got to Amy's flat she'd fished out a little black Chanel sunglasses box. The bright yellow body of Ava was laid out in it. I must confess it was almost impossible to keep a sombre face, but Amy was insistent that I help her bury her. Nearby, at the top end of Highgate Woods, there was some shaded woodland where I thought there'd be little chance of anyone disturbing us. Amy dug a rectangular ditch in the earth with a trowel I'd brought and gently placed the box into it. As she filled in the hole and smoothed the earth back over with her fingers she sang the chorus of 'Lullaby Of Birdland'.

However infuriating Amy could be, there were times when all I wanted to do was forgive her. She could be unbelievably sweet and thoughtful, even if it was in the most unexpected of ways.

That December Amy officially signed to Universal-Island Records Ltd, having worked with songwriters Matt Rowe and Stefan Skarbek in the Mayfair Studios in Primrose Hill and amassed enough songs for an album. However, I'm not sure how much time Amy spent actually recording. Nick Shymansky says that the only way they could get Amy to write songs was to call the studio and tell her Nick Godwyn and he were coming down that afternoon; suddenly Amy would spring into action and something would materialize off-the-cuff. She'd pretend she'd spent hours working on a song when in actual fact she'd penned it that minute.

Even if Amy could have spent hours in the studio, she worked so spontaneously that only twenty minutes of any session would have been knockout material. Instead of her later, more serious songs, at this time she would apparently write funny, jokey tunes. One was called 'I'm A Monkey, Not A Boy'. It was about a boy who was with her at Osidge Primary and who was always mucking around in class. She'd spend a lot of time in Camden too, rummaging through second-hand record shops looking for inspiration. One day she even went to London Zoo for the afternoon when she was supposed to be recording. Although it didn't seem like it on the surface, that was all work to Amy. She wrote so autobiographically that life itself was her stimulation. But, in the end, there was a certain amount of pressure on Amy from Brilliant 19 to create a more serious image, and deep down Amy wanted that too. She wanted to be up there with the jazz heroines she'd spent her childhood admiring.

It was A&R heavyweight Darcus Beese who signed Amy to Universal-Island Ltd, and straight away she was introduced to the Miami-based producer Salaam Remi who worked alongside her in the year leading up to *Frank*'s release. The meeting with Salaam was arranged through Guy Moot at EMI Publishing and had come about because she had loved a record by Lisa Left Eye Lopez that he'd produced.

Apparently Darcus had had an eye on Amy from the beginning. He had seen in her a career artist, not a one-hit wonder (a five-hit wonder, she always joked). Nick Godwyn had brought her to Island's offices to sing for a collection of the label's bosses. Footage exists of that performance, and in it Amy is sat on a brown leather chair looking as calm as anything. Her rendition of the jazz standard 'There Is No Greater Love' is truly stunning. After Amy passed away we started using it to promote the work of the Amy Winehouse Foundation. Appearing on that particular trailer were many of the teenagers the Foundation had begun to help, and who we are still helping. Right at the end it cut to that clip of Amy at Island Records that day, accompanied by only an acoustic guitar. Wherever we showed it, it never failed to leave audiences speechless.

Amy was due to sign on 23 December 2002, which was the last day of work before the Christmas break. Brilliant 19 had sent a taxi for her and Nick Godwyn was waiting with an assembled group at Island's offices. She was late, of course. When Amy finally called, she said, 'I'm here, I'm here, I'm at the publishing company.' Nick had to explain to her that she'd already signed her publishing deal in April; this was her record deal, and she was at the wrong offices.

I'm not entirely sure why, but Amy never wanted to sign any-thing. Although she'd held the dream of a recording contract for so long, there was a part of her that didn't ever want to commit. I always thought it was because she was afraid of succeeding. Signing on the dotted line might mean she'd done it. In her head she'd have nothing else to strive for. Amy had been rejected by most of the institutions she'd set foot in and now there were people suddenly saying, 'We accept you. We think you're special.' That became profoundly threatening to her because I don't believe she thought she was special at all. Without fail, Amy made life difficult for herself. If ever something looked like it was going to be easy, she'd sabotage it.

The deal Amy struck with Island was for £250,000. Before she received her first advance cheque of £83,000, Mitchell and I set up the company Cherry Westfield Ltd, named after the Westfield guitar that Amy loved which features in the song 'Cherry'.

In the new year she left for Miami to work with Salaam. I was so excited for her: everything she had worked for was coming together. I was also overjoyed that she was going to be spending six weeks in Miami. Whether it was by design or fate I don't know, but Salaam had moved his studios there from New York after the 9/11 attacks – the one place Amy and I loved together. It was almost as if her life was following the path I had taken at that age. Perhaps she had been taking notes all those years earlier when I told her that the world was her oyster. On that trip she was accompanied by Tyler James, who by coincidence was in Miami anyway, and Nick Shymansky, who flew with Amy from London. And where did they stay? Collins Avenue – the exact same spot where my aunt had opened the door to me at the age of nineteen, with my suitcase in my hand and not a care in the world.

Amy lived all-expenses-paid at the art deco Raleigh Hotel, and she and Salaam hit it off straight away. I have only met Salaam on a handful of occasions but he is a gentle giant. He had produced the hip-hop artist Nas, whom Amy loved, and she had a great deal of respect for Salaam as well as her second producer on *Frank*, Gordon Williams, who was based in New Jersey and who had worked with greats like Aretha Franklin and Whitney Houston.

Towards the end of her stay, Amy even made it to see my cousin Joan in Boca Raton. They had spent all week on the phone trying to figure out when they would get together and one night Amy and Nick finally turned up at around midnight having spent $100 on a cab from downtown. The day after, Joan took them to the mall.

Nick shopped on his own while she and Amy scoured Macy's and Victoria's Secret for clothes. Joan told me she was taken aback by Amy, now a slender nineteen-year-old with dazzling eyes and curly hair tumbling down her back, buying up skimpy lingerie like it was going out of fashion. To Joan, Amy was still the little girl who had splashed in her pool all those years ago. After Amy passed, I sent a picture to Joan of Amy and Nick during that visit. In it they are in a candy store looking confused as Amy debates what type of jelly beans she's going to bring home. Her cousins had always brought us jelly beans when they came over and Amy wanted to carry on the tradition. Knowing Amy's love for sweets, though, I can't ever remember if I received them.

Joan drove them back to Miami that night, and she recalls Nick insisting that Amy was going to be a huge star. He was always a great champion of Amy's, and if she ever brought him over to Cynthia's for Friday night dinner, Cynthia would be quietly (or not so quietly) trying to pair them up. I could see Cynthia's mind working overtime: a nice Jewish boy would be perfect for Amy. But, as far as I know, Amy and Nick always remained just friends.

It was after Amy returned from Miami and before she did her first showcase gig for *Frank* that my health took another turn for the worse. I had been undergoing all manner of tests but so far nothing had shown up as 100 per cent conclusive. One evening Tony and I went to a party at Richard and Stephanie's place in east Barnet to celebrate Stephanie's fiftieth birthday. Halfway through the evening I was standing and talking with a glass in one hand and a plate of food in the other when suddenly everything started to turn blurry. Just as before, the whole room seemed to be rotating around me faster and faster. The noise of music and people chatting started to feel disorientating, as if I was in a swimming pool with my head under the water. Conscious of my legs giving way I grabbed for any-thing around me but within seconds I was out cold on the carpet with my feet in the dining room and my head in the hallway. I couldn't open my eyes; it was as if they were glued shut. It was terrifying. When I finally came to I could just about make out Tony and Richard stooped over me and gently shaking me – 'Janis, Janis, are you OK, Janis?' Fortunately, one of Richard's friends had brought along his girlfriend, a woman called Angela, who happened to be a nurse. I was taken upstairs and as I lay recovering on a bed Angela checked my pulse and looked after me until a taxi came to take Tony and me home.

My doctor had told me that until they could find the cause it might be better if I cut down on my working hours, and I probably shouldn't drive either. But whatever the problem was, I still refused to see it as a problem and carried on as normal. Amy surely got her stubbornness from me. In typical Janis style, I still drove to work and didn't stop doing the things I had always done. In fact I only stopped driving in 2009 when I managed to demolish my garage door while parking the car. Not long after that I stopped work for good.

Other people noticed how I'd slowed down. Stephanie and I used to go shopping together, and while she was buzzing around Brent Cross I found the pace difficult. Shopping became a chore for anyone who was with me because it would take me twice as long to walk anywhere. That may have been the reason why after Amy left home we never really enjoyed those sorts of things that mothers and daughters do together. Amy always asked how I was if I seemed tired but nobody knew then what was wrong with me and I'm sure it must have been confusing for both children. Nevertheless, I'm pleased I forced myself to carry on as normal – I'd have missed out on so much otherwise.

I can clearly recall towards the end of 2003, when I was working in the Lloyds Pharmacy in Palmers Green, passing a huge billboard on one of the roundabouts on the way to work. I'd never really noticed it before but on this occasion I was driving towards it when I looked up and suddenly I saw Amy. *Amy?* It was the strangest feeling I have ever had. There she was, in a life-size poster to promote the album *Frank*, dressed in a bright pink off-the-shoulder sweater with her name below. Amy Winehouse. A huge grin spread over my face. 'You've done it, Amy,' I said to myself. 'You've actually gone and done it.' If I hadn't been so scared of losing control of the car I'd have pinched myself a hundred times over. It was Amy. My Amy. She was up there on that billboard. It felt almost unbelievable. Every time I left the house after that I always took the same route to work just so I could see her.

I'd tried to make it to every one of Amy's performances, but I could only be part of some of the build-up to *Frank*'s release. In mid-July, around a month after I'd collapsed, Amy played the Cobden Club in west London. It was a hot night and we'd all crammed into this small room set within this beautiful Grade II listed building. Amy was sat in the corner, perched on a stool with her guitar, singing jazz standards. That night the singer Annie Lennox was sat right in front of me. Amy looked a little nervous on stage, but she seemed to be enjoying the attention and she looked at home in the new world she was making her way in – although, to be fair, she still had the luxury of anonymity. I was smacked by another of those surreal moments: 'Is Annie Lennox really here watching my daughter sing?'

Amy played the Cobden Club several times that summer but it wasn't until late August that she finally gave me a sampler of six tracks from *Frank*, and that, as I said, was the very first time I'd ever sat at home and listened to Amy's music. I didn't really know what to expect, but it was what I call a 'wow' moment. I loved it. Her voice was the thing that shone out for me but it also struck me how accomplished and sophisticated the songs sounded. I'm no expert, but it didn't sound like anything I'd heard at the time. It had Amy's stamp all over it.

I took the CD into work the next day and played it to some of my colleagues in the back room. Most of them were completely dis-believing. 'Is that your daughter?' they said. 'Nah, it can't be.' But it was. Proud doesn't even come close to how I felt. I was often asked where Amy had had voice coaching lessons, but other than at Sylvia Young's, she hadn't. It was hard for people to believe that she had such a natural ear for music. I hoped and prayed the record-buying public would recognize her talent.

Amy had turned a corner personally. I always did feel a bit sorry for her ex-boyfriend Chris, though. It was evident that their break-up played a huge role in the writing of *Frank*. I suspect that Amy was referring to him as a 'ladyboy' in the song 'Stronger Than Me'. She could be very harsh but, the other hand, it was Amy's straight-talking that made that album so poignant and funny and brilliant.

As the excitement around *Frank* began to build, the lease on Amy's flat expired. She'd been talking for some time about wanting to get her own place. It seemed a sensible move, and Mitchell found her a home in Jeffrey's Place in Camden which she bought for £260,000. She put £100,000 down as a deposit and moved in almost straight away.

On the day she was due to hand back the Leopold Road keys to the estate agent I had gone over to help her with her packing. Of course, nothing had been done and, as ever, Amy's room was in a state. 'Amy, there's someone coming over to get the keys,' I kept reminding her. 'You need to be ready to be out.' What was going on in her head I do not know, but when the doorbell rang all of a sudden Amy announced that she couldn't vacate the flat yet because she'd run herself a bath. A *bath*? Bang in the middle of the living room, in front of Juliette and this poor estate agent, she dropped her trousers, yanked her top off, unfastened her bra and pulled her knickers off too. She stood there as naked as a jaybird before turning and casually wandering into the bathroom, shutting the door and climbing into the piping hot water. There followed a nervous half hour, with me trying to make polite conversation with the young gentleman who had quite innocently turned up for some keys but who now sat shell-shocked on the sofa. Talk about weird!

The flat in Amy's adopted home of Camden was perfect for her and she settled in straight away. She was off the main drag and set within a gated courtyard, with a living room and kitchen downstairs and two bedrooms and a bathroom upstairs. It was the first place Amy had ever decorated as a home and she had 1970s vintage wallpaper with bamboo shoots across one living-room wall and, above the stairs, 1960s Action Man wallpaper complete with helicopters, tanks and parachutes. Family photographs plastered her fridge secured with a multitude of fridge magnets.

Unfortunately Amy's flat didn't stay newly decorated for long. Soon after she moved in she left the bath running. I'm sure Tyler was staying there temporarily at the time and he was lucky not to have been caught under the falling plaster. 'Mum, my ceiling's fallen in.' It was never a straightforward phone-call with Amy.

Fortunately I had taken out home insurance for Amy's flat, but, as I recall, it took quite a few months for the damage to be repaired. In the meantime, every time she drained a bath half the water went down the plughole and the rest gushed through the hole in the ceiling. Not that it bothered Amy. Underneath she continued to hoard everything from books and CDs (that were never in their correct cases) to papers and newspaper cuttings. Amy could quite honestly have lived in a pig sty and not noticed.

I felt very little attachment to the places Amy lived in after Jeffrey's Place so even now this flat holds a special place in my heart. It was her first home and we still can't bear to part with it. There was one night a couple of years ago when I'd been out with Mitchell and Jane. The taxi dropped them at Jeffrey's Place before taking me home and, as soon as the cab door closed behind them and the car pulled away, I sat on the back seat and broke down in tears. It was the first time I'd been back there since Amy's passing and I couldn't stop sobbing until I reached my own front door.

Unsurprisingly, once Amy had completed all the work on *Frank* she seemed to lose interest in it. Frustratingly for her, there were a few differences of opinion over the mixes for some of the tracks and there had been a falling-out over whether the track 'Amy, Amy, Amy' should feature on the album. It was a song Amy had grown to dislike and she had wanted it omitted, but as nobody had been able to pin her down to finalize the track listing, all this was done for her in the end.

Whatever Amy's issues were with *Frank*, in my mind they were minor things that she'd blown out of proportion. During the making of the album she hadn't felt in control of the process, which I understand is often the case with emerging artists. Amy was a perfectionist. On the one hand she was meticulous about detail, and on the other hand she needed to be in perpetual motion. I always joke that she inherited the worst characteristics of me and Mitchell – my obsessive preoccupation with the world and his whirlwind drive and need for control. And both of us plough through life each day without necessarily worrying about what will happen tomorrow. Others have said Amy walked on the edges of both our personalities, and I think there's probably some truth in that.

On the flip side I could argue that those were exactly the traits that made Amy successful, only they seemed to sit together disastrously for her. She'd hardly have finished one thing before she was on to the next. That's done. Put it in the box. Move on. But underneath she was constantly dissatisfied with herself and the world around her. She could never achieve the ideal she wanted. And the only way she ever seemed able to sort things out in her head was through her songs.

Frank was finally released on 20 October 2003. I saved every single cutting about it I could get my hands on. I noticed Amy was being featured in a wide range of newspapers and magazines and getting some good reviews too. When she appeared on the Janice Long sessions on Radio 2, I sat and listened to her. She sounded so young and enthusiastic and bubbly. It was infectious.

There's no doubt Amy met the world with all guns blazing, but, if I'm honest, I'm not sure what people made of her. Everybody expected to see this rotund American black woman in her forties, but what they got was Amy – short, curvy, Jewish, white and only just turned twenty. What a living, breathing contradiction my daughter was.

7

Headline Honey

With *Frank* now released, Amy still had the hard work of promoting the album. As 2003 drew to a close she played her first major headline show at Bush Hall, where she was supported by her friend Tyler James. Although she was playing to a crowd of around three hundred it was a step up from the Cobden Club and the pubs and clubs she'd previously performed in. For years, the stage had been Amy's playground; now she was up there, performing for real. I sensed it was the fearless little girl who had propelled her there. It was where she'd found acceptance. But up there now was Amy the young woman, who felt unexpectedly exposed.

It was such a contradiction in Amy: she feared success, but she feared being ignored even more, and on that evening it showed. She was sandwiched between the members of her band on a tiny stage, dressed in a bright red cocktail dress. It took a bit of warming up for her voice to find its level. Also, Amy had a habit of nervously holding her Daphne Blue Stratocaster guitar into her as a sort of shield, and she tended to look down at it instead of making eye contact with the audience. After she'd made her TV debut on *Later With Jools Holland* with 'Stronger Than Me' in November there had been some discussion about Amy ditching the guitar for live performances, which eventually she did.

During the first half of 2004 her promotional and touring schedule was punishing: she was doing everything from playing to thirty teenagers in student union bars to supporting Jamie Cullum on tour. Suddenly it hit her that there was more to the job than writing music and mucking around in a studio. The work paid off: after a shaky start, in the middle of 2004 *Frank* peaked at number 13, selling more than two hundred thousand copies. But on one occasion when I visited her at Jeffrey's Place Amy opened up about how difficult she was finding the work that went along with being a musician. Structure was being imposed on her, and if there's one thing Amy kicked against, it was structure. She had to be places at certain times and there were record company demands to fulfil. Even though she was given a lot of free rein compared to other artists, it made her exceptionally anxious. Amy hunched her shoulders up to her ears, which was always a sign that she found something deplorable. 'It's too much,' she told me. 'I can't see why there's this attention and I don't see why I have to do these things. It's not for me.'

Committing herself to being a working artist was always going to be hard for Amy but part of the problem was also that Amy was finding it exasperating not being seen as an individual. She was a dynamo. I don't think for a moment she'd stopped to think before putting herself out there about how she might be perceived, or pigeonholed, or criticized.

In the end, *Frank* got mixed reviews. Some critics couldn't understand what Amy was about at all, but others got her immediately, describing her as a 'colossal vocal talent'. One of my favourite quotes was from the *Daily Telegraph* – 'writes like Cole Porter, sings like Billie Holiday, plays snooker like a pro'. But I don't know how much notice Amy took of these critics. Certainly at first all she cared about was making the music she loved; she seemed to bash all comparisons and criticisms aside and plough on regardless. But she'd always had romantic notions about being a singer and I suspect she was beginning to realize how tough it was to compete at that high level.

Now, if I ever flick on to any of the numerous talent shows on TV and see some of those young hopefuls with a quarter of the talent Amy had, I grimace. 'If the dream ever becomes reality, they won't have a clue what's hit them,' I think. Sadly, that thought comes from the bitter experience of losing my daughter, which weighs heavily on me.

Amy's album was released around the same time as work by other young artists such as Jamie Cullum, Katie Melua and Joss Stone, and there was a natural inclination to lump them all in the same category. Amy had a lot of respect for Jamie Cullum, whom she toured with that year, because she saw him as a consummate musician, but she didn't want to be associated with the rest, describing them as 'total rubbish'. Likewise, she hadn't wanted to be affiliated to Simon Fuller (who owned Brilliant 19) either, because he was synonymous with churning out pop and she fought the 'manufactured' label fiercely. In fact Fuller loved Amy's music, and when she first signed with Brilliant 19 he had been influential in getting her those publishing and record company deals as well as financing Nick Godwyn and Nick Shymansky to develop her before she made *Frank*. It was Amy's frustration. She was always striving to be better, to challenge herself, but sometimes she would come over as a petulant schoolgirl.

I don't know if Amy's management ever gave her advice on dealing with journalists, but if they did, it sailed past her faster than the wind. PR was not her game. She vented her dislike of other musicians openly, and publicly voiced her dissatisfaction with the final cut of *Frank*. On a good day, an interview with Amy could be great fun; on a bad day, journalists often met Amy in caustic mood – the same 'take me as I am' routine she'd perfected at school. One poor woman from the *Independent* newspaper turned up at a tapas bar around the corner from Jeffrey's Place to meet Amy, who greeted her with, 'No offence, but I could be at my nan's house right now, or waiting at home for the plumber to come and fix the washing machine.' Ouch.

Despite coming across as confident and opinionated, Amy was ill at ease talking about herself. For me, that hit home when I watched her on *The Jonathan Ross Show* in her first big television interview. She looked beautiful and she talked eloquently and assuredly, but her eyeliner was thicker than I'd ever seen it. And, as for her accent? It looked like Amy, but it didn't sound like Amy. It wasn't an accent she'd ever used at home. It was thick and cockney. Seeing it now, I can see it was Amy experimenting with herself. It was a persona that she went on to embellish, but there was no doubt in my mind that having a public face exacerbated an inner conflict for Amy. She was naturally provocative because it attracted attention, but once she'd got that attention she couldn't control what happened next and she then shied away from it. Half of the time she was playing games with people, but if Amy sensed someone trying to find out what made her tick, she turned up the dial on her attitude or she cut them off completely.

The songs that appeared on *Frank* had been written in Amy's private moments, just like she'd poured her heart into her notebooks and diaries as a little girl; now she was being asked to talk about herself with complete strangers. She was twenty, emotionally immature, and out there on her own. I don't think Amy ever really got to know herself; regrettably, she never got to appreciate herself or feel comfortable with herself. She didn't even own a copy of *Frank* at home. She wasn't wholly proud of it. All she saw were the flaws.

In those early days of fame I became increasingly aware that Amy was drinking more, particularly before she went on stage. I was seeing less and less of her too, which was doubly hard. I had lost Amy when she left home, and now, gradually, the music industry was taking her further afield. The people around her were becoming her second family. I wanted her to do brilliantly, of course. Singing was all she'd ever wanted to do. But I was very mindful of when I was a young woman having to cope with my mum leaving me. I had tried to make contact with Esther but she never made it easy, and I was determined not to let a similar gulf open up between Amy and me. I had always been available for her, I was always her constant, but now time and circumstance and Amy's own lifestyle were drawing us apart. I'd watched my daughter hatch into this butterfly. Now, just like a butterfly, she flitted around and only landed near me now and again. Every time I saw her she'd settle for a moment, then she'd be off.

Amy toured throughout April 2004 and into early May. Meanwhile, my hospital appointments continued. Every time I spoke with either of my children I downplayed my condition because I didn't want them to worry. But it was becoming increasingly obvious that I was changing, and in a way both of them doubtless would have noticed. They were used to seeing me active; now I was less sharp, more unsteady on my feet, and at times completely drained of energy.

Everything came to a head when I collapsed again at home. It was then that I was taken to Barnet General Hospital and given an MRI scan. It wasn't a pleasant experience being cocooned in this claustro-phobic machine which hummed and banged around me as it imaged my brain but I was made to feel comfortable. I was even given a private room until my scans had been analysed.

Tony was with me when the specialist arrived with my results. While the news was shattering it was not, by then, unexpected. The scan had revealed dark nodules on my brain which were lesions – the tell-tale signs of MS.

As I've discovered, MS is a complex neurological condition, but, put simply, the problem is that the substance that coats the nerve fibres in the central nervous system is under attack from the immune system and the lesions that creates interrupt messages from the brain to the body. MS had probably been present in me all along but the condition had been in remission for all those years. It was the virus with which I had suffered so badly in Italy that was the probable trigger for my sudden deterioration, according to the specialist. I had now moved from what is called relapsing and remitting MS to secondary progressive MS.

It is impossible to say today what might happen to me tomorrow. I could be walking one minute and unable to eat or speak the next, and, unfortunately, the condition's progression is irreversible. To help with feelings of nausea and to stabilize my balance I now take one drug called Cyclizine, but I am determined not to let MS beat me. It's the reason I try to pack as much into life as I can – because today, *I can.*

Although Tony and I moved soon after my diagnosis to a smaller two-bedroom flat in High Barnet it was, understandably, difficult for him to cope with my condition. Whatever other difficulties we had in our relationship, he'd lost one partner already and the fear of having to go through that again affected him greatly. I think it scared a lot of people. I remember Mitchell coming to see me in hospital along with my cousin Martin, and they all seemed so gloomy. 'I'm not finished yet!' I kept thinking. Richard and Stephanie visited too, and Richard and I talked about how my life would change, and how I might not be able to live as fully as I did before.

As usual, I was more concerned for the people around me. 'I'm fine, but are you OK?' I kept saying. Like Amy, I've never been very good at focusing on my own problems. Your children can fly the nest but you never stop being a mum, and when Amy came to see me with Alex that week I tried to reassure both of them. If there's one thing that's kept me alive it is my love for my children – it's human nature, I guess. My concern was always for them, and I know that Amy did, and Alex still does, find my deterioration excruciatingly painful. 'Please tell me you are going to be OK, Mum,' Amy said as soon as she set eyes on me. Alex has since told me that he and Amy were very scared by my illness, that they didn't want to confront it because it was too difficult to contemplate, and maybe that explains why they were both so subdued when they sat with me by my hospital bed.

'I'll be fine,' I told Amy that evening, even though I didn't have a clue what the future would hold. I still don't.

*

At the end of May, I didn't accompany Amy to the Ivor Novello Awards, but I knew that the Novellos were special to her. She'd been unsuccessful at the BRITs a few months earlier, but this was different. The Novellos recognized creditable songwriting and composition rather than performance or record sales, and Amy had spent so many years honing her poetry and lyrics that she saw it as *the* musician's award.

The ceremony was held at the Grosvenor House Hotel on Park Lane, and Amy had told me beforehand that she wasn't expecting to win anything. After all, she'd only released her debut album seven months earlier and she was up against megastars like Kylie Minogue in the Best Contemporary Song category. I didn't hear from Amy that night but early on the Friday morning I was in the flat when the buzzer went. In strolled Amy. She'd made her way to Barnet on the Northern Line and she stood in front of me in jeans and a T-shirt.

'Well . . . how did it go?' I asked her, not knowing whether to be upbeat or sympathetic.

'I got it, Mum!' she grinned.

'That's brilliant, Amy!' I went to hug her. 'So, what's it like? Where is it?'

She unhooked one strap of her over-the-shoulder bag, rummaged around in the make-up and notepads and yanked out this bronze statue. 'Here it is,' she said, gripping it in her outstretched hand. 'It's for you.'

It weighed a ton.

That memory is so vivid in my head, and it is one I hold very dear. Amy's sheer single-mindedness got her that award, but she also understood what we'd been through together. Somewhere in her absent-mindedness she was acknowledging all the times I'd found schools for her, or taken her to auditions, or sat in the audience at concerts, or simply supported her. My faith in Amy to come out winning was blind, and it tears at me now that the battle I wanted her to win the most – the battle to save her own life – was the one she couldn't overcome.

But as much as 2004 was a year of winning, it was also a year of heartbreak for my family. Winter was drawing in when Mitchell rang me one afternoon and asked if he and his sister Melody could come over to the flat and talk. Immediately I knew something was wrong, and, as I had feared, it was Cynthia. While I had been recuperating and learning to live with the knowledge that I had MS, Cynthia had also been undergoing tests. She had been a heavy smoker for much of her life – her voice rasped with it – and it had finally caught up with her. She'd been diagnosed with lung cancer, and the prognosis was not good.

I was heavy-hearted. We all were. Cynthia had remained a tower of strength in Amy's life, but she was my lodestar; I couldn't imagine a world without her. For me, she had not only been my mother-in-law, she was a friend too – a visceral connection to my past, to my children, to my family. Although he tried hard not to show it, Mitchell was very shaken by the news. Cynthia had been his rock too and had held everything together for him as a boy.

Cynthia never revealed her true feelings to me – she was a tough old bird. Instead, she was pragmatic. She gave up smoking immediately. I even accompanied her to a healing centre where she took advice on how to manage her disease. She acted positively, but my feeling was that in her heart Cynthia was also positive she was going to die soon.

All of our minds immediately turned to Alex and Amy. What a year they had had. I had just been diagnosed with a potentially life-threatening condition and now Cynthia was sick. Suddenly, the future seemed so uncertain. With Cynthia, we played down the inevitability of her diagnosis with the children, but they weren't kids any more and it shook both of them hard.

Cynthia's husband Larry had died a few years earlier. I had been there at his bedside when he took his last breath. So with Cynthia now coping with cancer alone, Alex moved in with her and helped care for her, until the experience of seeing his grandmother deteriorating in front of his eyes proved too hard for him. Amy took the news in Amy fashion. She was upset when Mitchell told her but outwardly she put on a brave face. My fear was that these changes at the core of Alex and Amy's family were causing more instability than there had ever been in their lives.

Happily, Mitchell and Amy had been developing a very close relationship, although Amy was old enough and independent enough for it to be on her terms now. I was glad he was taking a more active role in her life and they had time to be together more. Cynthia and I had been Amy's central support system, and instinctively, as a girl, she'd looked to us as her role models.

Since Amy's passing, I have read interviews where she stated that she learned everything she knew from Cynthia and me, and that gives me a great deal of comfort. When Amy's drugs problems exploded I felt utterly helpless, but I'm glad she recognized somewhere in her chaos that there had been an anchor, always ready and willing to listen to her and secure her when she needed it.

So with Cynthia declining fast and my own health uncertain, the ship was steering off course, and for me it was no coincidence that at this time Amy launched herself on a more determined path of self-destruction. Just at the very moment when Amy's star was ascending, the foundations of her family were shifting, and it was nothing she, or any of us, had the power to change. My feeling is that Amy frantically scrambled around for someone or something to secure her, but unfortunately all she found was Blake Fielder-Civil and hard drugs.

The moment in early 2005 when Amy met Blake is a story she would retell over and over as if it happened yesterday. 'I walked into the pub, strolled over to the pool table and there he was,' she would say. 'I knew he'd seen me out of the corner of his eye. I took a pool cue and played him. I wiped him out.' She'd often act the story out, as if she were on stage. It would have been a good story, if it hadn't been so tragic.

Believe it or not, I didn't meet Blake until after he and Amy got married a couple of years later. He was never around at Jeffrey's Place when I went to visit her. But she told me she'd met someone at the Good Mixer, a pub she went to in Camden, and she'd pointed Blake out to me one day from afar. She'd had his name tattooed on the top of her left breast, which I thought was vile, but what could I say?

He had an on-off girlfriend, something that Amy was never comfortable with. Although her gut feeling told her to stay away from Blake from the beginning, she was uncontrollably drawn to him. She'd always been a soft touch for a sob story, and Blake ticked all the boxes. He'd rebelled and dropped out of school in Lincolnshire before coming to London. He'd been a hairdresser and a fashion student and now he was working in music videos. But he'd also confided in Amy about the troubled relationship he'd had with his stepfather and there was a large part of her that wanted to help mend his broken wings.

When I finally did meet Blake in Amy's flat they had just come back from the Glastonbury Festival. It sounds so mundane, but I had gone over to take her a kettle. It was my wedding present to her, because there were times when I'd been round there and she'd boiled water for tea in a saucepan. She hadn't wanted me to come. Over the phone she kept saying she'd been travelling and she was tired, but I had insisted because I wanted to see her.

When I got there, Blake was lounging on her living-room sofa. He seemed quiet and introverted, averagely polite but scruffy and covered in tattoos. Like most of Amy's boyfriends, I wanted to take him and shake him from a window like a rag, he seemed so unclean. Perhaps it was optimistic of me to have expected it, but he didn't go out of his way to impress me. By then both he and Amy were mixed up in hard drugs, although I had no idea about that at the time. On that occasion I didn't stay more than ten minutes. I couldn't connect with Amy while he was there, and what struck me the most was how submissive she was around him. She kept asking him for his opinion or demanding he tell her what to do, and it was deliberate because she'd told me she wanted to build him up as a man.

Regrettably, all that happened was that Blake became another man over whom Amy sought control but who ended up controlling her. Blake clearly loved Amy but I don't believe he was ever emotionally there for her. That the media built Blake up to be an evil monster was laughable to me. He was a baby boy who had never grown up himself and who demanded unhealthy amounts of attention. Every time he pulled away from Amy, she chased him. It was infatuation. As far as I could see, their relationship had very little to do with kindness or care at that stage and everything to do with co-dependency.

It was around the time when Amy first started seeing Blake that her friends also noticed a marked change in her. Tyler James had suffered an horrendous attack, and Amy had taken him in and he was now living with her at Jeffrey's Place. Tyler was lucky to be alive. He'd been in east London one night when a gang of men tried to steal his mobile phone; they beat him so badly that both his cheekbones were broken, along with his nose and jaw. How people could be so violent towards someone appalled me. Amy offered him a room immediately while he underwent surgery and recuperated. Tyler told Mitchell after Amy's passing that Blake had brought out cocaine and heroin openly in the flat soon after he and Amy had started going out. If Amy had ever dabbled with hard drugs before, Blake was certainly the catalyst who reacquainted her with them. Through some hare-brained romantic notion she wanted to feel like he was feeling, but she also needed him to need her. Sadly, she ended up becoming more hooked than he was.

Amy meeting Blake also coincided with a time when she was doing very little. Her year of promotional work on *Frank* was done, and while her record company was looking forward to a next album for 2005, Amy wasn't looking forward to anything in particular.

She'd gone to the studio a few times but had fallen asleep on more occasions than she'd written anything. Worryingly, if I called her she'd often be in bed – that's if she answered the phone at all. She'd lost all the enthusiasm and focus she'd had when she started making *Frank* and I prayed that Amy wasn't slowly undoing all the good things that had happened to her, as she had done at Sylvia Young's. I was also concerned about what would make Amy *want* to produce another record. She needed something to happen in her life to spark her creativity, yet it was becoming clear that such happenings were usually catastrophes rather than positive experiences.

She fed off her lows as well as her highs, and her addictions made the situation worse. Whereas before Amy had largely hidden her drinking from me, now she was doing it more openly, and in a way she didn't seem able to control. On one occasion when I visited her she was drinking neat vodka and pretending it was water, and when I asked what she was doing all I got was 'Sorry, Mummy. I love you, Mummy.' I don't believe Amy ever set out to hurt me, but there were times when I left Jeffrey's Place feeling as though she had rubbed dirt all over my face. How could I continue to accept my daughter for who she was when she seemed determined to destroy her life?

Cynthia, as always, had a different way of dealing with Amy. When *Frank* was released she, like me, had been on cloud nine; it pained her now to see Amy throwing it away. 'You're an alcoholic,' she was now telling Amy to her face, and she had banned her from drinking in her flat. 'No, no, no I'm not – I'm not, Nan,' Amy would say defensively. 'I don't have a problem.' In only a few months, though, Amy's weight had noticeably dropped and at times I had to force myself to disengage from her because the anxiety of seeing her impacted severely on my condition. I would develop headaches, or barely sleep, and I was forced to realize that I had to start listening to my own body. It was yelling at me to step back. But Amy was on my mind every waking moment.

Amy never told me what happened between her and Blake when they split for the first time that summer, but Mitchell certainly became involved. The relationship had been destructive from the beginning and Blake had gone back to his girlfriend. In the aftermath, Nick Godwyn had called Mitchell and asked him to intervene.

Around that time, I believe a trip had been arranged for Amy to meet the producer Mark Ronson in New York but she didn't know Mark then and she'd refused to go. Instead she'd phoned Nick Shymansky and asked him to come over to Jeffrey's Place. When he got there Amy was completely broken. She was drunk and crying and a mess, and Nick ended up ringing Nick Godwyn who also came down to the flat. Both of them were trying to console Amy but neither of them had ever seen her in such a terrible state before.

Selfishly, I thank God I didn't see that. I think it might have destroyed me. Instead of ringing me it was then that they contacted Mitchell and asked him to pick her up. Apparently, her flat looked like a squat. He took her back to his home in Kent for a few days and both Nicks persuaded Mitchell that she needed to seek treatment for what was becoming a serious problem. It was agreed that they would drive Amy to a clinic outside Surrey after the weekend, and that's exactly what happened.

At first she was against going, but eventually she agreed – that's until she actually got there. The place smacked of authority; she began to feel she wasn't there on her terms and, like many people with addiction problems, Amy didn't even acknowledge the extent of her problem. She was aware she had an addictive personality because she would often say that to me, but in her head she was simply upset about Blake and she convinced herself that she would come through it.

A version of what happened is now immortalized in the song 'Rehab'. No sooner had the two Nicks dropped Amy off than she rang them. 'Right, done that,' she said, and they had no choice but to drive her back to London. She had spent fifteen minutes with a counsellor and decided it wasn't for her. 'He just wanted to talk about himself. He was the one with the problem,' she told me later.

I don't know whether this episode fuelled Amy's decision, but that December Amy and Brilliant 19 parted company, although they did so on good terms. Brilliant 19 had been Amy's home for six months longer than her initial contract and she was twenty-two now and able to make her own decisions about who she wanted to represent her. During those years Nick Godwyn had seen Amy change from the innocent teenager who had bust her guitar string the day they met. She was ambitious for something else, though I'm not entirely sure she knew what. But her creativity certainly seemed to become unlocked when she finally made it to New York to meet Mark Ronson.

I always think of Mark as another of Amy's brothers. I don't think he was what she expected at all. 'He's probably an old Jewish guy with a long beard' was what she said to me, rather than a young, hip DJ and record producer. But, in the same way that Salaam Remi and Amy had hit it off, so Amy did with Mark. They had a lot in common. Mark had been born in London and he understood implicitly the connection between Jewish music and the black music of soul, hip-hop and jazz that Amy loved. He also seemed to understand her enough to bring out all the pain of the last few months and help her turn it into music. He is shy and softly spoken and seemed to have the knack of steering Amy in a non-confrontational way, which allowed her to flourish. They wrote *Back To Black* in three weeks during that trip.

But with no management behind her, Amy was at a loose end. I know she would have been happy for Nick Shymansky to leave Brilliant 19 and have him manage her, but by his own admission he was too young and inexperienced. I suspect, too, that he had realized what a handful Amy was. She had taken to Raye Cosbert, though.

Raye wasn't a manager, he was a promoter at Metropolis Music, but he'd already been involved in promoting some of Amy's gigs. I had seen Raye backstage a few times – he's hard to miss being well over six foot with long dreadlocks – and he and Amy shared a love of similar music. He had high expectations for their future partnership, which seemed to appeal to her. *Frank* hadn't been released in the States, a decision that had disappointed Amy, but he saw that a future album could crack the American market.

With hindsight, not releasing *Frank* there was a wise decision. So few artists make it in the US that Amy knew, in her heart, she only had one shot at it. My apprehension was always that despite Amy's growing ambition she had never personally matured. It was as if her talent was miles ahead of her and she'd missed out on a stage of development. Whenever I saw her perform she'd be reaching out for me in the audience. 'There's my mummy. I can see my mummy!' she'd call out into the crowd almost as if she was trying to bridge the gap between us and the surreal world of fame. I suspect that she was both exhilarated and completely terrified that life was moving so fast for her.

Mitchell had come on board as part of Amy's management team, and I was happy for him to do that. With MS I could never have been on hand for her, and besides, what did I know about the music industry? Amy wouldn't have wanted me to interfere either. And I don't think I could ever have enjoyed socializing in her industry – I hated all the fake smiles and the handshakes. I was always very proud of Amy, but I never wanted to be part of the entertainment world in the way that Mitchell did. I was a pharmacist, for God's sake, and her mother.

Even so, I was always interested in what she was doing and I couldn't wait to hear the new album she kept telling me about. I felt sure that Amy knew what she wanted and I knew that once she'd set her mind on something she'd achieve it, just as she'd done with *Frank*. But, as usual, she kept everything under wraps until the last minute.

In between recording in New York with Mark and also working with Salaam in Miami, Amy took a holiday in Israel with Cynthia, Mitchell's sister Melody and her husband Elliott. Cynthia had never been to Israel, and perhaps she realized this would be her last chance: she now relied on tubes to support her breathing. I'm so pleased that Amy and Cynthia finally got to share some time together because on 5 May 2006, Cynthia died.

I was in Italy with Tony at the time so I wasn't at Cynthia's bedside, but I'd called for regular updates on her condition once I knew she had been admitted to Barnet General Hospital. Cynthia had left very specific instructions in the event of her death. She was petrified of being buried so, against Jewish tradition, she was cremated at Hoop Lane Cemetery in Golders Green. She had also requested that her ashes be interred among twelve trees in north London parkland.

Not for a moment did I, or any of my family, think that only five years later we would be filing past Amy's coffin in the exact same chapel. Later we would decide that the best place for Cynthia was beside Amy, and they now rest together in Edgwarebury Cemetery: nan and granddaughter reunited, but, tragically, both gone too soon.

Amy sat with Mitchell and Alex at Cynthia's funeral and cried and cried. She was inconsolable. I remember her hugging me and she had mascara smudged across her face. I also remember that she was not wearing black; instead she'd turned up in a leopard-skin print dress, which Cynthia would have loved. She always wore such bright colours.

What Cynthia would have hated, though, is the tattoo that Amy went on to get of her on her right shoulder. I have to confess, I hated Amy's tattoos too. She had her first one when she was fifteen – a Betty Boop in the small of her back – and she'd periodically added to the collection. 'So you're responsible!' I joked when I met Henry Hate last year, the artist who'd drawn some of them. Actually Henry is far sweeter than his name would have you believe. It was at his studio in Shoreditch that Amy had Cynthia tattooed on to her. It cost her £120 and she went back a week later to have the word Cynthia and two love hearts placed next to it.

Having lost her phone, she'd introduced herself to Henry by using his without permission, and then proceeded to pick up one of the many books on his shelf and began ripping out the pages she liked. The book was called *1,000 Pin Up Girls* and she was looking for a likeness of Cynthia. She had been a Sophia Loren figure, she told Henry, beguiling and vivacious. Eventually she found the picture she was looking for and Henry had started to make some sketches of the image. He'd wanted to add his own touches but Amy stopped him. 'I don't want your doodles, that's exactly what I want,' she said, pointing at the page. On it was a black-and-white photograph entitled 'Headline Honey' featuring a 1950s model called Marge, curvy and smiling and dressed in black stockings, high-waisted knickers and with a front-tie shirt covered in newspaper print pattern not unlike the pattern covering the Moschino shift dress Amy went on to wear later that year on *Later With Jools Holland*. The blurb beside Marge read 'Getcha mawnin' papers fellas, all the news you wantta read! It's the whirl before your eyes brought by cuddly Marge Wilson, a neat 5'4" of flash from Pittsburgh, Pa.'.

Perhaps it wasn't only Cynthia who could see into the future.

8

Puttin' On The Ritz

In mid-May 2006, not long after Cynthia's death, the Winehouses had a wedding to go to. My friend Phil's sister Hilary, with whom I'd often gone out to Jewish singles nights, was getting married in Whetstone in north London. Phil had made the journey from New York with his family for the occasion and it was lovely because Hilary was sixty and she was getting hitched for the first time, to an Italian called Claudio whom she'd met at salsa dancing classes.

Amy brought along her latest boyfriend, a sweet young man called Alex Clare, but she spent much of the meal huddled into my side, not really wanting to mix with the other guests. That was unheard of for Amy because she absolutely loved gatherings when all the family were together. 'Are you OK, Amy?' I kept asking. I knew how badly she was taking Cynthia's death and I knew her well enough to know that when things really mattered, she kept her feelings bottled up. Over and over again she reassured me she was fine, and she sang that evening. But, later on, once Amy had left, one of the guests took me aside to tell me that Amy had been heard being sick in the toilets. Once again, I was beside myself with worry.

Bulimia had never been diagnosed in Amy and it wasn't ever formally diagnosed throughout her life. I was aware of a creeping problem, though, because she had lost all that weight; whenever I saw her I would make a mental note about how thin her arms and legs were looking. Amy didn't want to speak to me about her weight. 'I'm dealing with it, Mummy, it's fine,' she'd say. Again, perhaps I was too close to the situation to push things with her, but that evening I was reminded of a conversation Amy had had with me at the flat in Leopold Road, shortly after she first left home.

'I've got this amazing new diet,' she announced.

'Oh right, what is it?'

'It's called eating and throwing up!' she laughed.

'Oh, Amy, don't be so ridiculous,' I said, brushing the remark aside.

It was the sort of outrageous thing Amy liked to come out with all the time, but in the light of her obvious weight loss that conversation took on a whole new meaning. Had that been Amy's way of confessing her secret? She was still just a teenager then, with no record deal, no paparazzi following her and no public interest in her whatsoever. But, like most young women, she was conscious of her appearance, even though she always looked beautiful to me.

I remembered, too, the very rudimentary self-portrait she had drawn as an eight-year-old when I'd been struck by how harsh an image she had of herself. Was that a clue to something more deep-seated?

I started furiously grabbing at every insignificant memory as a way of trying to piece the clues together. I needed to understand the situation and to explain it to myself.

Amy certainly saw herself differently, and once *Frank* had been released and she was being photographed regularly she became even more self-critical. 'For God's sake, I'm a singer, not a model,' she would often say, but, sadly, what woman is judged on her talent alone? Although Amy was developing a strong sense of how her look could attract attention, my own feeling was that by the time *Back To Black* was released, her image had become a mask that she hid behind.

Back in 2003, around the time of *Frank*'s release, Amy had

appeared on the cover of the weekly magazine *Time Out* and Richard recalls asking her to sign a copy for him.

'Are you changing your name now you're a big star?' he had teased her.

'No!' she'd replied with a frown. 'I'm Amy Winehouse and that's who I'm staying.'

But a few years later she was doing everything she could to hide the Amy Winehouse I knew. At the same time it grew harder for her to break her self-destructive habits because they were becoming deep-rooted. I think she'd convinced herself that what she was doing was normal, but whether it was alcohol or cannabis, everything Amy did was to excess. I saw this as Amy trying to control her anxieties – in particular, now, after Cynthia's death – but I also saw that she took comfort from these same habits. They were becoming what she knew best.

I had known for some time about the drinking and the smoking. I also knew that her periods had stopped, and I'd put that down to bulimia. But whenever I tried to discuss it with her all I got was the 'I'm fine, don't worry about me' routine. 'Mum, she's not telling the truth,' Alex would often say to me. But, what was the truth? Amy could never give a straight answer. There were aspects of her spiralling problems that were difficult to understand, but they were always made worse by the lies she told to the people who loved her most. And, worst of all, the lies Amy told to herself.

In the summer of 2006, the eyeliner Amy was so fond of wearing took on a life of its own, and I noticed that she'd started back-combing her hair. If I'm honest, I'm not sure I liked this meta-morphosis. Granted, it certainly gave her presence, but occasionally I had a fleeting feeling that it wasn't really Amy sitting in front of me. That sounds weird, I know, but the Amy I knew was a regular tomboy; now it was as if she'd turned up in fancy dress. Did Amy even know who she was any more? In the hectic life she'd now been catapulted into, I don't believe she ever had enough time to find out. I found myself in the bizarre position of watching my own daughter on screen and trying to figure her out too. And when Amy appeared on several TV shows later that year, those feelings escalated into what felt like a public execution.

Amy had put the finishing touches to her second album *Back To Black* at the Powerhouse Studios in west London during the summer, and prior to the album being released she appeared on *The Charlotte Church Show* performing a duet with the show's presenter. As a finale they sang Michael Jackson's 'Beat It'. It was a song Amy used to play time and again as a child. Apparently the filming of that track took three takes because Amy had been drinking all day and was almost paralytic by the time she needed to perform. The band had played in a key that was right for Charlotte Church, but it had been too high for Amy, she told me later, and that was the only reason she'd slurred and shouted her way through the song.

Believe me, without some gallows humour I would have fallen apart long ago. I can joke about it now, but I was thrown off balance at the time. The whole thing reminded me of the famous scene in Mel Brooks' spoof horror film *Young Frankenstein* when the Monster, played by Peter Boyle, duets with his creator Dr Victor Frankenstein, played by Gene Wilder. When the duo attempt to sing the 1929 Irving Berlin classic 'Puttin' On The Ritz' in front of an expectant audience the inarticulate Monster wails and strangles every note of the title line.

But, unlike *Young Frankenstein* – a film that has always had me in stitches – I sat there open-mouthed watching Amy. To start off with I shrugged it off as Amy sticking two fingers up to the world, which was in lots of ways the gutsy part of her that I loved, but by the time the credits rolled it was a different story. 'Please don't do this, Amy,' I kept saying to myself. 'You have no idea how much it hurts me.' Watching her felt like watching a car crash. I had no idea then that her public appearances were about to get a whole lot worse.

Amy hadn't always been like that on TV. She'd first appeared onscreen as a panellist on the BBC2 quiz *Never Mind the Buzzcocks* in 2004, just after *Frank* was released. She was on the comedian

Phill Jupitus's team, and I'd loved watching her back then. She was bright and funny and I could hear her laughter throughout the show. But by November 2006, when she was invited back, she was out of control. Her shiny brown hair had disappeared and the back-combed bird's nest had sprouted into a full beehive which to me looked completely askew.

This time Amy was part of Bill Bailey's team, and the pro-gramme's host was fellow comedian Simon Amstell. The show is supposed to be anarchic so Amy's razor-sharp wit fitted in well, but as the half hour progressed Amy got louder and more raucous the more tipsy she got. I don't for a moment think she was embarrassed. I'd never known her to be embarrassed by things she said or did in public – that's if she could remember what she'd said or done. Amstell tried to make light of her behaviour and some of his comments cut to the bone, but he appeared to be genuinely concerned about her, at one stage even remarking, 'This isn't a pop quiz any more, it's an intervention, Amy.'

There was one excruciating exchange that struck me at the time as being profound but, looking back, was an omen of worse to come.

'We used to be close,' Amstell said jokingly, leaning over to Amy.

'We were close, but she's dead,' Amy retaliated.

'Can we resuscitate the old Winehouse?' he pleaded. 'I loved you when you were sober.'

'She's dead,' Amy repeated.

That Amy could say something so perceptive about herself and yet say it so flippantly sent me reeling. Perhaps that moment resonated so deeply within me because there was so much truth wrapped up in it, the sort of truth no outsider would have under-stood. I had become conscious of losing part of my daughter way before then, and there she was, on national prime-time TV, confirm-ing it.

I have always allowed my children the freedom to be their own people, but it was as if it had become Amy's task in life to bury the girl I raised. Now, even I couldn't get a handle on her. Sometimes seeing Amy was like having an out-of-body experience. I started seeing her from a distance, as if I'd become desensitized. It went against my mothering instincts, so I then became conscience-stricken about my own detachment. When I later talked about it with my counsellor Jacky, she explained that what was happening was OK and that my numbness was my mind protecting my body. It was becoming physically harder for me to face Amy because she was becoming so emotionally distressing to watch.

What made life all the more confusing for me was that *Back To Black*, which had been released in October 2006, was absolutely incredible. A couple of months before the album came out Amy had given me a sample CD which had on it a mixture of stripped-back versions of songs like 'Some Unholy War' and others like 'Back To Black' which had only the beginnings of production work by either Mark Ronson or Salaam Remi (the two producers had split work on the album in the same way that production on *Frank* had been split between Salaam and Gordon Williams). Because the instrument-ation was so bare on the demos it was again Amy's vocals that leaped out at me. Whereas *Frank* had youthfulness about it, *Back To Black* struck me as shatteringly adult. I was gobsmacked at how slick Amy sounded, and taken aback by the maturity of her lyrics. All this was my little girl! I've heard commentators say since that Amy's writing on the title song 'Back To Black' is as good as any Shakespearian sonnet. That puts the biggest smile on my face. If only she knew.

To me, the album was such a bold statement. I know she was proud of it too. She'd felt more involved in the process from start to finish and to her it was more her creation. The Dap-Kings, the 1960s backing singers who appeared on the final version, were the perfect accompaniment to Amy's retro sound too. But, honestly, none of us had any idea how it would capture mainstream audiences in the way it did.

Where Amy got her love of the sixties girl-group sound that dominated *Back To Black* I am not sure. When she was younger, Richard used to make up tapes for her. He has an eclectic vinyl collection and on the cassettes would be American musicians like Laura Nyro and Willy Deville, but he'd always include some ska music or music by the Shangri-Las or the Supremes. I don't know if she listened to them closely but something might have percolated through. The dark melodramas played out in the lyrics of these songs certainly gripped her, even though the Shangri-Las' harmonies often sounded sugary sweet. After all, *Back To Black* was all about breaking up with a boy who was no good for her (even if he was someone who at this point I'd never even met).

And the beehive? It was Amy's modern twist on that era too – Ronnie Spector meets Sweet 'n' Sour. As far as I know, the beehive was an idea that came solely from her and was created over time with her hairdresser Alex Foden. In one of her later flats in Camden she kept the wigs in the cupboard under the stairs. Whenever I opened the door I could see three beehives lined up and laid out in their boxes. I called them her 'litter of beehives', to match her growing litter of cats. Although she rarely wore her beehive indoors, the hair extensions were becoming such a vital part of her appearance that I remember asking myself in the run-up to Christmas one year, 'Should I buy the beehives a present?'

It was around the time of the release of *Back To Black* that Amy started employing stylist Naomi Parry, who worked alongside her to develop her look. Apparently she and Naomi had met in a club in Soho a couple of years before and they'd bonded in front of the mirrors in the ladies' toilets while back-combing their hair. Amy was brilliant at making friends with people she'd only just met and, not unusually for her, the pair kept in touch. Naomi had just finished her degree at Camberwell College of Arts when she got a phone-call from Raye Cosbert asking her, 'Are you actually a stylist, or one of Amy's mates?' Amy had requested that Naomi come on board, but Raye was wise to check. You could never be sure who Amy was asking to do what, or whether they were even qualified for the job. Poor Naomi was thrown in at the deep end, but then it was always going to be a shaky start with Amy.

Naomi's first job was to dress her for the pre-recording of Jools Holland's *Hootenanny*, on which Amy sang a duet with the musician Paul Weller. Naomi had found a strapless black number by Julien Macdonald sewn in with feathers that looked like something Shirley Bassey would wear. Of course, Naomi's job was made much harder by Amy refusing to be fitted before any performance, so dressing her was often guesswork on Naomi's part. Amy detested all that fuss.

On this occasion she tried the dress on only minutes before the recording was due to start. She loved it but it was too long and she wanted it above the knee and much more fitted. So Naomi pulled it in under the bust and pinned it down the back. Unfortunately, that now meant the silk bodice didn't sit right on her and kept slipping down once she was on set. As Amy and Paul Weller sang the most beautiful rendition of 'Don't Go To Strangers', the song made famous by Etta James, Amy was constantly adjusting her dress, but the final footage was amazingly well edited. Off camera the dress slipped down so far that her breasts kept falling out. Paul Weller certainly saw more of Amy than he'd bargained for.

Naomi was waiting in the wings watching the 'boob malfunction' with gritted teeth, and she fully expected to be sacked afterwards. 'Who cares?' Amy told her as she walked off set. 'It's only a boob.' She found it hilarious rather than embarrassing. Amy had always been completely comfortable with nudity, which was strange for a girl who hid so much underneath.

As Naomi recalls, Amy regularly got her to take a pair of scissors to the hems of her dresses a quarter of an hour before she went on stage so they could be made shorter. A dress could have been from Primark or Prada, Amy wouldn't have cared, and I guarantee she would have ripped them shorter if Naomi hadn't been there to make the cut. Typical Amy! In her drive for perfection she managed to create the most imperfect image of all her contemporaries, which in a weird way is why I think her look has become so iconic. In the same way that fans could identify with the emotions behind her lyrics, ordinary girls could relate to her thrown-together wardrobe and could easily emulate it.

There was no doubt in my mind that *Back To Black* was a fantastic achievement, but it was interesting to me that everyone saw the album as an outpouring of Amy's heartbreak. It was also an album about revenge. It was Amy saying 'screw you' to Blake, who had abandoned her for his ex-girlfriend.

If there's one thing I instilled in Amy it was never to behave like a victim. 'Always turn a negative into a positive,' I'd tell her, and boy, did she show him. She turned that experience into a record that reached the top spot in the album charts in less than two months. By the second week of its release *Back To Black* had sold more than seventy thousand copies, and by the end of 2007 it had sold 1.85 million copies, becoming that year's best-selling album. It was unbelievable.

Whereas reaction to *Frank* had been mixed, the reviews for *Back To Black* were unanimously positive, some writers even tipping the album as an instant classic. There was no bigger 'screw you' to Blake than that. I only wish that *Back To Black* had been Amy's final word to him.

Thinking back on that time now, it felt like being pulled along by a runaway train that kept picking up speed. I hardly saw Amy in the months after *Back To Black*'s release, yet she was everywhere around me. I bought every newspaper and every magazine, and friends and family sent me cuttings of her. I still have them. I'd been forced into behaving like a fan rather than Amy's mum.

Even though I could see Amy losing her footing in a way I'd not experienced before, I could never have predicted the perfect storm that was brewing inside her, a storm that would send her into a kind of freefall. I loved her so much but the hardest part of the next few months and years was that that wasn't enough to stop her. At first I thought that if I willed it enough, someone or something would scoop Amy up and make her OK. It sounds naive, I know, but it was the only way I could keep hoping she would reconnect with me. I also genuinely don't know to what extent Amy realized how agonizing it was for the people closest to her to witness her harming herself in such extreme ways. Because she refused to acknowledge her weaknesses, I don't believe she saw the chaos she created. She was now instinctively making a beeline for the next drama or disaster and I fought an ever-shifting battle in my mind about how to – or whether to – react to every irrational move she made. Still, without fail, for every trough Amy hit there was always a peak that she climbed.

On Valentine's night in 2007 we all gathered as a family to support her at the BRIT Awards. She had been nominated in the category of Best British Female alongside artists such as Lily Allen and Corinne Bailey Rae. It was the first big industry bash I had been to. Amy had called me earlier in the day. 'You're coming, aren't you, Mummy?' Nothing could have stopped me.

That day is so clear in my mind. I went to get my hair done in Barnet in the same hairdresser's Amy used to run into as a child and announce that she was going to be a star. Now that she actually was, it felt very peculiar. People tapped me on my shoulder. 'Fingers crossed! Good luck, Janis!' they wanted to say, and it was lovely that there was so much support for her.

That night a car came to pick me and Tony up and we were driven to Earls Court where the ceremony was taking place. I was made to feel very special. This year Amy was performing, which was a real treat because she now had the ability to command an audience in a way she'd not been able to before. I was so thrilled that we would be there to experience it with her. Given that it was St Valentine's Day, Amy had been asked to perform in a red dress, which Naomi had only managed to come up with at the last minute. Because Amy was so insistent about her dresses being tightly fitted, her style often defied what was currently on the catwalk, and as a result it was a mad scramble to find clothes that she actually wanted to wear.

Other than at Amy's concerts, it was the first time I'd properly stepped into her world. 'Don't hope for too much, Janis,' I kept saying to myself, but it was a superstitious thing. If I told myself she was going to win, it was bound not to happen, so I tried to keep my cool. It wasn't easy because the atmosphere that night was electric. Our table might have been set with the most God-awful kosher chicken, but without doubt, being sat in that room was exhilarating. But there was also an element about it that disturbed me. When I took a look at the other tables, the celebrities occupying the seats near to us completely passed me by: all I saw was champagne chilling in silver buckets and bottles of wine and spirits on the tables. It niggled with me. This was a world of alcohol. It was all part and parcel of being in Amy's circle, and it wasn't a freedom, it was a trap. If she was surrounded by all this, how was she ever going to sort herself out? Did she even *want* to sort herself out? She'd not shown any intention to do so. She was twenty-three and riding the crest of a wave.

It was difficult to put these questions to the back of my mind, but for a short while my anxieties gave way to elation. The DJ Jo Wiley was up on stage and Amy was back at our table with yet another dress on – a black and white number by Giorgio Armani, she told me. I took a deep breath as the nominations were called, and then the moment came when Jo Wiley opened the envelope. I smiled at Amy whose eyes were wide open with anticipation. She was usually so self-deprecating, but this meant so much to her.

'Way more rock 'n' roll than Liam Gallagher, it's the one, the only . . . Amy Winehouse!'

Wow! Now *that* was something else. We were up and on our feet cheering and clapping and the arena seemed to ignite around us. 'I love you, Mummy!' Amy shouted in my ear over the noise as she made her way round the table to hug me. I had a grin from ear to ear that I don't think left me for days.

'I'm just glad my mum and dad are here, to be honest,' she said up on the stage, nervously holding the microphone.

I wouldn't have missed it for the world, Amy.

*

My daughter had an amazing gift, on display on occasions like these BRITs, but she didn't seem to handle well the pressure of performing, and I watched as she used alcohol more and more to hide behind. I had long suspected that Amy's dependencies were the signs of something more deep-seated than youthful rebellion, and I've come to learn that is the case for most people with addiction problems. Amy's success was certainly an added layer we had to navigate, but famous or not, families coping with an addicted child oscillate between feelings of shame and embarrassment and worry and dread, and these feelings shift rapidly from day to day. Whether it was my counsellor or those closest to me, I found it so important to have an outlet where I could discuss what I was feeling. Although it seems counterintuitive – and it's one of the toughest lessons for any parent to learn – I had to look after myself. It's no accident that when the ship is sinking the advice is to secure your own lifejacket first. In whichever way I could, I needed to be strong for Amy.

After the BRITs it was interesting to observe how people behaved around me. With my old friends and family, nothing whatsoever changed. 'That's Amy, she always had balls,' we would say when we were together. Even when Amy's drug problems became obvious, I never hid what was going on – how could I? I'm forever grateful to the people who made up the support network on which, at times, I relied heavily. It was with strangers that my life took an interesting turn. All these people now recognized who she was and who we were. 'Oh my God, you're Amy's mum!' I'd get occasionally. 'Yes, but I'm just a regular person,' I kept thinking. I'd be out having a coffee with a friend and suddenly I'd find myself being harassed. 'Please, bring Amy in,' one woman in a local café would always plead with me. I'd smile politely and shrug, saying to myself, 'But you don't know her.' It's funny how people become blinded by fame.

Of course, I would be lying if I said it wasn't hard at times not to be seduced by what fame can offer. During the time after *Back To Black* hit the charts and Amy was in the newspapers a lot, my friend

Stephanie and I went on a spa weekend to Champneys in Hertfordshire for a bit of girlie pampering. Stephanie booked ahead and, because Amy was now being followed continually by photographers, she thought it best to warn the staff that I was a 'Winehouse' in case there were any reporters or photographers sniffing around. Suddenly Stephanie wasn't dealing with front-desk staff any more – she'd been put through to a special line presumably reserved for VIP guests. Our room was immediately upgraded to a luxury suite and we were treated like queens. I can't deny that it was lovely. It was a tiny fraction of what Amy was now getting used to but it was enough for us to get a taste of the high life. I took it – who wouldn't? – but there was always a part of me that knew it was artificial. Mitchell certainly felt more comfortable with that part of Amy's life than I did. I always said to myself, 'Janis, keep your feet on the ground,' and I like to think I always have done. Inside, Amy never really forgot who she was either; I think it was the recognition that this life in the spotlight was one great illusion that became the most dissatisfying for her. It was all she'd ever wished for, but the reality was so different from how she'd imagined it.

Certainly the sheer joy of her BRITs win was short-lived. Instead of propelling her to a better place, it seemed to tip Amy into another black hole. Whereas before she had been seeing Alex Clare steadily and living with him on and off in Muswell Hill, Amy was now hell-bent on thrill-seeking. She wasn't usually the kind of girl to let things go to her head but success and the public attention that came with it created a fear in her far deeper than the euphoria of winning. All this expectation placed on a girl who couldn't even convince herself that she could deliver, let alone anyone else. I was always surprised how little she valued what she did. Occasionally she'd ask, 'But Mum, do you honestly think it's good?' That self-doubt was always eating away at her, under her bravado.

Alex Clare was left heartbroken when Amy started seeing Blake again in the spring of 2007. Blake had never really gone away for Amy. I didn't know much about their previous relationship but I knew it wasn't a stable one. As soon as I learned she was seeing him again full-time, my heart sank. Amy was back on the knife edge that she always seemed to balance her life on. Unsurprisingly, she didn't call me. She wouldn't have wanted to hear my opinion. She was an adult now and she needed to be responsible for her own choices.

However, when Amy and Blake got engaged that April I didn't ever think she would be foolish enough actually to go through with it and marry him. She'd always said to me, 'Mum, I don't think I'm the marrying sort.' I had no idea what location Amy's brain was vacationing in. It was Amy's money that was now paying for Blake to travel with her and, although I didn't know it at the time, it was her money that was fuelling their drugs habit. If I'm honest, we were all guilty of brushing the subject of Blake's connection to hard drugs under the carpet. We didn't want to believe that that's what was happening.

It was his opportunism that I hated the most. Amy held all the keys to Blake satisfying his own addictions, and he was everything destructive that she craved. They deepened each other's wounds. I think Amy still harboured a lot of anxiety about her father. I didn't know much about Blake but there was one occasion when he really made me recoil. He was with Amy while I was in Italy that year and Amy put Blake on the phone. Whether or not it was a joke I'm not sure, but he called me 'Mummy'. *Mummy?* It felt like he'd stuck a knife in my belly. That was what Amy called me affectionately, and I loved it.

'I'm not your mummy,' I replied.

But, if life felt like it was moving too fast for me, God knows how it must have felt for Amy. Paparazzi had started camping outside her flat in Jeffrey's Place full-time now, which was another odd experience. When it first started happening Amy embraced it. What else could she do? She made the photographers cups of tea and chatted to them. She was generous and friendly, and their interest in her also satisfied Amy's need for attention. But it didn't take long for her to feel powerless in the face of it.

For me, it was just surreal. Now, whenever I went to see her I'd have to walk through strangers to get to my own daughter's flat. Sometimes when Amy's friends walked to her front gate they were shoved aside so the mob could get their pictures. It was a scrum, and it was scary too that suddenly people considered it OK to grab Amy if she was walking down the street to pose for a photograph. It was that noise that struck me the most, that 'click-click-click' that now became a normal part of visiting her. I took it on board because I had to, but I was never comfortable with it. And once Amy began to be known in the States it only seemed to get worse.

9

Behind the Beehive

In April 2007 Amy had performances lined up for her in the US which she was very excited about. After her disappointment at *Frank* not being released there she wanted to put all her energy into launching *Back To Black*, and she'd done a couple of gigs at Joe's Pub, a tiny venue on Lafayette Street, back in January, which had gone well. But it was on 8 May when New York got the measure of her. Amy kept the audience at the Highline Ballroom waiting an hour before appearing on stage, and she drank her way through the whole set. My American relatives sent me reviews – one described her as a 'talent teetering on the edge of destruction'. You couldn't have got a more accurate description. 'That's Amy,' I thought. But, despite several nerve-racking appearances, America received her well. Unexpectedly, too, Amy discovered in New York that she had a huge gay following: apparently there were men in drag hugging each other by the end of her concerts.

I had no idea that ten days later Amy had travelled to Miami for a holiday until I was woken by a phone-call. It was a distant-sounding Amy on the line.

'Amy?' I shouted. 'Where are you?'

'I'm in Miami, Mum.' She giggled sheepishly. 'We're married.'

Later, I discovered that she'd phoned Mitchell half an hour

earlier and told him before she'd braved me. Every inch of me wanted to shout 'You *stupid* girl!' but I contained my anger.

'Lovely, Amy,' I replied through gritted teeth, then wished her good luck: 'Mazel tov.'

'We're going to have another wedding in London – a big party,' she said quickly. I think it was her way of apologizing and saying 'I want you to be part of it', but as soon as I replaced the receiver I just stood there feeling like I'd been smacked in the face with an iron bar.

My mind was racing so fast that my body could hardly keep up. What was she doing? Why was she doing this? Nobody had been told. Nobody had been invited. It had just been Amy and Blake on the morning of 18 May 2007 in the Miami-Dade County Marriage License Bureau. I almost choked when my cousin Joan rang me from Miami later that day having seen the news reports on TV. 'If we'd known, we all could have gone and wished her well,' she said, innocently, as if it was some normal family celebration rather than this toy wedding.

'I don't think it was *that* kind of service,' I replied flatly.

I boiled for days. Not only did I hate the fact she'd married Blake, but I hated the fact that of all the places on the planet, she'd chosen Miami. Not for a moment do I think that Amy would have made the connection. She was in her own 'Amy bubble' without a care for anyone other than herself.

Miami? When I had landed there thirty-five years earlier it had been about me finding freedom and fulfilment through working and experiencing the world. I have held on to that positive experience throughout my entire life, steadily improving my confidence and my self-respect no matter what. Now here was Amy, with more professional and financial power than I could ever have imagined, and what was she doing? She was throwing all that away by getting hitched to some no-hoper.

I tried to put my bitter disappointment to one side, but I would have been superhuman had it not affected me. I'm not sure I would ever have accepted Blake, but in another lifetime I would have wanted to be involved in the preparations and the excitement building up to the event; just like any mum I would have fussed over the dresses and the bridesmaids and the party. Talk about a reality check. All I wanted was for Amy to make choices in her life that offered her true happiness, but now any romantic notion I'd ever had of that had been smashed.

The most disconcerting aspect of it for me was that the whole world saw my daughter's wedding pictures before I did. It was horrible: Amy in her white anchor-patterned dress plastered across the tabloids with a smiling Blake. I found the public appetite for news about Amy as she lurched from crisis to crisis overwhelming – although, interestingly, I was about to get caught up in it myself. 'The whole thing is a big performance,' I kept saying. In fact it was only a dress rehearsal.

That summer continued as it had started, Amy wrapped up in her own bubble with Blake and running to catch up with herself. She'd won another Ivor Novello award in May for 'Rehab' in the Best Contemporary Song category. It should have been a time for celebration, and it was, but as ever it didn't take long for that celebration to turn sour.

I can't say Amy's marriage was the moment when any one-to-one connection between us was severed, but our relationship certainly became strained. It felt like another light had been switched off in my life. I thought about whether, because of my MS, Amy was shutting me out, out of kindness or even fear, but I concluded it was more because she just couldn't stop herself doing what she was doing and she didn't want to face me.

When I went to Jeffrey's Place and met Blake for the first time, with the kettle I'd bought Amy as a wedding present, I came away with the strangest feeling. She'd taken on another role. She'd assumed this other persona, like an over-the-top gangster's moll. Whether she'd got it from a film or from Mitchell's childhood stories of the East End, I don't know. She called Blake 'my man', but she would never have heard me speak like that, nor Cynthia. It was a character conjured from her imagination. Added to that, some part of her warmth was missing. Something had a bigger grip on Amy than her love for her family, or our love for her. What an unsettling reality that was for me to accept. If I'm honest, I didn't accept it until later that summer, and even then not completely. I didn't want to. It was just too difficult.

I kept thinking back to the time when Amy was sixteen and we'd first sat in that office with Nick Godwyn and Nick Shymansky to discuss a possible contract. She was a little girl, stubborn and determined, but with all the potential to fly. Now she was out there soaring like an eagle but without a full set of feathers to keep her airborne. Could I have stopped the juggernaut once it had started rolling? Could any of us? The answer is no. Fame takes on a breathtaking momentum of its own.

I hardly saw Amy after her marriage to Blake. I would have to turn up at Jeffrey's Place because Amy continually lost her mobile phone or failed to stick to arrangements. She was impossible to pin down, and it struck me that she was living her life as if she wasn't connected to it. She'd simply lost any emotional connection with herself.

She had no awareness of, or perhaps just no care for, how she looked either. She now had a tooth missing, and at times her skin looked blotchy and pimply. If only I'd known then what I was soon to discover – that the quantity of drugs she was taking was blocking out anything real. Was this the only way she could now deal with her life?

Mitchell and I had very different ways of dealing with her: his approach was far more combative, whereas I had always taken a steadier, quieter line. We all made mistakes, but it was a learning process for us too. With any form of addiction, you don't wake up one morning and have all the answers. It doesn't work like that. You take each day at a time, trying bit by bit to understand more of what's happening, trying all the while to navigate your way through the onslaught. Even in the darkest of days I always tried to pin a hope on something.

That summer Amy played the Isle of Wight Festival and sang the Motown classic 'Ain't Too Proud To Beg' with the Rolling Stones. I wasn't there, but I did see it. It was like watching a thoroughbred bolting out of the starting blocks. Amy sashayed up next to Mick Jagger without a care in the world, but she was out of it and it showed, although at that point I thought she'd been drinking rather than taking drugs.

A couple of years later, when Richard was filling up a jukebox Amy had bought with Blake, she stopped him putting a 45 of the Rolling Stones' 'Honky Tonk Woman' in it.

'You performed with them!' he pointed out to her.

'I only did it to out-Jagger Jagger, and I did, I out-Jaggered him,' she hissed back.

My God, as a woman I loved Amy's chutzpah at wanting to out-rock a Rolling Stone, but by then she'd become paranoid and displayed an aggression deeper than she'd ever had.

It sounds strange, but back in 2007, knowing that Amy was performing with bands like the Rolling Stones did make me feel optimistic. Although they were men, no doubt more able to put their emotions to one side, all those musicians had gone through the same experience when they started out, and they had all made it to the other side – they'd survived the pressures, the unwanted attention and the addictions. Maybe being in a band protects you; Amy was a woman, out there on her own. Although her world was not a world I understood, I kept thinking, 'When Amy makes it through this, she can get back to concentrating on the music.' I was always searching for that chink of light. 'She's tough like me, she'll get through it.'

But on the morning of 7 August that hope was dashed like never before. I don't know whether it was Mitchell or my cousin Martin who rang me. I don't even remember what was said, but Amy had been taken into University College Hospital the previous night after suffering a seizure. Blake had been with her at Jeffrey's Place when she had gone as white as a sheet and started trembling. He had apparently placed her on her side and phoned Juliette for help, but I still don't know if I believe that story. Up to that point, I couldn't see that Blake had much kindness about him.

I spent most of that morning fighting back waves of nausea. My mobile phone kept ringing, and picking it up became a practical diversion from my own emotional torment. Between my son, Alex, and Martin I was being kept updated. 'Don't come in, they're releasing her soon' was the message.

Amy had been admitted to the emergency ward at around one a.m. She'd had her stomach pumped, and we later discovered that her collapse wasn't just alcohol-induced. She'd taken a cocktail of drugs that included heroin, cocaine, ketamine and marijuana, all of which had brought on the fit. The minute she was discharged, Mitchell took her to the Four Seasons Hotel in Hook, Hampshire, which was set in its own grounds and could provide her with some respite, even though within hours it was crawling with journalists.

It wasn't until the morning of Wednesday the 8th that I drove there with Alex. As we turned into the gravel driveway I experienced a familiar feeling of panic. What was I going to find there? What state would Amy be in? Over the past few months I'd been in complete denial that Amy was a serious drugs user, even though with hindsight the evidence was staring me in the face. It's peculiar the way the mind can shut out painful realities. Thinking back on it, I didn't even use the word 'overdose' it was so distressing. I called it Amy's 'accident'. From now on, though, there'd be no hiding.

We passed the reception desk and I was directed towards Amy's room. The door was open, and as I approached it the world seemed to shift into slow motion. When I did eventually focus on Amy, it was with confused feelings of worry, fear and anger. She was skeletal, like something out of Belsen concentration camp. Hunched over the bed, she was sitting with a white towel wrapped around her. I could see the scars on her arms where she'd cut herself. She was like an apparition. How could it have come to this?

Amy went to hug me. She was grabbing on to me.

'What's happening to you?' I said to her.

'Mummy, Mummy, I'm so sorry, Mummy,' she kept repeating.

I sensed that she was very scared. In her head, perhaps this was her first wake-up call. However, I was to discover that Amy's rock bottom was like nobody else's rock bottom. It was impossible to know where she would draw the line because her behaviour was so wildly inconsistent.

I could barely utter a word to my daughter. My body had gone into some sort of overload. I sat beside her in silence. We both knew that in one form or another this was history repeating itself. For a moment my mind flashed back to when Amy was a toddler and I'd yanked the cellophane out of her throat while she'd convulsed in her buggy. Here I was, twenty years later, still wondering how to save her from disaster. 'I can't keep rescuing you, Amy,' I kept thinking. 'You have to save yourself.'

Several commentaries from that time describe me as cold or without emotion. I've learned to bat such judgements aside. I don't know why people feel they have to comment on a situation they know nothing about. It's human nature, I guess, but nothing could have been further from the truth. I was terrified, but I was trying to be pragmatic. Me crying or pleading with Amy or even me becoming wrapped up in the highs and lows of her dramas was not going to solve anything.

I felt so badly for Alex. I know how incredibly tough he found it seeing his sister like that, and I sensed his frustration. He was the one to give Amy the warning. 'You're going to kill yourself,' he was shouting. 'You're not going to live to twenty-five, you know that, don't you? Are you happy with your life like this?'

Amy didn't answer. She didn't say a word.

'You need to go to rehab, Amy,' Alex carried on.

'No,' she snapped. Rehab might mean she'd have to stop what she was doing and that was not an option that appealed to her. Something powerful was willing her to carry on.

Amy was not choosing to die, that I know, but neither was she choosing to live. Her battle with addiction was not simply a battle that raged in her body, it raged continuously in her mind too, which is why it was so difficult for her to end it. It's a mistake to think that people suffering with addiction can be suddenly cured of the condition. Even under treatment they remain prone to relapses all of their life, to a greater or lesser extent.

The other obstacle to Amy seeking help was Amy herself. If fame resembled a juggernaut, Amy was like a supertanker: it was almost impossible to turn her around. She'd been like that since she was a child, but now she was worse than ever. She dug her heels in hard before she ever decided to move forward. God knows, I can be strong-willed, but Amy really was her own worst enemy.

Click. Another light switch went off in my life. Seeing Amy on that hotel bed became a sort of epiphany for me. Consciously or not, from that moment on I made a decision to practise some tough love, though I didn't ever manage to maintain that course. I've met parents coping with addiction who have been forced into cutting off contact with their addicted child, until the point when that child decides to become drug-free, and I know what an agonizing decision that must be to have to make. That was just too hard for me. I wanted Amy in my life, regardless. I couldn't shut her out completely. I just couldn't do it.

What I did do was let Amy know that I was there for her when and if she decided she wanted my help, and that I loved her. What I couldn't do was allow myself to be continuously sucked in by her. This young, successful woman forced everyone around her to worry about her, and I'd been manipulated to the point where I didn't have a shred of energy left in me. I had to say 'no' now. 'Enough is enough.'

It's so hard for me to say this, but Amy's first seizure was the point when I ceased to be the fully functioning parent I'd always wanted to be. She had apparently asked for me to be at the hotel, but she didn't ask for help and she didn't want my opinion – the last thing she wanted was my opinion. Perhaps for her I was a vital connection, but, as her mum, I couldn't 'fix' anything. This wasn't like mending a broken-down bike or finding another school for her. I'd been reduced to this person who was just 'around', a powerless bystander watching my child kill herself. It was sickening.

Even though from that day I physically stepped back, it quickly became obvious that my mind could never turn off from Amy. She occupied my thoughts day in, day out. I'm positive she didn't know it, but if she wanted my attention she had it whether I was with her or not. She had Mitchell's too, but he preferred to stay there, at times in the thick of the drama, living it with her. I don't judge him for that, but I personally didn't see that that was going to alter the course she was taking.

Over the years Mitchell has come in for criticism about the way he handled Amy. For different reasons we have both been charged with failing to 'save' her. I read something particularly cruel recently which was based on total ignorance of the situation. 'If he couldn't save his daughter, what's he doing starting a charity?' one internet commentator had written. No one could have saved Amy except Amy. We started the Foundation not only because we wanted to help others who don't have the same access to treatment that Amy did, but because we wanted to understand more about addiction ourselves. We lost our daughter and we are still trying to learn from this devastating experience.

Perhaps such judgements simply reflect one of the most difficult aspects of addiction for outsiders to understand: no matter how any-one approaches the situation, the only person who can really save an addict is themselves. Amy knew that too, though perhaps she never saw that it applied to her.

I left the Four Seasons Hotel that afternoon. Every time I left Amy it was the hardest decision to make, but I had to make it. Alex phoned me the next day to tell me that Blake had turned up that night, and he and Amy had taken crack cocaine. It was just before Mitchell called in consultant psychiatrist Dr Marios Pierides from the Capio Nightingale Hospital in Marylebone, one of London's leading psychiatric hospitals. Amy's 'Sorry, Mummy' washed off me like rain.

I went back to work the next day and I was not present when Blake's mother and stepfather arrived towards the end of the week. I didn't ever meet Blake's mother Georgette Fielder-Civil or his stepfather Giles. I chose not to. I had a pretty good idea of the kind of people the Fielder-Civils were, though. Amy had talked about them enough, and in May of that year they had both been convicted at Grantham Magistrates Court for disorderly behaviour. An argument had broken out between them and a football coach because the coach had told off their youngest son.

Although I never witnessed it first-hand, from what I knew of Blake's parents' behaviour around Amy it was nothing short of bizarre. His mother seemed overawed by her success rather than wanting to deal with her son and Amy as addicts who needed support. Mitchell said that when he first met them she was waving around a designer handbag that Amy had bought her and had refused to acknowledge that her son had a problem. She was behaving like a child, not like Blake's mother.

If I sound dismissive of the Fielder-Civils, I'm sorry, but there it is. I am just not at a stage where I can feel conciliatory towards them. I don't know if I ever will be.

Georgette and Giles Fielder-Civil stayed on at the hotel until Saturday, 11 August, when Mitchell arranged for Amy to be flown to the Causeway Retreat, a rehabilitation centre on Osea Island, a remote place off the Essex coast (closed in 2010 after an investigation by the UK health watchdog the Care Quality Commission which found that the owners had been treating psychiatric patients without a licence). Blake travelled with her, and no sooner had they arrived than they arranged for drugs to be smuggled into the premises. Tragically, the two of them couldn't be together without using drugs, and it didn't surprise me when Amy called for another helicopter to get them out of there. She had no intention of staying for any length of time, although why on earth they had to travel by helicopter and not by road I will never know. Was it another act for the cameras, or just Amy's way of saying a big 'stuff you'? My feeling is that it was both.

It wasn't long after Amy's seizure that I had my first encounter with the press. To say that I was naive is one of life's great understatements. Journalists found me through my synagogue. One journalist in particular had a connection with me: his father attended my synagogue and my telephone number was passed around without my knowledge. Mitchell was able to talk to journalists throughout, but I was different. Now, though, the privacy I had up to that point maintained was about to be shattered.

It wasn't the first or the last time I let it happen, but to this day I'm not sure what my motivation was for letting reporters into my life. Amy had always said to me, 'You don't have to talk to them, Mum,' but there was something about the way that I was approached this time round that hit my weak spot. 'It could just be the one thing that turns her around,' I remember one reporter saying to me. Another reason regularly offered was that talking to the press might help other families to cope with addiction. I was part of a family desperately searching for an answer to Amy's addiction problems and, looking back, that left me wide open to persuasion and incredibly vulnerable. If there was the slightest chance that I might alter the course Amy was taking, what mother wouldn't take it? In the end I concluded that I had nothing to lose.

It's taken me a long time, but I've come to realize that in the same way that Amy became fodder to fill pages, I believe so were we. When I made that decision I had no PR machine around me or anyone advising me. I still don't, and the reality was that I felt very powerless in front of the media. I didn't take payment for that first article; instead I asked for a donation to be made to the MS Society. It seemed to me that someone should benefit.

Two journalists came to see me in my flat in High Barnet. There, I had Amy's platinum discs on the wall and her awards on display. It was so odd, because on the one hand I was incredibly proud of everything she had achieved, and on the other I was being asked to talk about the fact that she could have died. You couldn't have got two more contradictory emotions.

It was the *Daily Mail* who ran that first story, but when I picked up a copy I was horrified to see my family photos plastered across the pages. During the visit I had been asked if I had any snaps of Amy as a youngster, so naturally I'd brought out an album. What mum wouldn't? There was Amy in her little pink ballet outfit and pumps, and Amy at my graduation – happy moments of our lives that now seemed a world away. Without asking, the photographer started snapping my photographs. It didn't immediately sink in what he was doing, so instead of stopping him I innocently assumed that any newspaper would ask me what photographs of Amy I wanted in the public domain. No such luck. I felt gutted that pictures I'd taken all those years ago were splashed across an article about Amy's overdose. What was worse, as soon as those pictures were published they appeared under the *Mail*'s copyright. In effect I no longer owned these cherished parts of my life.

Today I am happier giving interviews because it's my task to promote the work of the Foundation and to raise awareness of MS. But back in 2007 I wasn't on as sure a footing. Undeniably too, in the midst of the craziness there's a part of you that gets swept along by events. Once I'd let journalists into my home, I found it difficult to say no again. Perhaps by then I didn't have the strength to resist. That is one thing I would have done differently, but I've lived and learned.

What I really hated was that I'd often get paparazzi loitering around outside my block. I'm not sure what they were hoping for: Janis Winehouse carrying a bag of shopping? My friend Stephanie was much more forthright about sending them packing. One young man she found sniffing around outside definitely got more than he bargained for – a tirade about him being lower than a worm's bum, I seem to recall.

'Vermin' was the word Amy used to describe the photographers who were now camped outside her home day and night. Whereas in the beginning she'd tried to make friends with them, now they scared her. I'll never forget that feeling of being inside her flat knowing they were out there. They'd be leaning up against the car or hanging around outside the gate. I likened it to a column of ants swarming around their prey. Although it sounds insignificant, I do remember Amy's upset at not being able to travel by public transport any more because she was so besieged.

Then again, she could never just sneak out. It's another thing about Amy I never understood: if she went out, it was always in her full beehive and make-up. Either she needed to be in character just to cope with stepping outside her own front door or she craved the drama too much to leave it off. It was a constant puzzle to me. I suspect even she would not have been able to give an answer to that riddle, though I think, deep down, it was dawning on her that she may have created her own monster.

Alex went to see Amy and Blake when they arrived back from Osea Island. They had checked themselves into the Sanderson Hotel in London's West End on the night of Wednesday, 22 August.

After Amy's seizure Alex hadn't known where to turn, but he wasn't blind to what was now surrounding his sister. From drug dealers to paparazzi, she was drawing in parasites that feasted off her every move. Like me, Alex didn't quite recognize who Amy was any more, but his natural instinct was to protect her – who could blame him? He'd often offer his home in Hornsey as a temporary sanctuary should she want to step out of the fray. 'You can come for an afternoon or a day and be safe here,' he would say to her, but back then she had no intention of stepping out of anything.

That night, Alex argued with Blake and then Amy about their drug use. He voiced what we were all feeling inside, but Amy reacted badly to being told what to do. Alex probably knew that it wasn't going to change anything but he needed to say his piece and go. It wasn't until the early hours of the morning that all hell broke loose. An almighty row erupted between Amy and Blake – the whole thing was drugs-fuelled. Amy ran out of the Sanderson with Blake chasing after her. In the photographs from that night they looked wild on drugs. She had mascara smudged all over her face. Both of them had scratches and Amy had a deep cut in her arm and a gashed knee. Blood had soaked into her ballet pumps.

The newspapers got their story, but I doubt Amy was even conscious of the photographers. She was hurtling from one disaster to another and God help anyone who got in the way. Among all the cuttings I have, the pictures of Amy from mid-August 2007 are absent. I can't bear to look at them. She was my daughter. It hurts too much.

Soon after that, Mitchell began arranging meetings with the Fielder-Civils, Amy's doctors and Amy's record company, but neither she nor Blake was ever present and without them there I didn't believe anything would be achieved. Mitchell just needed to react. I'm sure he meant well, and I wouldn't want to put words into his mouth, but he was terrified too. We could have lost Amy only weeks before when her life had hung so perilously in the balance.

We were out of our depth, dealing with incidents while never being able to anticipate what might happen next. I knew Amy was out of her depth too, however tough she thought she was. I saw a girl whose life was overwhelming her, more than she had ever anticipated. It wasn't just bigger, it was uncontrollable and ugly.

For me there was now an issue over her safety, which I could hardly bear to think about. Unlike most users, Amy didn't ever have to go out and find drugs. Drugs came to Amy. For legal reasons I can't point towards any of her suppliers; let's just say some surprising visitors came through Amy's life – and that's the fraction I knew about. They certainly weren't people any parent would want their daughter to be in contact with, especially not a girl who displayed the openness and blind trust Amy did at times when she was 'out of it'.

No matter how off the scale Amy's behaviour was, she cared about people. She was capable of such love, even though what she was doing to herself hurt everyone who loved her. 'It doesn't matter where you are from as long as you're a decent person,' she would say, and if Amy wasn't out of it she could be a good judge of character. It was becoming clearer to us that she was surrounding herself with some very dodgy characters because her mind was programmed solely towards the next fix. There were certainly 'friends' who used her, and the fact that Amy was independently wealthy made it a thousand times worse. As fast as Amy's royalty cheques were coming in she was giving her money away. I'm not sure whether she was doing it to feel in control or to feel accepted, but aside from her true friends, her generosity always seemed misplaced to me. As a child she'd not had much respect for money or for possessions and she'd never pursued music to be rich. Now, though, Amy passed her credit cards around people she hardly knew and let them run up large bills on them. She acted as though she didn't care, and I'm honestly not sure she did. Mitchell told me after her passing that he'd once found her giving away a £20,000 watch to a friend's mother backstage when she was drunk. Money went through her hands like water.

But the financial cost of it all pales into insignificance for me, because I paid the ultimate price of losing her.

Had Amy been older and more mature when she met success, would things have been different? I believe it all happened too fast and she was too young. I was acutely aware that Amy didn't have a stable enough support system behind her to keep her centred. What made me incredibly sad, though, was that she'd got to the top because she was outstanding and because, professionally, she compromised on nothing: Amy was nobody's pawn. Now, without even realizing it, she was becoming everybody's pawn, and kidding herself that she was still on top.

10

Fly Me To The Moon

In the days after the Sanderson Hotel furore a story started to circulate that Amy's blood-soaked ballet pumps were the result of her injecting drugs. I didn't know what Amy was capable of now, but there were some stories I chose to disregard. As far as I know, Amy only ever smoked heroin or crack cocaine – a belief later confirmed by Blake in an interview he did on *The Jeremy Kyle Show* in 2013, after Amy's passing. Not that that made it any easier for me to accept. I'd found myself with a whole new set of questions to wrestle with. If Amy was drinking, was it better than taking hard drugs? If she was smoking drugs, was it better than injecting? It became a case of take your pick. If I'm brutally honest, what did any of us really know back then?

When I finally caught up with Amy after the argument in the Sanderson she simply refused to discuss it. It had become a regular pattern for her never to talk about what had gone before, as if secrecy had become her best friend. I no longer seemed to be dealing with a rational person.

'Amy, I hate seeing you like this,' I said to her.

'Leave it, Mum, I'm fine,' she replied. 'Don't worry about me.'

Thank God Cynthia wasn't alive to see this, I thought. She wouldn't have understood. Although if she had been alive, would she have been the only person able to talk some sense into her?

Amy and Blake flew to St Lucia that week. Mitchell had wanted to confiscate Amy's passport, but Amy had asked Juliette to bring both hers and Blake's to the hotel along with money so that they could leave. Amy would have found a way no matter who tried to stop her. It sounds awful to say it, but that week was a relief for me. There were times I didn't want the phone to ring. I didn't know who or what was going to be on the other end of the line. I was scared of what newspaper stories would emerge next. How had my love for Amy, our love for each other, become so distorted?

It was while Amy and Blake were out of the country that the Fielder-Civils decided they were going to have their say. In what can only be described as a bizarre interview on Radio 5 Live they pleaded with the record-buying public to stop financing Amy and Blake's drugs habit by not buying Amy's records, saying that 'her addiction and her behaviour is not acceptable'.

Seriously, what good would a boycott of Amy's records have done? It was clutching at straws. Whether Amy was a millionaire or living in a cardboard box, she and Blake would have found a way to satisfy their habit come hell or high water. They were now regular users of crack cocaine, one of the most addictive illegal drugs. The intense highs they were experiencing were quickly followed by intense lows followed by an even greater craving for the next hit. Were a few less album sales going to curb that need? I don't think so. I could completely understand their desperation – Blake was their son – but I always felt they craved attention themselves and, unfortunately, I had little faith in them as decent people.

In those few months I'd lost all sense of why Amy had been catapulted to fame in the first place or why our lives were suddenly in the spotlight. The even weirder thing was that Amy was still performing brilliantly and winning awards. Tabloid newspapers only ever wanted to feature her crashes, and I don't think that ever changed, but there was a lot more in between, and every now and again there came a reminder that one day she might want to put all this behind her.

That year, Amy picked up a MOBO award for Best UK Female Artist, having been nominated in four categories. She also won Best Album at the Q Awards, which Mark Ronson collected on her behalf – at the time it was anyone's guess where she was. Her European tour had been cancelled, but she did appear at the Mercury Music Prize awards ceremony at London's Grosvenor House Hotel. Only a month after her seizure she sang the most moving rendition of 'Love Is A Losing Game'. Accompanied only by an acoustic guitar, her voice sent tingles down the spines of all the assembled guests. Mitchell was there to support her that night and it was her old friend Jools Holland who had welcomed her on to the stage. He was such a fan of Amy's music and he made sure to remind guests why. 'Please welcome the truly amazing voice and the person that is . . . Amy Winehouse!' he shouted. I longed to see that person again too. But, that was Amy: just when you thought it was over, she'd pull a rabbit out of a hat and remind us of how gifted she was.

On 14 September it was Amy's twenty-fourth birthday and a chance for some respite from the pandemonium of the last few weeks. Amy seemed more relaxed after her holiday. As usual she came back not knowing what all the fuss had been about. The fame, the drink and the drugs may have convinced her she was invincible, but she was anything but. She was Amy, and she was very human.

Mitchell had arranged a party for her at the Century Club in Soho. She was late, of course, but when she did turn up she ran towards me and gave me a huge cuddle. 'Mummy, Mummy!' she squealed as she wrapped her arms around me. Amy was naturally petite, but suddenly I felt how painfully thin her frame had become. I could feel her ribs as she hugged me, and the bones in her elbows, but I kept my concerns to myself. Whenever I saw Amy I tried not to let my shock at how she looked show on my face. I didn't want her to know the pain I was experiencing inside. That familiar feeling of paddling, paddling, paddling furiously under the surface just to stay afloat never let up in me but I willed myself to appear strong for her. It was the only way now that I could be a parent. Whenever I saw her the instinct to protect her was far greater than any fear.

Although Mitchell and I rarely decided anything together in relation to Amy, there were a few aspects of how we dealt with her that we did agree upon. In theory we were both overseeing Amy's business affairs, and one decision we made jointly was to limit Amy's personal allowance to £300 a week to try to curb her spending. Amy seemed to accept it, although we learned that ultimately it didn't change a thing: all she did was run up IOUs with drug dealers – one for a whopping £12,000. It was an impossible situation.

By October we were back on the merry-go-round again. Amy and Blake moved from Jeffrey's Place into a modern apartment in Bow, east London, next door to Amy's hairdresser Alex Foden (though Amy kept Jeffrey's Place and they moved periodically between the two). Alex was also a drugs user so it couldn't have been a worse move for Amy. I'd met him a few times at Amy's concerts. He was polite and affable but not someone I wanted Amy to be around. They were 'drugs buddies', not what I would call friends.

Alex Foden was with Amy in Norway midway through that month when she and Blake were arrested in Bergen for smoking cannabis in Amy's hotel room. They were released after paying a fine of around £350. *Back To Black* had only made number 1 in Norway in February and now she had a criminal record there. And there was an even more serious problem looming.

Back in June 2006, Blake was one of two men who had badly beaten James King, the landlord of a pub in Hoxton, east London, called the Macbeth. Nobody knew what the argument was about but it was on a summer's night after the pub had closed that Blake had helped his accomplice Michael Brown stamp on the man and kick him to the floor. They'd left him lying on the pavement with a broken cheekbone and a shattered eye socket. And this was my son-in-law.

After the incident Blake and Brown had been arrested and charged with grievous bodily harm but they had pleaded not guilty to the charge and a trial was set at Crown Court for a later date. The first I knew about any of this was on the evening of 8 November 2007, when Amy's flat at Jeffrey's Place was raided by the police.

The day had been a strange one. Tony and I were due to visit Amy, but just as we were about to head off, the phone rang. It was Amy. 'Don't come to the flat, Mum, I'll meet you in a pub,' she said. She sounded panicky, and she said she'd call back. It wasn't until mid-afternoon that I eventually heard from her, but instead of meeting her at Jeffrey's Place she asked me to pick her up from Hackney in east London. I could rarely keep up with Amy's constant chopping and changing, but I was determined to see her. Her mobile cut off before she could tell me the meeting place, though. I tried to call her back several times but she wasn't picking up. It was my son Alex who eventually got through to me. 'Jeffrey's Place is being raided,' he told me. 'There's plainclothes police everywhere.' I stayed put, but my stomach was churning. What the hell was happening now?

Neither Amy nor Blake had been at Jeffrey's Place when the police used crowbars and a battering ram to smash open the door. They spent three hours sifting through her belongings and walked out with three boxes of papers and computer equipment. Mitchell eventually sorted out the mess and was with her in Bow when the police finally caught up with her and Blake. Amy was apparently distraught when Blake was arrested and led away in handcuffs. She wanted to go with him, but the officers wouldn't let her.

The police hadn't been looking for drugs, as I had initially assumed. Shortly after charges had been pressed against Blake and Michael Brown, James King had been pressured and bribed into withdrawing his statement: he'd been offered £200,000 and an all-expenses-paid trip to Spain in return for the charges being dropped.

Allegedly it was Amy's money that was paying for it, and it was evidence against her that was now being gathered.

When I spoke to Amy the next morning she sounded disturbingly remote.

'How are you?' I said, treading carefully.

'You haven't said anything about Blake,' she snapped, as if that was the only reason I'd wanted to speak to her.

'That's a bit like saying the sun is out, it must be daytime,' I replied. 'I know he's been taken in. What more is there to say?'

But she was so focused on herself and Blake now that nothing else in the world mattered, and I was left once more facing another catastrophic situation.

It was such an unnerving feeling knowing that Jeffrey's Place was a crime scene where officers had combed through cupboards, drawers and wardrobes and pored over Amy's life. It was the place where she'd started her career, a place I was enormously fond of. Amy was capable of a lot of things, but I was certain that bribery was not one of them. I took a deep breath and prepared myself for the next bombshell, but in truth I was numb now and largely acting on autopilot.

Blake's trial for GBH was due to begin at Snaresbrook Crown Court on 12 November but it was delayed following the allegation against him that he had attempted to pervert the course of justice. Blake was remanded in custody in Pentonville Prison pending a further hearing. It was the first time Amy and Blake had been apart in months.

Amy had decided to carry on with her UK tour which was booked throughout November and would see her playing some of the largest venues she'd ever played in the country. She was beginning to hate touring but desperately wanted to honour her commitment to the thousands of fans. At heart she was a professional – she didn't ever want to cancel or let her management down – but she had no idea of what her limitations were.

Touring took a physical and mental toll on Amy. Aside from the relentlessness of the travelling there was also the strain of playing a different venue every night. Because most of Amy's performances were at night and after-show parties went on into the small hours, much of her day was spent sleeping or with no real structure. Her body clock was now programmed to a dark-hours setting, which couldn't have done anything to alleviate her depressions. Neither did having to pour her heart out again and again. *Back To Black* had been made in the aftermath of personal turmoil, and when she sang its songs she was pulled back to that every time. For her, the problem was that once the show was over she just couldn't cut loose from it.

I was texting her regularly at this time but I would only get the occasional text back. 'Fine, Mummy. I'm fine.' It was an act, and I knew it. Even when Amy was a teenager, whenever she sang her mind seemed to go to another place, so wrapped up was she in the adrenalin of the performance and the emotions behind the lyrics. The process of writing certainly exorcized demons for Amy but constantly having to revisit those songs never allowed her to move on. With Blake now in prison I was worried that touring would be a mistake for her rather than a focus. It turned out to be both.

After a discussion with her doctors, Amy had begun a course of the opiate blocker Subutex before her first gig in Birmingham, and although for me that was a positive move, I knew from past experience it was dangerous to hope. If Amy came crashing down, so did those around her. Even so, it was the first time Amy had even tip-toed towards any sort of recovery. With Blake in prison I thought that some breathing space might give her the clarity to see the person she'd become and call a halt to it. It would never be too late to stop, I kept encouraging her.

But coming off drugs and staying off drugs are two very separate things. More often than not it has to be done little by little. As a pharmacist, when I was dispensing methadone it could be months, sometimes even years, before an addict's dosage could be taken down by even just a milligram. The problem too is that, contrary to belief, blockers like methadone and Subutex don't stop a user wanting to take drugs, all they do is alleviate some of the physical cravings. The mental addiction remains. I was under no illusion about the nature of the task that Amy faced, and I couldn't see how she would get through that without professional help.

My biggest frustration was that although Amy resisted psychiatric help, it was clear in my own mind that that was exactly what she needed. Before I sought counselling it had been difficult to admit that I couldn't cope, but once I'd cleared that hurdle everything got that bit easier – I'd faced a problem. Sadly, I don't think Amy ever got to the stage where she thought she had a problem. Another possible reason, which I learned from my daughter-in-law Riva after Amy's passing, was that Amy had continually resisted the idea of medication or therapy for how she was feeling because she was terrified that she would lose the highs and lows that fuelled her creativity. Devastatingly for me, either might have saved her life.

Despite her best efforts, that first gig at the Birmingham National Indoor Arena on 16 November was a disaster. She'd seen Blake in prison the day before the show; that evening she talked about him and 'standing by her man' and forgot the words to her songs before falling over on stage. Instead of quitting while she was ahead, in typical Amy fashion she began attacking the audience for booing: 'First of all, if you're booing you're a mug for buying a ticket. Second, to all those booing, just wait till my husband gets out of incarceration. And I mean that.' When it came to performing the song 'Valerie' she dropped the microphone and stormed off.

She'd recorded that song, originally written by the Zutons, with Mark Ronson earlier in 2007 but it had been released as a single that October. Despite reaching number 2 in the UK charts, she hated it. She hated that it had become her signature tune because it wasn't a song written by her. It's funny, but whatever mess Amy was in, it was her material that she wanted out there. But where was her inspiration going to come from? Alcohol and now drugs had become her only experience of the world. They defined her existence, and her connection to reality; I think they were the only things that allowed her to feel anything. What a destructive form of self-medication.

Two days after the Birmingham disaster, Amy played Newcastle Academy. It was a surprisingly good gig. My sister Debra had met up with Amy in her dressing room beforehand as the venue was on Debra's doorstep. Debra's husband Eugene had had a car accident only a few days before and he was the first person Amy asked after. Throughout the show Debra stood with her son, Sam, next to the sound engineer who couldn't stop enthusing about Amy and the polished performance she put on that night.

In the ups and downs of those few weeks Debra had been nervous about how well the concert would go; she certainly didn't expect Amy to be her sweet and funny self when they met afterwards in her suite in the Malmaison Hotel. Eugene joined them there too and, although by then it was more difficult to spend private time with Amy because of the entourage surrounding her, they chatted until two a.m. Debra told me what a lovely evening it had been, catching up on family news. Although Amy didn't say it, Debra sensed she was keen for them to stay and talk because it stopped her from taking drugs; it was as if she was looking for a distraction and was trying to hold herself together. For Amy, even momentarily touching base with family became more important when she was successful because we had no ulterior motive for loving her. To us she was never that megastar girl on the posters or the album covers – she didn't even look like that: she was far more petite in the flesh.

Just like everyone else in my family, Debra remained very supportive. 'Hang in there, Jan, hopefully she'll be OK,' she would say, as sisters do. Along with my brother Brian, whom I spoke to a lot, she kept me sane, even though there were some days when I couldn't see a future. People had begun stopping me in the street. 'Are you OK, Janis?' they would ask. 'I'm either OK or I'm crazy,' would be my reply, because I feared that each day could suddenly turn into my worst nightmare. Underneath, I longed to be plain old

Janis Winehouse again, the pharmacist from north London who lived an ordinary if topsy-turvy life but who was proud of everything she'd achieved and loved her kids with all her heart.

Amy's tour was cancelled soon after she'd returned to London to attend a preliminary hearing set for Blake at Snaresbrook Crown Court. The Subutex had made her sick and she'd stopped taking it. It was one step forward, two steps back, but I had to keep reminding myself that that was always going to be the case with Amy. Most of the time the cravings she experienced were so strong that she forgot she ever wanted to get clean. It was such a vicious circle.

Crack cocaine and heroin had now become Amy's way of dealing with anything bad that happened in her life. I don't blame the fans for booing at her concerts – they'd paid to see Amy Winehouse, not her shell. She gave the impression that she didn't care, but she did. Even so, instead of that triggering in her a desire to get better, the anger and frustration she felt about her performances just got worse and she'd get high to cope with the anxiety.

November spiralled into December, and on the 2nd Amy was photographed in her red bra and jeans crying outside her flat in Bow. It was reported as if she had been 'wandering the streets' but I understand she'd simply opened her front door. Again, I can't look at that picture. I still feel a tremendous amount of anger that it was published at all. It wasn't necessarily the shock of seeing Amy like that that upset me the most – I'd seen Amy scared and distressed before – it was the fact that someone somewhere had decided it was OK to continue photographing a girl who was clearly battling with her own mental health. To me, she looked like a frightened child – *my* frightened child. It was such a savage assault. I still wonder if any of those people ever stopped to ask how they might feel if that were their child. I doubt it.

Along with Amy, I could feel myself reaching my own rock bottom. I try not to dwell on my darkest days, but there were certainly times when I pictured Amy in a room on her own, just lying there not breathing, someone having to smash in the door and scoop her body up from the floor. During those months I replayed Amy's death so many times in my head, even though I fought constantly with myself not to think like that. She was hardly recognizable to me as my daughter. But for all those days when she seemed far away, there were others when I caught a glimpse of my Amy and I thought, '*Come on*, you can get through this.'

It was after those pictures appeared that I was contacted by an agency journalist and asked whether I would write an open letter to Amy that would appear in the *News of the World*. I mulled it over, and discussed it with friends. I rarely discussed anything with Tony as he had long before taken a step back. Understandably, he didn't want to be sucked in by the drama, though I'm not sure Tony had the gumption to put his foot down with press intrusion. I felt very alone in the decisions I was having to make.

My initial reaction was that I didn't want to go ahead. I'd been appalled when my family photographs were splashed across the tabloids. But, in the situation I found myself in, I'd had to learn to let so much of what I valued in life go. Somewhere along the line I'd lost my bite too, and I think my MS was largely responsible for that. I am the worst judge of exactly what this condition has taken from me but people closest to me tell me it's a lot.

I think by that point I also had little sense of what was the right thing to do. Coping with the problem of addiction is bad enough, but I always had several more added layers of public scrutiny to deal with which complicated every decision I made. And I had Alex to think of. Throughout all of this I was still his mum and I did worry about how my involvement in Amy's crises would impact on him. In the aftermath of the Bow pictures, my emotions were pushed and pulled in all directions. If there was a chance that doing *something* might help Amy, should I do it? Could I counter what was out there with a mother's perspective, or would I simply make the situation worse?

In the end, another factor tipped the balance. Soon after the initial phone-call I received another call to let me know that Blake's mum Georgette was writing an open letter to Amy. If there was one thing I wasn't going to do, it was let Blake's mother publicly plead for my daughter. The fact that she'd even offered to – if indeed she did offer to – was evidence enough that she didn't know Amy, or me, or anything about our relationship. In the end her letter never materialized, and I can only think it was a way of manipulating me into agreeing.

It worked.

But I didn't write the letter. I believe the journalist did. I briefly saw a copy of it before it was published in the *NOTW* the following Sunday. I'm not a person to have regrets, but nothing whatsoever was gained by its publication other than the *NOTW* getting their story. I realized I should have listened to my gut instinct. It didn't even sound like me. And as much as I would have wanted Amy back home, my condition made that impossible; there was too much in which she was involved for that to be a realistic prospect anyway. I did want her to seek help, however, and perhaps the sentiment rather than the facts reflects something of how I felt at the time. Here is the letter that appeared in the *NOTW*:

Dear Amy,

I hope you understand why I'm writing this. We have spoken recently but many people will wonder why I haven't run down to whatever hotel you're staying in, scooped you up and taken you home for a hot bath and a steaming bowl of chicken soup. It's because your father and I know what you're like, Amy. We want to help you, but we know that unless you want to be helped, unless you come to us, anything we tried would be in vain.

So this letter is my way of making sure that you know that all you have to do is come to us, Amy, and we'll do everything in our power to get you well again. After all, you are still my baby and you always will be.

I pile hope upon hope that you will make that decision, Amy, and your strong will can bend for just a moment to make that decision and come home to me.

You were never a wayward daughter but you always had a strong will and a mind of your own – qualities your father and I were so proud of. You were well brought up, you had a keen sense of right from wrong and you understood the values we always impressed on you as a family.

But you would never be pressured or influenced into doing something if your heart wasn't in it. I know there's no point in me ringing you, fussing over you or ordering you to do something. I need you to take that first step, darling. I need you to call me, to pick up that phone and tell me what's troubling you.

Your father and I would like nothing more; wherever you are, whatever you need, we're here for you day and night. I hope you know that. We were terrified after we saw those pictures of you earlier this week, wandering the freezing streets of London at dawn in your underwear. All I wanted to do was rush into those pictures and wrap you up in a big, warm blanket . . .

Because I know that however big, grown-up and successful my Amy gets, she still needs the love of her Ma. Do you remember on January 14 this year, when your album got to number one? Do you remember how overjoyed your father and I both were? We shed tears of joy for you that night.

And not just because we were delighted for your success, that you had finally fulfilled that childhood dream of singing your heart out in front of millions. But also because finally, the whole country thought our little girl was just as special as we knew you were. Some wonderful things have happened since that night, darling, but also some not so wonderful. Blake, your husband, might not be my favourite person – you know that, Amy, but he's your choice and I would never say anything about him to hurt you.

When I was quoted recently as saying 'Thank God Blake's inside' what I meant was that putting him in jail might help him to clean up HIS act and change HIS life. It wasn't said out of viciousness or to upset you. If your relationship is meant to be, it will survive. I'm a great believer that everything in life happens for a reason, a purpose. And if you two are destined to be together forever, then so be it. But I want you to love Blake for who he is, Amy. Not because you feel sorry for him, or because he can get you doped up. Not for any other reason than that you have respect for him . . .

Having to cancel your tour, as well, has been very sad. But I know it's happened for the best. Despite disappointing all of your fans, who I know you treasure so much, maybe it will pull you up and make you stop and think and take stock of where your life is going. I pray it does. I hope it makes you realize that although you might be a superstar, you're not superwoman. Early fame has overwhelmed you, it's dizzied you and muddled your mind. For a moment, forget you're a superstar. You're also young and vulnerable. Remember you're just an ordinary human being, no stronger than any of the rest of us. You think you're strong enough to get through this on your own, darling, but you're not.

I want you back, and I'll make you fitter and stronger. I'd like nothing better than to have you home and help you put on a bit of weight with some wholesome home cooking. You're at your happiest in family situations, I remember. It's part of that strong Jewish tradition you were raised in. Remember how you spent time with my sister before the gig in Newcastle the other week? You felt comfortable and at ease. That's how I know family is important to you.

But I can't force you to do something you don't want to. You have to want it to happen, darling, you have to ask for it. Me and your father, and your brother Alex all want you to be happy and quickly restored to full health. For the moment, that's all of our priorities.

We are concerned, but we're not panicking. You've got to see things in your own time and I'm sure you will. You are a brilliant talent, of course, and if you get yourself well, you'll be able to go on and fulfil your destiny.

You're a true professional who thrives on work and you need to get back into that routine. We know you don't want to let your fans down. We know how important they are to you and how once you're over this present setback you'll give them a show they'll never forget. You know I'm an optimist, and that I think, with our help, you will get back on top of things. But I know you must come to me first for that to happen.

I just hope that, because of this letter, you do. Pick up the phone.

All my love, Ma

I soon got word that Amy wasn't pleased about it at all, but she never brought the subject up with me. I also couldn't bring myself to discuss it with her. Perhaps somewhere deep down she understood why I'd done it. Ordinarily I was the calm, rational parent. Perhaps she would see that she'd pushed me beyond desperation, although I didn't know what she understood about anything any more. Over those months our relationship had become largely an unspoken one; her problem had become the problem that could not be talked about. I just hoped that one day, when she was well again, she'd see that anything I had said or done had one sole purpose: to stop her from dying.

The upshot, though, was that I found myself in a state of perpetual confusion. No course of action was the right course of action and my tough love was wavering at every turn. A week or so later, when it became clear that the police were about to arrest Amy in relation to Blake's bribery charge, I felt compelled to accompany her.

Blake had now admitted that he had intended to pay £200,000 to James King to stop him testifying in the GBH case, and Amy's solicitor Simon Esplen had advised that it was only a matter of time before Amy would be taken in. Rather than wait to be arrested, it would be better if a statement was prepared, and her solicitor arranged an interview with her at the police station. Mitchell and I would have had to be counter-signatories to an amount as large as £200,000 so I knew that the allegations against her were completely false. Until that point I had resisted stepping in and going to court with Amy on the occasions she had been there to support Blake, but I simply couldn't let her face this alone. Amy's life was a mess in so many ways, but bribery was a step too far.

An interview was set up at Shoreditch police station for Amy on 18 December. Under English law, a formal suspect has to be arrested by police before they can be questioned and Amy attended voluntarily. I arrived at her flat in Bow just before she was due to set off and we sat together in the back of the escort vehicle. She was visibly agitated, but she was trying hard not to show it. Expect the unexpected was always my motto with Amy, but, thank God, the trip turned out to be a rare moment of light relief.

Even before we arrived, Amy had the officers wrapped around her little finger.

'I was about to buy some sweets before you turned up,' she said.

'I'll get you some, Amy,' the female officer replied without hesitation, and a five-minute stop outside a newsagent's followed during which she ran in and returned with several packets of the Haribo chews Amy loved.

She sat there munching on them in the interview room.

'Can you confirm your name?' the officer requested.

'Amy Jade Civil,' Amy replied politely.

'I'm afraid we're going to have to measure you,' he continued.

Amy stood up and followed him to the wall. She straightened her back against it, but the officer feigned confusion.

'Do I measure here, at the top of your head, or here, at the top of your beehive?' he asked.

'The beehive, definitely,' Amy grinned back, and the room erupted with laughter.

The photographs were the next rigmarole. She was put in position and we all waited while the camera was set up. I could see Amy was anxious and bored, and as soon as the bulb started to flash she launched into the song she used to sing while standing outside the headmaster's office at school:

Fly me to the moon,
And let me play among the stars,
Let me see what spring is like
On Jupiter and Mars

The officers turned to me and I shrugged. 'You've not met Amy before, have you?' I thought to myself. If she could have flown me to the moon at that moment I would have happily packed my bags that second.

Amy, me, her solicitor and two officers spent the next two hours in that interview room but the atmosphere seemed more like a celebration than an interrogation. It became obvious that the whole thing was nonsense and that we were just going through the motions.

'Were you with Blake on such-and-such a date, Amy?'

'Nope,' she replied.

'Did you give him the £200,000?'

'Nope.'

And so it went on.

'Do you want a sweet?' Amy interrupted at one point, opening a fresh bag of Haribo which she began offering around.

'Don't mind if I do,' one of the officers said, reaching over.

I was half expecting streamers and balloons to follow.

Suffice to say Amy was released on bail, and the charges against her were finally dropped in January 2008 due to lack of evidence. But the episode had shown us what a vulnerable position she now found herself in.

11

Two Steps Forward, One Step Back

After Christmas, on 28 December, Amy travelled to Barbados and on to Mustique to stay at the home of rock musician Bryan Adams. Tyler and Juliette accompanied her and I hoped that with good friends around her the idea of recovery might sink in. Amy had struck up a friendship with Bryan Adams in London while doing a photo-shoot and he was understanding of the position she found herself in and genuinely wanted to help. The problem was that Amy still didn't want help on anything other than her own terms, and although she was only in Mustique for around a week it was hard for her. Mustique was a clean, quiet, calm environment. She managed to stay drug-free but unfortunately she was sick constantly from withdrawal and her weight plummeted again.

As soon as Amy arrived back home, it was back to square one. She returned to the flat in Bow, next door to Alex Foden, and was unable to detach herself from that drugs world. I rarely went to that flat to see her, but Mitchell told me it was filled a lot of the time with hangers-on and drugged-up people. I now feared the long-term damage Amy would do to herself. She clearly wasn't eating – her diet was drugs and Haribo sweets – and how she was ever going to manage a structured programme of rehab I really didn't know. It was impossible to raise Amy during the day as she was often asleep, and if I did see her there were times now when I could barely look at her without her slow, painful death staring back at me. She looked ravaged. She was jittery and agitated much of the time, and her doctor, Dr Paul Ettlinger, had prescribed Valium to help her to relax. But it had never been easy for Amy to relax.

And there was a prestigious deadline looming. Amy had been nominated in six categories and invited to perform at the 50th annual Grammy Awards in the Staples Center in Los Angeles. She had phoned to tell me just before Christmas, and although she sounded incredibly excited, not to mention astounded that she'd been nominated in so many categories, reality hit home again as the problem of her getting a visa to perform in the States now arose. In order to qualify for an artist's visa her body would have to be free of all drugs, including prescription medication, for a week before being tested. If Amy tested positive she would automatically be refused entry. The appointment for the drugs test had been made for 22 January 2008, but Amy didn't live week by week. She didn't even live day by day. Amy lived minute by minute.

On the very morning of her appointment a shocking story appeared in the *Sun* newspaper. Apparently photographs of Amy taking crack cocaine had been sold to the newspaper by two of Blake's friends. Mitchell had been warned about it by Raye Cosbert beforehand but the news didn't reach me until the story broke. By that point I had pretty much stopped buying newspapers, but if there was something awful I needed to be warned about, my cousin Martin would often ring me to tip me off. There was a video that went along with the story, I understand, but I have never watched it.

That morning I went out and bought a copy of the *Sun*, and I sat in my car and stared at the cover. A frozen feeling crept through my body. For the first time after months of trying to keep my emotions in check, I broke down and sobbed uncontrollably. I had seen Amy drunk; I had seen her looking anything other than human; but I had never seen Amy actually taking drugs. I thought I was going to throw up there and then. It was absolutely mortifying.

The crazy thing is that my life felt so outlandish I was now unsure what was real and what was fiction. Did Amy know she was being filmed inhaling crack cocaine from a pipe? Did she agree to it? Was it even set up by her? Or had some low-life filmed her without her knowing? She maintained to Mitchell that she hadn't been set up, but if she hadn't then was the whole thing another of Amy's performances, another of her manipulations? Or if Blake's friends were involved, who was manipulating whom? I don't even know if Amy knew. The lines were so blurred now between the Amy I thought I knew and the Amy that stared at me from the front page of the *Sun*, it was terrifying.

There were occasions in the past when Amy had bad press when she'd say to me, 'Look, Mum, I'm still here! They said this and that, but look, I'm still here!' I always said to her, 'If you're going to be there, Amy, make sure it's for your talent.' So to be in the headlines because she was a crack cocaine addict was something I found very hard to accept. To me, she'd become a caricature. God knows what the public thought when they saw those pictures but it seemed to me that Amy's life was being reported as if she'd chosen a path of drug addiction, that she was somehow enjoying it.

Thankfully I was spared much of seeing Amy at her absolute worst, but I saw her enough times looking emaciated, fragmented and hollow to know that none of it was enjoyable for her. No person chooses to destroy themselves like that; no addict chooses to be an addict. Sadly, the condition is often presented as if the person has made a conscious choice – unlike other diseases, cancer for example, which never have the same stigma attached to them. I can only assume it's because addiction is so closely tied up with mental health. Amy was a slave to drugs. However much she may have wanted to be free of them, her mind and body had become trapped. Her addictions had started to take on a life of their own. What may have begun as an escape or something she thought she could handle was now a habit she couldn't control. She'd started to look like the addicts who came into the pharmacies I managed, and my greatest fear now was that she'd already gone too far to reverse the habit and change her life.

Although my focus was to stay strong for Amy, these other voices undoubtedly gnawed away at me. I don't think any parent survives something like this without questioning themselves and the part they may have played in their child's problems, but I stopped short of asking what I could have done better for Amy: throughout our life together I did the best I possibly could with the know-how and the resources I had. But at the time, and since then, I have continually asked what I could have done *differently*. Could I have realized sooner that this would happen? Was there a point in Amy's life when this course could have been avoided, or altered? Could *I* have altered it? I still think about those questions now, but the answers are always beyond my reach.

The reality, of course, is that there's a myriad of possible answers. I fight hard in my own mind to stop heaping guilt upon myself because I know it's neither rational nor productive. It's taken many years, but I've come to the conclusion that blaming myself or my MS or Blake or anyone else is simply destructive because Amy's life wasn't 'normal' – it was pushed to the extreme in every way. For all I know this might have happened even if she hadn't become famous. After all, Amy was set on a different path from adolescence onwards. Addiction destroys the lives of thousands of ordinary people and thousands of families every day and it happens for a multitude of reasons, not just one.

It was the chairman of Universal Music, Lucian Grainge, who finally hauled Amy into a meeting to discuss her upcoming appearances at the Grammys. Amy's career was at stake, but I knew even that was unlikely to prevent her spiralling downwards. Mitchell took her to the meeting, which she was late for, and I'm positive that if he had not been there she would not have gone at all. Lucian's no-nonsense approach had some effect. He laid it on the line: either she sought help or he would stop her from working. He'd already cancelled a gig she was due to perform in Cannes on 24 January because he believed Amy would make a fool of herself. Amy had some good people around her who, like us, believed in her, and we are eternally grateful for their attempts to intervene.

There was also a very real possibility that Amy would face criminal charges over the *Sun* crack cocaine video, and I was concerned that it would be difficult for her case to be seen objectively because it was a tabloid newspaper that had broken the story. It was a question of which disaster to worry about first, but as I had no input into Amy's career, I felt it was more important for me to continue to support her in her journey away from addiction. If that couldn't be done, nothing would follow.

The same day as her meeting with Lucian Grainge, Amy was admitted to the Capio Nightingale Hospital, but she almost changed her mind on the journey there. In my heart I had my doubts about whether it would last, but in my world everything happened in small steps now, and this was one small positive step. If only she could put on some weight, I kept thinking. That would be a start to her acquiring the physical strength to cope with recovery.

At Capio Nightingale Amy was again under the supervision of consultant psychiatrist Dr Marios Pierides. For the first two days she spent much of her time sleeping and she was allowed only a few visitors. Around three days later she was transferred to the London Clinic in the West End for rehydration because she had been vomiting.

I saw Amy when she was moved to the London Clinic but it was only a brief visit. Doctors had put her on a cold turkey programme which was physically exhausting for her and she looked tired and drawn and wasn't in the mood to talk. The process of withdrawing completely from drugs is one of the most unpleasant experiences an addict can go through. Amy had a range of symptoms from flu to sickness, diarrhoea and severe stomach cramps, but I saw in her a slight change in mindset. For the first time in a long time she seemed to want to get better.

Then, just days later, she had drugs smuggled into the Capio

Nightingale hidden in a teddy bear. Whether it was because there was prior knowledge of the *Sun* story breaking I don't know, but Amy's management had arranged to have her US visa drugs test delayed by one week, until the storm died down and there was more hope of Amy passing. In the end, the US Embassy declined her application because traces of cocaine were found in her blood. Two steps forward, one step back.

This was a bitter blow for Amy. She had desperately wanted to go to the US. The Grammys were a big deal and I could understand her disappointment, but I was secretly pleased her visa had been declined. I would never have said it to Amy, but I thought it would all have been too much for her. It wasn't just the travelling and the performance; I was terrified that in her frame of mind she wouldn't have coped well with the entire experience. I pictured this little girl lost in the enormity of the occasion, unable to hold herself together.

In the end it was Raye who came up with an alternative plan. Instead of Amy going to the Grammys, the Grammys would come to her. In an unprecedented arrangement, Amy would perform by live satellite link-up from the Riverside Studios in Hammersmith, west London. However, Raye warned her that if there were any signs that she had taken drugs before the performance, it would be pulled.

On the night of 10 February, to coincide with the ceremony starting in LA, our London show was due to start at 11.30 p.m., so it was around eight when a car came to pick Tony and me up from Barnet. I couldn't remember the last time I'd actually felt excited about seeing Amy, but she had certainly started to look better in hospital and my fingers were firmly crossed that her progress would continue. Perhaps because of her age, Amy had an amazing ability to look at death's door one week and radiant the next, a state which constantly lulled us into a false sense of security.

The enormity of the Grammys hadn't yet sunk in but I was a bag of nerves none the less. Thankfully, although the decision to remain in London had been made under dire circumstances, Amy performing in the UK meant that all of her family could turn out to support her at what was a crucial time for her in her career and her recovery, and that made me very happy.

I could feel the intensity of the atmosphere as soon as I walked into the main auditorium. The stage had been done out like a night-club, with huge ruched curtains as Amy's backdrop and dimmed floor-lights, and red-tasselled lampshades dotted around. It was a hive of activity when we walked through. As I headed towards back-stage, the technicians were still setting up and testing the microphones. I took a deep breath. This felt different. Although the last few months weighed heavily on me, something had lifted, and that was confirmed as soon as I saw Amy.

The first thing that struck me was how alive she looked. She'd put on some weight and there was something about her beautiful eyes that sparkled again. She had a nurse with her and it was obvious that she hadn't taken any drugs. I could see she'd had a drink, but that seemed very much like the lesser of two evils. It was an Amy I hadn't seen for a long time: not only was her health returning but there was an enthusiasm too that the drugs had stifled. Even now, the memory of that evening brings me so much joy.

And then came the awards. First up, Amy won Best New Performer. Later she took Best Pop Vocal Album for *Back To Black*, Best Female Pop Vocal and Best Song of the Year for 'Rehab'. By the time Amy was due to perform it was around three a.m. our time. I can only describe the studio as buzzing – and I mean *really* buzzing. I don't think I've ever been with Amy when the sparks fizzed throughout an auditorium like that.

Amy was to perform part of her show for the invited guests and then sing two songs for the live broadcast. She started with 'Addicted', and three-quarters of the way through the show there was a pause while Amy was connected via satellite link and intro-duced onstage by the actor Cuba Gooding Jr, who had been in London at the time. She launched into 'You Know I'm No Good', which moved into 'Rehab', and she laughed and danced her way through both. 'This is fantastic!' I thought. 'She's going to come through this, I know.'

It was just after that performance that Tony Bennett appeared with soul singer Natalie Cole to present the award for Record of the Year. Not only was Tony Bennett Amy's childhood hero but she was up against some very stiff competition that included the female vocalists Beyoncé and Rihanna. When the announcement came through that she'd won for 'Rehab' it took a moment to sink in.

Only on very rare occasions was Amy speechless, but she just stood there shell-shocked. I was beaming and clapping and staring up at her face, but it was obvious the penny still hadn't dropped for her. The room exploded. All around me everyone was chanting 'A-my, A-my, A-my!' over and over. Mitchell rushed onstage to hug her and I followed, having to be helped up by Amy's band members. She walked over to hug me, and the squeeze we gave each other . . . there was so much attached to it that no one else could have understood.

'I love you, Mum,' she said into my ear.

'I'm so proud of you,' I told her.

Amy pulled me into her as she moved towards the microphone, but at the last moment she leaned over to me and said, 'I know I've won, Mum, but I have no idea what to say.'

Always the pragmatist, I advised, 'Just keep calm and thank everyone.'

She just about managed to compose herself. As she addressed the audience I stood beside her, and she held my hand, just as she had always done as a kid.

It didn't come any bigger than the Grammys, and by the end of that night Amy had won five. A single light had been switched back on, and it was the light I'd needed to help me to look forward again. When I think back on that evening now, it is with both elation and longing. It was a moment of reconnection. Amy was my little girl again, for however brief a time. If only I could have even a second of it back. It would be enough just to touch her again.

*

That February, just after the Grammys, Amy moved back to Jeffrey's Place. She had been talking about doing so while she was in recovery at the Capio Nightingale and she wanted to make a fresh start. In particular, she wanted to move away from Alex Foden, her 'drugs buddy' in Bow. She had paid £130,000 for him to go into rehab at the same time as her, but together both of them were a disaster. Despite the change of scene, however, Amy struggled to stay clean, and despite the progress she had made before the Grammys it turned out not to be the watershed moment in Amy's life I had so hoped for.

In the middle of February, Amy appeared on stage with Mark Ronson at the BRIT Awards. She had been nominated in the British Single category for 'Valerie' but she came away empty-handed. She was drunk, and her performance was shaky, but she just managed to hold it together. She had also contracted impetigo, a highly contagious bacterial condition, and she had blisters across her cheeks. Again, I worried about how her weight loss along with all the substances she was pumping into her body were affecting her immune system. Strangely, she'd become obsessed with her health, almost to the level of hypochondria. She constantly complained of a sore throat or a cold or a stomach bug – but it never stopped her abusing her body. As a pharmacist I was always very health-conscious, but Amy never seemed able to make the connection between her substance abuse and her health.

In March, Amy moved from Jeffrey's Place into a house around the corner, in Prowse Place, which I believe she rented from the Specials' singer Terry Hall. She was looking forward to it and I saw it as another of her periodic searches for an environment where she could get off drugs. Personally I didn't see that moving from place to place was the answer – Amy needed instead to work out what was constantly driving her back to drugs – but I hoped against hope that it might make a difference. Even though her actions didn't often make sense to us, they made sense to her, and she was adamant that she wanted to do things her way.

Shortly after the move to Prowse Place, I went over to see her. She seemed steadier than I had seen her for a few weeks, and as I stepped through the door she pointed to the right, where the garage had been newly converted into a guest bedroom with its own en-suite bathroom.

'That's your room, Mum,' she said, and I laughed.

'There's always a place for you at mine too,' I said, hugging her, but somewhere in my heart I knew she wouldn't take up that offer.

I had my doubts about whether Prowse Place would give her the privacy she needed thanks to the sheer number of photographers who soon took up residence outside, but decamping there did have a good, albeit temporary, effect. Shortly afterwards she told Mitchell she wanted to get clean. She didn't want to go into a rehab clinic but instead she wanted to detox in the house. It was important for Amy to do whatever she felt was the most comfortable, and she was in the very fortunate position financially to be able to make that choice.

Dr Ettlinger and his practice partner Dr Cristina Romete would preside over the drug replacement programme, and two nurses would work shifts to administer Amy's medication. This time methadone would be used as the replacement rather than Subutex and, as with any programme, Amy needed to be clean for a number of hours before it could begin.

Amy's attempt failed before she'd even started. She smoked heroin before the treatment began which made it impossible to administer anything. I felt sorry for the nurses. They were there to do a job and, God knows, I knew how difficult Amy could be. There was only so much we could do as a family but there was also only so much the medical profession could do too. In the final analysis it had to be down to Amy.

Although Amy was locked in her own world she was still aware of what everyone expected of her. There was no pressure from Amy's record company Island to produce a third album, but at the back of her mind Amy knew that couldn't last for ever. No pressure created a different kind of pressure for her, and now with her Grammy wins she'd been built up to such great heights that her success threatened to become counterproductive. Amy's need to challenge herself didn't go away, but could she produce an album that was better than *Back To Black*? She was terrified. She'd reached a pinnacle and was scared that there was nowhere left for her to go. Amy just wasn't the kind of person to churn out pop hit after pop hit. She would never have been satisfied with that. She had to believe in what she was writing and singing, and she always wanted her new songs to be better than the material she'd produced before.

Throughout Amy's career I didn't ever watch her at work with her band, but I do know the respect she had for them, in particular her bassist and musical director Dale Davis, with whom she'd been working since 2003. But even the people who were creative sounding boards for Amy could not alter her inability to work.

On one occasion Richard's son Michael dropped in on Amy at Prowse Place while her band sat with her trying to work out some new material. The property had a mezzanine bedroom just above the living room, and halfway through the session Amy picked herself up off the sofa, walked up the stairs to the bedroom and lit up a crack pipe within earshot of everyone below. She came down again, and a minute later she was nodding out on the sofa, unable to speak or think or work. Michael has since described her as empty, as if she were a living sarcophagus. It's what I found the most disturbing thing to observe in Amy too, that she'd become this ghost, this fractured person, trapped in the hell of addiction.

Mark Ronson was beginning to get the same treatment. Just after Christmas, Raye Cosbert had arranged for Amy to sing the title song for the next Bond film *Quantum of Solace*, which she was due to record with Mark around April. He and Amy were to work together after her replacement programme had failed; lyrics were Amy's department and Mark would put together the music. But after four days of waiting for Amy in a studio in Henley-on-Thames in Oxfordshire, Mark had almost had enough. When Amy eventually did make it they had one good working day together but for the rest of the time Amy was out of it. Apparently she looked like a homeless person − grubby and, at times, talking nonsense.

Over the next few weeks Amy's life fell apart. She slapped a man who refused her his pool table at the Good Mixer pub in Camden, and head-butted another who was helping her into a cab. At the end of April she was taken to Holborn police station, kept in overnight, and was released the next day with a police caution for common assault for the incident in the Good Mixer. Raye accompanied Amy to the police station on that occasion. Usually it was either Mitchell or Raye or me (if I was asked to) who'd be there for Amy, but more often than not her management now took care of all these situations.

During this period Mitchell and I did occasionally speak to each other about where to turn next, or what might stop this. But going over the 'ifs' and the 'whens' and the 'buts' always felt like we were wading through the unknown. 'What will be, will be,' I remember saying to myself over and over, and Amy was similar to me in that respect. 'Fate will take its course, Mum,' she would say, even though all of her habits were about controlling herself and the environment around her. Perhaps she never thought it would be too late for her. Rightly or wrongly, I too had blind faith at times that she'd suddenly turn herself around.

At the beginning of May, just as Raye was on the point of cancelling the Bond recording, Amy made it back to Henley and to the studio there owned by Barrie Barlow, the former drummer and percussionist in the progressive rock band Jethro Tull. The building was self-contained with two bedrooms, a kitchen and a bathroom upstairs and a studio downstairs, and it sat within his property in the village of Shiplake just outside Henley. Instead of writing lyrics to the Bond theme as Amy had been asked to, she had written both lyrics and music and had clashed with Mark over how the song should be developed. Before Mitchell arrived, she had had an argument over the phone with Blake. She was in constant contact with him while he remained in custody, and it was after that argument that she had what can only be described as a psychotic episode.

Mitchell didn't always phone to tell me everything that had happened to Amy but on this occasion he did. He could barely describe to me the state he had found her in. By the time he arrived at the studio Amy had been on a two-day drink and drugs binge and she had flipped out completely. She had cuts on her arms and her face and had stubbed out a cigarette on her cheek. Her hand was badly cut from punching a mirror and she was crying and screaming hysterically. A nurse had been called to attend to her. Mitchell was sure it was the most distressed he'd ever seen her.

Mitchell's sister Melody had also phoned me, very upset at the state Amy had got herself into, and together we went to Henley. It was a routine I'd practised before – stay calm, try and deal with the situation practically, and don't punish Amy for what she was doing – but I honestly wasn't sure how many more times I could go through this.

I remember that day clearly because it was unusually hot and the journey to Shiplake was filled with apprehension. The possibility of sectioning Amy under the Mental Health Act had been raised several times before and I remember Mel and I discussing it on the journey down. It would mean Amy being admitted to hospital without her consent and being treated against her will. But her behaviour was not extreme enough for her to be considered a danger to herself or to other people. To make an assessment, a GP, a local health authority representative and a clinical psychologist would have to be present, and usually by the time medical help arrived Amy's episodes had subsided and she was calmer.

Although I wasn't always part of those conversations, I found the idea of sectioning my daughter hugely difficult to come to terms with. I'd dealt with her from childhood; I knew exactly how uncompromising she was about taking charge of her own life. It would be so distressing for her to have even a fraction of that independence taken away. It was harrowing enough watching her do what she was doing to herself, but to think of her being restrained by strangers was a scenario I could barely contemplate. In practical terms I wanted to do what was best for Amy, but emotionally, being forced into a decision about whether or not to have her sectioned was agonizing. As far as I was concerned it could only be a last resort. We were now in a worse position than before the Grammys. How could that be possible?

By the time we arrived Amy was in better spirits than we'd expected, which was something at least, but her body was shaky and she was highly agitated. As soon as Mel and I stepped out of the car we could hear that familiar click-click-click. 'Photographers are everywhere, Mum,' Amy warned us, and she wasn't wrong.

She was dressed in just her bra and shorts with bare feet on the gravel path.

'You shouldn't be out here without something on your feet,' I remember telling her, and I laugh at that now. Of all the things Amy was doing to herself, not wearing shoes was a minor offence, but I guess it's how mums think.

'I'm all right, Mum, I really am, but I want to give up drugs,' she kept repeating, but she looked pale and drained. Her skin looked awful and there was a part of her that was not really with it at all.

Later that afternoon, when Mel and I went for a stroll on the grass bank along the Thames, Amy joined us with her guitar. As we enjoyed the sunshine she sat there strumming, but there were photographers with huge lenses lined up on the bank opposite continually snapping us. I will never forget that. When we left Amy in Shiplake – it's what she wanted – I was completely lost as to where to turn next.

The following week Amy was back in London. While she had been in Henley, Mitchell had attended a meeting with Amy's solicitors and two police officers who were handling the crack-cocaine video case. It was made clear at that meeting that Amy would be arrested and charged with 'allowing her premises to be used for taking drugs and the intent to supply drugs'. As had been the case with the bribery charge she attended Limehouse police station by prior appointment, accompanied by Raye and her solicitor. Amy was drunk and had apparently taken drugs when she was interviewed under caution and she was bailed to return later that month.

Fortunately, only a week later the Crown Prosecution Service informed us that Amy would not face charges as it couldn't be proved whether the substance she had been smoking was crack cocaine. However, the police did know who'd shot the video and sold it to the *Sun*, for £50,000 – a pair called Johnny Blagrove and Cara Burton, who ended up going on trial later that year for offering to supply class A and B drugs. Blagrove was handed down a two-year sentence, Burton escaped jail, but a 'hit list' of other celebrity targets had been found in their home. When Mitchell asked Amy about the pair she claimed they were her friends. What kind of world was she living in? It was one less problem for us to worry about, but there were a myriad of others still to face.

That same week, something shifted again in Amy. She took it upon herself to make an appointment to see Dr Mike McPhillips at the Capio Nightingale and claimed she wanted to start on a new drug replacement programme. The visit was unprompted and it was the most positive sign yet that Amy wanted to be free of drugs. I don't know for sure, because Amy didn't discuss it, but heroin and cocaine had become routine for her, something she had to do every day like a job, and she was bored with it. Whatever the trigger, drugs were certainly losing their appeal for Amy, and she began on another Subutex programme, this time because *she* wanted to.

Thursday, 22 May was a day when there was at least something to look forward to: Amy had received nominations for two songs at the Ivor Novello Awards in the category of Best Song, Musically and Lyrically. I felt it was important to be there for her that night, to keep encouraging her, to remind her that she had my support. Tony accompanied me and we sat with Mitchell at a table at the Grosvenor House Hotel in Mayfair, but as the evening rolled on, one place remained empty – Amy's. She had told Mitchell she would meet us at the hotel but time was ticking on and she hadn't arrived yet.

As everyone sat checking their watches, I thought back to four years earlier when Amy had stood in my flat with an outstretched arm gripping her first award. How different she looked, how different she was, how proud she had wanted to make me. Where had those four years gone? How could a person – a woman – change beyond all recognition in such a short space of time? How could someone value their achievements so little? Tonight, she might not even bother to turn up. Well, I'd gone past the point of getting anxious about Amy's no-shows. If she came, fine. If she didn't, I'd live with it.

She won, for 'Love Is A Losing Game', one of the most accomplished songs I think Amy has ever written, but it was Mitchell who accepted the award.

Amy appeared at our table shortly afterwards, just in time to hear David Gilmour of Pink Floyd receive a lifetime achievement award. 'It's been a long, bumpy and exhilarating road,' he said, adding, 'in twenty or thirty years, Amy Winehouse will get one of these.' I looked over to see if Amy was listening. Her beehive was pinned with the most outrageous large red heart clip which had the word 'Blake' written across it. She was back playing another of her stage creations. She laughed, but it was obvious to me that her mind was somewhere completely different.

12

Maybe

In early June 2008, Blake's trial was due to begin. Amy was confident he would be released, but this seemed like another of her delusions, some kind of happy-ever-after scenario created in her head that bore no relation to what was actually happening. She bought a new suit and attended court on a couple of occasions but turned up late and left early. On 6 June she was present at court with Mitchell when Blake pleaded guilty to the charges of GBH and conspiracy to pervert the course of justice. His co-accused, Michael Brown, did the same.

Both Blake and Brown were remanded in custody for sentencing at a later date, but because Blake had already served seven months there was a chance he could be released sooner than we expected. If there's one thing I feared most it was Blake being back in Amy's life full-time. She had visited him regularly while he was in Pentonville, and they were constantly in touch by phone, but this was coming at such a crucial stage for Amy, just when she'd made real progress in her recovery, that I didn't want her tipping into another abyss. Amy had continued with the Subutex programme, although she was drinking a lot and still struggling with her weight.

On 12 June, she rang me just before she flew to do a gig in Russia. She said she was looking forward to performing again. Richard's son

Michael rang her once she'd arrived that night and said she seemed in good spirits. Apparently they spoke for a good half hour, but when he asked her what she was doing in Russia she had no idea who she was performing for. 'Something to do with Chelsea,' she'd told him. In fact she had been invited to sing at a private party Chelsea FC owner Roman Abramovich was throwing for his girlfriend, but Amy always played down everything, more so now than ever.

Distressingly, Amy didn't need Blake to be freed in order for her to tip into another crisis. On the 16th, two days after she flew back, she suffered another seizure. This time she was at home in Prowse Place and was caught by a friend just before she hit the ground. It was unclear whether the seizure was drug-induced but Mitchell was called and he took her to the London Clinic where she was kept in for several days to undergo tests. I visited her soon after she was admitted and we sat together for a while. She looked better than I'd expected, but I steered clear of the subject of recovery. We talked about Prowse Place and what colour she was going to paint the walls – she'd spent a lifetime redecorating her rooms, and finding her with a roller in her hand was not an uncommon sight. Concentrating on the everyday stuff brought some kind of normality to the situation, even though we were further away from normality than anyone could imagine.

Mitchell was dealing directly with Amy's medical team. I know now that a lot was kept from me, and perhaps that was for the best. It was Dr Cristina Romete and a Dr Glynne who sat Amy down the day after she was admitted and spelled out the prognosis to her in no uncertain terms. Her CT scan had revealed mucus all around her lungs, her voice had almost gone completely, and there was a possibility that she had nodules on her vocal cords. Doctors were also worried about a growth that had appeared in Amy's chest cavity. She underwent a PET scan to ensure it wasn't cancerous, which it wasn't, but at the very least it needed to be monitored. The most worrying aspect for Amy was that she now had early traces of emphysema brought on by inhaling crack through a pipe and years of smoking cigarettes. She was only twenty-four and she'd been told that it might only be a matter of time before she developed full-blown emphysema.

I remember sitting with Amy by the side of her bed just looking at her. Of all the things to have happened to her, this was probably one of the saddest for me. For a singer, it would mark the end of her career. All that work I'd watched her put in over the years could be gone, just like that. 'You've got a gift,' I used to tell her when she sat singing with her feet dangling from the window in Greenside Close. 'You should do something with that one day.' Those words choked me now. But this wasn't the first wake-up call Amy had had and, from experience, I doubted it would be the last. She'd covered herself in nicotine patches, though, and she was quiet and visibly shaken, so maybe something had sunk in.

Although at times I felt a great anger towards Amy for what she was doing to herself, and to us in the process, I also knew that her desire to come off drugs was strong and that lapses are part of the treacherous journey. So I continued to be positive, but I never shook off a deep-seated fear that she could so easily throw it all away at the last hurdle.

Amy left the London Clinic briefly to perform at Nelson Mandela's ninetieth birthday celebrations in Hyde Park. The sickly person of a few days before was nowhere to be seen: Amy had once again bounced back to life. She beamed on stage, smiled and waved at the audience but I could still see a glazed look in her eyes, as if underneath she was trying hard just to get through the performance. Just as at the Ivor Novellos, she wore the hairpin with the word 'Blake' written on it, and instead of singing 'Free Nelson Mandela' in the chorus of the final song she'd sung 'Free Blakey my fella' – a very 'Amy' thing to do, and I could only roll my eyes when she told me a few days later. It was an amazing, historic event to be part of, and an honour to be given a lead role in it, so how sad that Amy appeared to have made little connection with it. Her emotions and everything going on in her world continued to consume her to the point where I think she was oblivious to the occasion.

I'd stopped trying to work out what was going on in Amy's mind. To try and make sense of everything was both exhausting and impossible. Whatever Amy felt at any given moment, those feelings were real to her and she acted on them. But to be around her often felt as if I'd been given a role in a melodrama where she was playing the lead part. I went along with it and reluctantly accepted that that was the way Amy expressed herself. But then, a lot of the time Amy was playing a character I didn't recognize. Her brother rarely let her get away with this and would often confront her about the multitude of personas she brought out at any given time. 'Who are you now?' he'd ask her. But all she ever did was pause momentarily before carrying on.

It wasn't long after Amy entered the London Clinic that a decision was made to place security guards around her twenty-four hours a day. I'm not sure whose idea it was, and of course Amy resisted it at first, but it made a lot of sense. Mitchell couldn't be with Amy all the time, nor could her management team, and I had never been able to fulfil that role, and wouldn't have wanted to. Andrew Morris was employed as her chief security guard and four others worked a shift rotation. They were good guys, there to protect Amy from the outside world and the outside world from Amy.

The guards all called me 'Mum', which I didn't mind at all. It was affectionate, and it felt comforting to know there was another surrogate family around Amy, even if they were employees. But their presence did have the unnerving effect of putting greater distance between us. I didn't just turn up to see Amy now. If I couldn't get hold of her, which was often, I'd ring one of her security staff and see what the state of play was. Sometimes it was fine, but there'd be other days when they'd tell me not to come over, or that Amy was asleep, or that she didn't want to see anyone. I never knew the real reasons, and with hindsight perhaps it was better that I didn't know.

I certainly stopped asking, and accepted that if Amy wanted me to be there, I would be.

As Amy's protectors, the security team tried their best to police whatever was coming in and out of the house. Drug dealers had always found a way to get supplies to Amy, and Mitchell had learned over the years to take nothing for granted. It could be flowers being delivered to the house, or packages thrown over her garden wall. Intercepting them was never an easy job, and if Amy wanted to she would find a way to bring heroin or cocaine in. Early on she wanted the guards removed, probably because they were doing a good job: as soon as she was back in Prowse Place she made a fuss about them living with her round the clock, but Mitchell insisted they stayed, and they remained with Amy throughout the rest of her life. In some ways they became the closest people to her, brothers even, and although I was happier knowing that they were there, yet again I had to put trust in others to look after my daughter. From her first record deal, this had always been a tough reality to accept. As her mother, I could see what Amy needed, but that wasn't always what she wanted.

In July, as far as I was concerned there was at least one piece of good news that related to Blake's trial. Amy was not present in court, but at his eventual sentencing on the 21st, the judge, David Radford, handed down a twenty-seven-month prison term to him. Blake's QC, Jeremy Dein, had asked the judge to suspend his sentence, saying he was determined to rebuild his life with Amy without hard drugs, but I couldn't see that was in any way possible while Amy was still using. I didn't know whether Blake was drug-free or not, but as drugs had been so integral to their relationship in the first place, it all smacked of delusion once again.

It was still unclear how long Blake would actually serve in prison, having already been inside for around nine months, but at least it gave Amy a little more breathing space. The longer she could continue on the path she'd started, the better the future seemed. We'd spoken by phone a few times since she'd gone back to Prowse Place.

'I don't want to take drugs, Mum, I don't want to do this any more,' she'd said to me on several occasions, and though it was hard to put faith in anything Amy said while she was still addicted, I quietly sensed another shift in her. Deep down, Amy's life scared her. She desperately wanted to make changes, but I'm not sure she knew how to.

It was just after Blake's sentencing that Mitchell and I were invited to Madame Tussaud's for the unveiling of a waxwork of Amy. Initially it was Amy who had been asked, but she had refused to go – she didn't give a reason. My life seemed so mixed up back then: while holding down a locum pharmacist's job, one minute I was receiving news of Amy's progress, the next I was dealing with news on Blake, then suddenly I was stepping in to unveil a waxwork of my daughter. When I say I put events into a 'surreal box', I really mean it. It's as if I have a file in my brain that has 'Deal With Later' stamped on the front of it. Partly because of my condition and partly because our lives had become so bizarre, I couldn't process a lot of what was going on. In fact I'm not sure that feeling has ever gone away.

I approached Madame Tussaud's optimistically, none the less. Moments that were about what Amy had achieved I'd learned to cherish, because over the past two years reminders of them had come few and far between. It irked me that the press wanted only to portray Amy's failures and setbacks, and this gave me an even greater impulse to accentuate the positive whenever I could. Amy's recovery was far more complex than it was portrayed as being and her addiction problems were not the only story.

It felt most disconcerting walking through the room Amy's figure stood in. There was Jimi Hendrix to one side, the Beatles to another, and even Michael Jackson – Amy's own childhood hero. She was in incredible company, but because she was my daughter I'd never before had the chance to see her from an outsider's perspective. I had very little sense of where she stood in relation to other artists, and this was the first time I'd ever caught a glimpse of her place in musical history. That day I was looking at Amy among my own teenage musical heroes. It was another of my 'wow' moments.

As soon as we were ushered towards Amy I had to do a double-take. 'That's my child,' I kept saying to myself. She was dressed in the yellow Preen dress that she had worn to the BRITs party the year before. Amy had of course refused to pose for the artists so to create the waxwork they'd had to use photographs. I found myself checking her face to see if they had her dimples correct, and just to observe how close a likeness of her it was. They'd even kept in the piercing on her upper lip. But it was her small hands that struck me the most. Amy had my fingers, and I held my hand up to her wax hand to see how they matched. She was my baby, my flesh and blood, and here I was comparing myself to her waxwork self. I smiled politely for the photographs, but odd doesn't even come close to describing the way I felt.

Following Blake's sentencing, Amy sank into a deep depression and refused to leave the house. I didn't know whether the agoraphobia had set in because of the photographers outside or because she simply couldn't face the day. When I rang, much of the time I was told she couldn't be woken, or that she was in her room, so that summer I don't remember spending much quality time with her at all. Throughout Amy's life her room remained her sanctuary, the place she took herself off to, to work things out in her head. As a teenager she'd read, write or draw in there; now, I didn't know what she was doing.

In all the flats or houses Amy lived in after Jeffrey's Place I didn't ever go into her room without her permission. It was a boundary I chose not to cross, and a boundary that Amy's security guards now regulated. Because Amy had so little privacy in her life, I figured being alone was important to her. I was also scared of what I might find there. A lot of the time when Amy came downstairs it looked as though she'd been sleeping, but I often wondered how she managed in those quiet times when her body must have been going through turmoil and her mind racing.

In the week following the Madame Tussaud's unveiling Amy was again rushed to University College Hospital. On the evening of 28 July, Mitchell had dropped in to see her at Prowse Place and found her upstairs in her bedroom, coughing and wheezing and struggling for breath. Jevan, her new PA, had been downstairs and had checked on her five minutes before, but it was clear to Mitchell that now she was in the throes of another seizure. He lifted her off the bed, put her on the floor and placed her in the recovery position. Thank God, I never had to witness Amy in that state; it must be a memory Mitchell finds very hard to live with. If he hadn't walked in that night, or if an ambulance hadn't been called immediately, she would almost certainly have died.

Amy's doctor arrived shortly before the paramedics. The newspapers reported a suspected cannabis overdose, but in reality nothing could be ruled out. Amy was also drinking heavily on a daily basis, although at that point all of us still regarded hard drugs as the greater evil. When I think about it now, there was probably not a single moment when Amy didn't have some toxic substance in her system. Apparently just getting her outside Prowse Place on a stretcher and into an ambulance with the paparazzi surrounding her front door was a task in itself. A blanket had to be put up to shield her from all the flashing bulbs. It was bad enough that photographers wanted to document Amy's everyday life; in my view their interest had reached the level of being utterly grotesque.

It wasn't until the next day that Mitchell rang me with more information. Amy was stable. She'd woken up and wanted to eat her favourite KFC, which in Amy-world was a good sign. The hospital wanted to keep her in for observation. I saw her shortly after her bodyguard Andrew brought her back to Prowse Place.

'You scared me,' I said to her.

'Please don't bug me about this, Mum,' she replied, and the subject was changed.

My inclination was always to keep treating Amy as if she was a clear-thinking person, but her body said it all. Her hands trembled and she couldn't keep still. Perhaps, again, because of her youth I could always sense the fighter in her – an inner determination that never left her. Others tell me I've always had that too.

Amy continued with the Subutex, although by now she was beginning to reject her doctors. It was school all over again. Amy's respect for authority had always been lacking and she continued to refute any kind of diagnosis connected to her deteriorating mental health. Against her will, it was decided that it would be better if she did not fulfil some of the gigs she had lined up that summer. She did go on stage at the V Festival, but how Amy felt about performing now I was never sure. My feeling was that she'd lost so much confidence with the drugs that having to bare her soul in front of thousands of people left her too exposed.

Her gigs in France were cancelled at the end of August, and her appearance at the GQ Awards. For every gig that was cancelled Amy lost thousands of pounds, and at every gig she did do it was anyone's guess as to how she was going to behave. Although everyone around Amy had their work cut out coping with her she was still trying to maintain her place in the industry. There were times when I thought she wanted to turn her back on all of it, but so much was at stake, and that really mattered to her.

At the end of that summer I took a much-needed holiday in Italy with Tony. As much as Amy needed to make changes in her life, I was beginning to realize I needed to make some in mine too. Tony shared a holiday home with a friend in a very beautiful town called Ceglie Messapica in the southern tip of the Apulia region and I'd spent much time there over the years. Perhaps it was the openness of the beautiful Italian countryside and the sunshine that prompted some soul-searching of my own, although, with hindsight, I had been changing for some time. What was happening with Amy bore no relation to my eventual decision to end my relationship with

Tony, but I do think it impressed on me the need to be happy again.

Tony and I had been grinding to a halt for some years, but it was on that holiday that I finally made the decision to move out of our flat in High Barnet and embark once again on my own life path. Tony and I didn't give each other the support we needed: we'd never really been able to communicate properly, and our relationship eventually became an isolating experience for us both. I suppose part of me thought that leaving might re-ignite something, but that never happened.

Both Alex and Amy knew my life with Tony had never worked. They'd lived with us and Tony's children before leaving home and were therefore armed with first-hand experience of what an imperfect arrangement it was. I had been putting off confronting the problems in our relationship to avoid the inevitable. If I was working a distance away I would often stay in bed and breakfast accommodation just so I didn't have to go home, or I would go to a friend's place to avoid being in the house. It was an impossible way to live – for everyone.

Unbeknown to me, Alex and Amy had been discussing for some months how they could help me leave. I didn't know about all the conversations they'd had together until recently, and looking back I'm amazed that with everything Amy was going through both she and Alex had the inclination or the time to talk about my situation, but they had. Apparently Amy had suggested putting down a year's rent on a flat for me, and Alex agreed it was a great idea. When they approached me they were worried about me being on my own again, but I reassured them I would be fine. I was still driving so I wasn't completely isolated, and I had lots of good friends around me too. 'Mum, I've taken enough from you over the years,' Amy told me. 'It's time for me to give to you.' I've always been grateful to Alex and Amy for giving me that opportunity to help me live my life to the full.

I found a new home in Potters Bar in Hertfordshire. It was a bungalow, which meant I didn't have to worry about stairs any more.

I'd had several accidents in the flat in Barnet while climbing the stairs, one of which landed me in hospital. I'd had to come to terms with being partially disabled, and although I've never been one to work within my limitations, having only one floor to negotiate did make me less anxious. I knew my concentration and reaction times were impaired, but I was also struggling with an embarrassing and debilitating aspect of my MS which was that my bladder was overly sensitive. Put bluntly, I was becoming incontinent. I couldn't even hop on a tube or bus, or drive for any length of time. Having to think about sanitary wear and worry about what I could and couldn't do undoubtedly affected my self-esteem and physically limited me further. It wasn't until 2012 that I discovered that Botox injections into my bladder could solve the problem. I now have annual injections and it's been a life-saver for me. I've never looked back.

Alex and his then new girlfriend Riva helped me transport my belongings from the High Barnet flat, and Amy donated two of her cats from Prowse Place, Moggy and Minty, to come and live with me for company. A fresh start was always going to be daunting but it didn't take me long to settle in and I very quickly felt that it was the best thing that could have happened to me. When I think about it now, it was the first home I'd been in for a long time that I'd felt comfortable in – since the children were little in fact. Riva helped me put out all of my books and my ornaments. Suddenly I felt I was in a far better place emotionally to deal with my own ill health and take on board everything that was happening around Amy.

Around the time of my move, in November 2008, Alex, Riva and I went over to see Amy at Prowse Place. Because Alex and Riva had only just started dating, Riva hadn't met Amy before, but she'd loved Amy's music and she'd seen her occasionally in the bars in Camden Amy used to go to. She confesses now that she had naturally assumed Amy would be intimidating and that she hadn't been sure of what to expect. But Amy was infinitely more nervous about meeting Riva. We were let in by one of the security staff, but Amy was upstairs in her bedroom on the mezzanine floor and when Alex called up she refused to come down.

Riva laughs about it now – four years later she married Alex – but God knows what she must have thought. The three of us ended up chatting in the living room below for a couple of hours with Amy occasionally interjecting comments from above. When Riva talked about her family in Blackpool and how she missed being near her own mum, suddenly we heard 'Awww, that's sooo sweet!' from upstairs. Occasionally Amy would bob her head over the balcony. All Riva could see was a mass of beehive hair, but whenever Riva looked up Amy would quickly disappear back behind the mezzanine wall. Riva had to wait another couple of weeks before Amy would meet her properly. Fortunately they hit it off straight away. Riva, like all of us, simply had to get used to Amy's unconventional ways.

Amy's health had steadily improved. Unbeknown to me she'd even started putting together a collection for the fashion store Fred Perry, a partnership which had been initiated by her stylist Naomi. It was typical of Amy never to reveal successes like that, just like she was always so secretive about her music. Amy had always sketched and drawn figures of herself, and this was just another facet to her creativity; perhaps in the long run a career in design might have materialized, but that's all speculation now. Her collection for Fred Perry was eventually launched in March 2010, and Fred Perry continue to work with the Foundation today.

Even though Amy's life was slowly changing, media interest in her refused to subside, and I was faced with another decision to make. Mitchell had been approached by an Israeli-American journalist called Daphne Barak whom he had already met and who wanted to make a documentary about Amy and us. I had more or less taken a back seat in terms of interviews, especially after the *NOTW* letter and the lack of impact it had had on the situation. Although I hadn't read any of them, I had been warned that 'exclusives' had been appearing in the newspapers that spring and summer from Blake's mum, Georgette, on how Amy was going to destroy Blake and how Blake wanted a divorce from Amy, but the last thing I wanted was to become involved in a tit-for-tat war of words, especially one that raged publicly. Mitchell had responded, but that was down to him, and no one could have dissuaded him. Daphne, however, was a very charismatic character, and she'd clearly already charmed Mitchell. She was with him when she phoned to ask me whether I would come to the Intercontinental Hotel in central London, where she was staying, to discuss the possibility of a film. As ever, I was open-minded about finding out what she was about.

I too found myself swept up by Daphne's enthusiasm, but again, I wonder now why I went along with it. Daphne promised a lot but, looking back, I don't think she really delivered. Her premise was saving Amy – in fact that was to be the title of her proposed documentary. She spoke very forcefully, as if a cataclysmic shift was going to happen in our lives as a result of her being there. It's difficult for me to admit this but, in retrospect, I was taken in by her. Perhaps back then I wanted to believe anything if it would lead to an improvement in Amy's health and outlook.

Mitchell had already agreed to talk on record and I also agreed to be formally interviewed by Daphne about having a daughter with addiction problems and about some of the dilemmas and decisions that sprang from living with that. Daphne's film never actually materialized, but I wouldn't have wanted to see it anyway. I began to seriously doubt whether she was interested in saving Amy at all – I began to suspect that she was currying favour with us to get a scoop on Amy.

At the end of November she threw a party for Mitch's fifty-eighth birthday at a very fancy club in Mayfair called Les Ambassadeurs. Before the party, Daphne's assistant, a sweet man called Erbil, drove me to the London Clinic where Amy had admitted herself for the week. Daphne had insisted I go and invite her, and I went along with it, but it wasn't something I was comfortable with at all. Amy hadn't even wanted to be at the unveiling of her own waxwork so I knew she would say no. And, of course, that's exactly what happened.

At the party, which Alex and Riva briefly attended, Daphne pushed me forward during Mitchell's speech to say a few words in front of the invited guests. I'm not a person to be rude so I politely agreed, but it became Mitchell, his wife Jane and me facing the crowd. A microphone was thrust in my hand and I couldn't have felt more awkward.

By the beginning of December my new bungalow was still covered in unpacked boxes, and I was dividing my time between work and visiting Amy, who was in and out of the London Clinic. She was in good spirits, and instead of talking about her treatment we talked about family and recounted funny stories of when she and Alex were younger. Her black sense of humour was back. One time I walked into her room to find her collapsed and feigning imminent death. 'I'm dying, I'm dying!' She was prostrate on the floor, writhing around. 'Ha-ha, gotcha!' she burst out giggling as I rushed towards her.

Please don't ask me to explain that one. Amy, bless her, was just being Amy.

I do remember one evening, though, when I just sat with her. She wanted to sleep and I held her hand as her eyes began to close. I watched her. It was as if she was a baby again and I was up on the bed at Osidge Lane reading stories, with her and Alex tucked under each arm. That was a whole universe away, but I still had that same urge: to hold her just like a child, to kiss her goodnight, and stay there until I knew she was safely asleep.

When it looked as though Amy had drifted off, I let go of her hand and quietly moved to tiptoe out of the room.

'Mum, where are you?' she called out drowsily.

I turned back immediately. 'It's OK, Amy. I'm still here.'

13

Island In The Sun

Although she had had several relapses, Amy was starting to turn a corner, and it was encouraging to see. Our lives had been stuck in a horrible limbo for more than two years, only nudging forward occasionally, but I still longed for the day when she would announce, 'That's it, Mum, I'm clean.'

But even as the problem of hard drugs was subsiding, another one was becoming more prominent. The London Clinic is not a detox facility and Amy knew she could always get a room there, which was why it was her preferred choice. If she wanted to she could order in wine and champagne to her room from the hospital menu, and she was doing so, drinking it openly and offering it around to anyone who came in. There had already been complaints from the medical staff. 'This is a joke,' I said to her on one occasion. 'You're here to recover.' I got the silent treatment.

Alcohol had been a constant companion for Amy for a long time, but now it was taking centre stage. A lot of people said, 'If Amy's drinking, it's not as bad as hard drugs,' but I was beginning to see that there was no difference between the two. Alcohol is legal and readily accessible, but it is still a drug with a different name. I was terrified that she had replaced one kind of dependency with another. We were still on very shaky ground.

Right: Amy during our trip to Paris. She tore around the city with us, taking in all the sights with her usual irrepressible energy.

Below: Growing up so fast – Amy aged sixteen.

Bottom: A card from Amy when she was going through a French phase. That's me on the front, complete with lab coat and pens in my pocket!

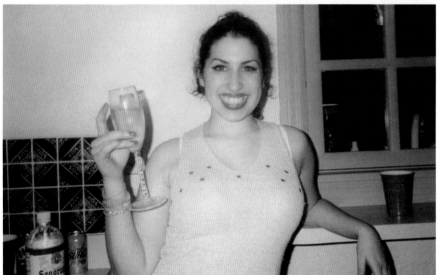

Maman ..... °

Chére Maman!
BONNE FÊTE MAMAN!

Je suis mechante quelque fois,
mais tu es trés patiente!

Je te donne, un
dîner delicieux!

Je t'embrasse

Grosses bises
Amy
x

Maman!

Above: On holiday in Florida. Amy spent most of that holiday playing guitar and writing her own compositions.

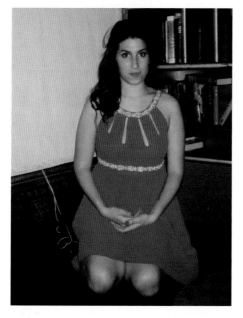

Above: My beautiful daughter, at home.

Right: Amy visited my cousin Joan in Boca Raton shortly after she signed her record deal with Universal.

Right: Amy loving life, around 2000.

Below: Amy adored her grandmother, Cynthia. I'm not sure she'd have let many others near her hair!

Below: This is the bedroom wall that Amy painted in her garage room at Guildown Avenue.

Above: Doing what she did best – Amy at an intimate gig, before the release of *Frank*.

Below left: Happier times for mother and daughter. **Below right**: Jools Holland was a fan of Amy's music right from the start. Here she's performing for the *Later With Jools Holland* Christmas special.

Above left: Amy with her Ivor Novello award in 2004. This award was so special to her – she saw it as the musician's award. I was thrilled when she turned up on my doorstep the morning after the ceremony with the award. 'It's for you,' she said.

Above right: Hustler! Amy regularly played pool with her friends.

Right: The infamous Amy look, with trademark beehive. This was exactly how she was reproduced when Madame Tussauds created her waxwork.

Amy wasn't allowed to travel to the States for the Grammys, so the Grammys came to her, and she performed by satellite link from the Riverside Studios in Hammersmith. The atmosphere was electric when it was announced that she had won in multiple categories. No one apart from Amy and me could have understood the meaning attached to the hug shown in this photo, though.

Above and below: My trip to see Amy in St Lucia. It was great to see her looking tanned and much healthier than she had been in the months before she took off there.

In April 2014 I did a parachute jump to raise money for the Amy Winehouse Foundation. I'm still recovering from it!

'One day at a time, Janis, one day at a time,' I kept telling myself.

One thing that made the ground even shakier was Blake. In the first week of November he had been granted early release from Edmunds Hill Prison in Suffolk where he was serving out his sentence, on condition that he attend Life Works, a rehab clinic in Woking, Surrey. Amy had paid for it – around £30,000 – which was something I was unhappy about because it meant that they continued to be dependent on each other, but in the end it was Amy's choice. Apparently Blake had told her if she loved him, she'd pay. What could we do? It was her money after all.

A month into his treatment Blake absconded from the centre after failing a drugs test. He turned up at the London Clinic to see Amy. Mitchell was called immediately by the security guards and he spoke to both Amy and Blake by phone. God knows what Blake was thinking, but eventually he agreed to turn himself in at Limehouse police station and he was taken back into custody. I only learned of this incident afterwards, but it demonstrated to me that however much I thought Amy was out of the woods, she wasn't. Blake was still her husband, but until they understood what was driving them to drugs, I didn't think it would be safe for them to meet.

In the midst of all this, what was also fascinating to me was that whenever I saw Amy in the London Clinic she would always have stories about other patients. There was the woman down the corridor who refused to take her medicine, or the man in another room who was taking such-and-such medication for his condition. She knew everything about everyone and she talked endlessly to other people. They loved her being there, but she never referred to her own treatment. Everyone else had a problem except Amy. I often wondered how much she blamed other people, including her own family, for her predicament, and whether she ever truly took on board how much she would ultimately have to reach inside herself for the solution.

Just before Christmas, Amy got restless. Her hospital room was small and windowless and she often complained of feeling cooped up. She was undergoing treatment voluntarily so nothing could stop her leaving: she discharged herself and flew to St Lucia, taking Jevan and a couple of her bodyguards with her. She continued with her drug replacement therapy abroad. We could do nothing but trust her, but unfortunately Amy and trust didn't sit too well together.

Amy wanted to stay on in St Lucia into the new year, so I planned to go out towards the end of February 2009, and I invited my brother's wife Jann to keep me company. Jann was a great travelling companion and it had been a while since we'd caught up with each other. I'd also wanted our arrival to be a surprise for Amy. I don't know why, but it seemed like a nice idea, one that would make the whole trip a bit more special.

It was my first time in St Lucia, and as we flew in I was awestruck by the lushness of the island and the tall mountains rising like pyramids into the blue sky. We felt the warm Caribbean breeze brush around us as we stepped from the plane and into a waiting helicopter that shuttled us above the palm trees and white sands to the crescent bay where Amy was staying. Cotton Bay Village, on the very northern tip of the island, is a secluded resort, and I understood immediately why Amy had fallen in love with the place. The salty sea air was healthy and clean and it felt uninhibited and friendly.

As it turned out, we were staying next door to Amy's villa in a beautiful colonial mansion with a beachside view. No sooner had we checked in than word must have got to Amy that I was there, because suddenly I heard a familiar voice. 'Mummy! Mummy!' Amy screamed as she rushed in and wrapped her arms around me. 'You're here!' She giggled and looked puzzled. She looked like a different person. She'd put on weight and her skin was tanned. That hug was like the hugs she gave me when she came back from holiday as a child. She would burst through the door shouting, 'I missed you, Mummy!' and we'd hold on to each other tightly.

Our places being next door meant that we could move easily without press intrusion. Stories had already been published in the British tabloids about Amy crawling around on her hands and knees begging for drinks in beachside bars, but that's not something I ever saw her do. I never believed any of them anyway. Why would Amy need to beg for drinks when she could pay for them? But as it turned out I didn't see much of Amy. No sooner had she said hello than she popped her head round the door and said she was going to the gym. A few days later she announced she was trying to book a flight back home.

Admittedly I was a little taken aback by that. I didn't bring it up, but it did seem strange to me at the time. I understood that Amy was in St Lucia to find her feet. I certainly wasn't expecting her to spend every minute with me, neither did I demand that of her. The atmosphere was so far removed from the prison she'd had to endure in London that I could see St Lucia had been doing her good. If she wanted to spend time with us, she could, but she had her friend Violetta Thalia with her now. I just didn't put two and two together at all. Amy must have found out that Blake was being released from prison at the end of February to attend the Phoenix Futures Rehab Centre in Sheffield. Only afterwards did it dawn on me that this was why she had had such a sudden change of heart.

Mitchell had been dealing with the Blake situation behind the scenes and had had several messages from Blake saying that he wanted a divorce. I didn't discuss it with Amy because I understood that she knew, and that Mitchell was talking to her about it. As a family, our concern was that Blake would demand a share of Amy's money. Ultimately that didn't happen. Despite this, the impression I got in St Lucia was that there was no change in their relationship at all. The newspapers were reporting that Amy was seeing the actor Josh Bowman, but if she was, I wasn't introduced to him.

I didn't always understand Amy's romances. I could never fathom what she saw in Blake. As far as I could see, the relationships Amy pursued were all about momentary pleasure, and the drugs and alcohol were part of that package. None of it was about finding lasting happiness. She'd always been like that – trying to satisfy a deep emotional need through quick fixes. It makes me sad that Amy never lived long enough to discover that she could love and be truly loved by someone.

In St Lucia, something else struck me as peculiar too. Amy had befriended a woman called Marjorie, the owner of the bar on Cas en Bas beach, a warm and friendly woman I also hit it off with straight away. She had taken to Amy soon after she arrived on the island, and there were a few late afternoons when we sat there with the sun on our backs watching the waves roll in. I would look up and Amy would be lying across Marjorie's shoulder. She called her 'mumma' and she draped her arms around her neck. I was reassured that someone was looking out for Amy but it did sit uncomfortably with me. Amy had a mother, me, and I was there. I may have been limited in how involved I could be in her life, but I was always her mum. I loved her, and I told her that, even when she made it impossible to be loved. I wonder if she ever truly heard it.

It was midway through our stay and Jann and I were having an early afternoon lunch in the beachside restaurant when Amy found us and announced she was leaving. She'd managed to find a flight home via Barbados and a car was arriving to pick her up in an hour or so. As ever with Amy, it was a case of no surprises, but I did feel deflated. We said an emotional goodbye, she kissed and hugged everyone else, and then she just vanished.

The next time I gazed up at the horizon Amy had reappeared, astride a shiny black horse. Both the horse and Amy were bowing. 'She's called Black Beauty!' Amy shouted. 'Bye, Mummy, I love you!' It really was a most magical moment, like a scene from a movie. She'd arranged it all with the owner of the horses that were for rent in the bay, and it was such an Amy thing to do. I suspect she was feeling guilty for disappearing, so there was an extra show of affection. No matter what, Amy had the ability to sprinkle that shower of gold dust on you that made everything melt away. I called Amy's world 'my other life' because whichever way I experienced it, it was unbelievable.

It didn't take long for me to return back to earth with a bump.

While Amy had been away, Mitchell had found a house for her to rent, in nearby Hadley Wood, the rationale being that when she returned from the Caribbean she could concentrate on her music and be out of Camden and the limelight for a while. Amy was against the idea, but she did want to continue with her recovery. She'd not stopped taking Subutex the whole time she was away and she'd sworn that she hadn't taken any hard drugs; the alcohol, on the other hand, was a different issue. I tended to believe her about the hard drugs. She certainly looked a thousand times better than she'd done the previous year. 'You're doing really well, you're looking great,' I would say to her.

All the same, the circus couldn't wait for Amy to come back to town. On 6 March she was charged with assaulting a fan at a charity ball, and a burlesque dancer called Sherene Flash was claiming that Amy had punched her backstage at a fundraiser for the Prince's Trust on 25 September the previous year. In fact it came to nothing. There was always jostling around Amy. Fans and photographers could be incredibly intimidating. I felt frustrated for Amy and was also worried that this would arrest all the progress she'd made. She tolerated being at home for a while, but a month later Amy was back in St Lucia.

While Amy was in the Caribbean between December 2008 and February 2009, I had been finding my feet following my separation from Tony. After a decade of not being on my own I was getting used to it again. But in life things often happen when you least expect them to, and perhaps Amy being abroad had provided the necessary space.

Richard's marriage to Stephanie had broken down the previous year so both of us found ourselves at a loose end. As Amy was boarding a flight back to St Lucia during Passover festival in April 2009, I guess you could say we found each other. To be honest, we didn't have to think too hard about it. Richard and I had known each other since I was twelve. He went to Victoria Club with my brother Brian and he was even best man at Brian's wedding. We'd all been friends for so many years that getting together was a bit of a no-brainer.

I had already planned to go back to St Lucia to visit Amy. Even before Richard and I started going out he had said he'd come with me as a friend; in the end we used the trip as an opportunity to tell Amy that we were an item. After all, Richard was her Uncle Richard whom she hadn't seen now for a few years, and his son Michael and daughter Jessica had known Amy since birth. I would have hated it if she'd heard about our relationship through the grapevine. Both of us wanted to break the news to her properly.

On 3 May we flew in to Hewanorra Airport and made our way to Cotton Bay. We'd timed the trip so we could watch Amy perform at the St Lucia Jazz Festival, but with a few days beforehand to unwind and enjoy the sun. We dumped our bags in our villa and Richard went off exploring while I rested on the double bed: travelling takes it out of me physically, and when my body says rest, I force myself to listen to it. Amy couldn't be far away, and we agreed that you could always hear her before you saw her so there was no point in ringing her mobile, which she probably wouldn't have answered anyway.

Richard had walked for two minutes down the main street, Atlantic Drive, when he heard a voice shouting, 'Uncle Richard! Uncle Richard!' Amy was racing towards him, and she launched herself at him, wrapping her legs and arms around him.

'What are you doing here?' she asked.

'I'm here with your mum,' he replied. 'Come on. She's desperate to see you.'

I was sitting on the bed unpacking when Amy bowled in. All I saw was this whirl of flower-patterned dress and two arms diving towards me. 'Mummy!' she was screaming. We cuddled and cuddled. God, it was great to see Amy like that.

'Which room are you staying in, Uncle Richard?' she asked.

There was an uncomfortable pause.

'Here,' Richard said.

Amy burst out giggling. 'Here?' Then her mouth dropped open. And that was that. She turned and disappeared out of the patio doors.

I now know that she ran to phone Michael. 'Can you believe it? It's too weird,' she had said to him. 'Does that make us brother and sister?'

Richard caught up with Amy a little later and they walked on the beach, just the two of them. Richard felt it was important to tell Amy that he was serious, that this wasn't a fly-by-night fling. We'd decided that it was better it came from him because of the way Amy might see it, and he wanted Amy to trust him. However chaotically Amy behaved, she was always protective of me, especially when it came to relationships. Apparently she screwed her face up in sheer disbelief during most of the conversation. When she joined us for dinner that evening she kept staring at Richard, then at me, then back at Richard. We ended up laughing about it – what else could we do?

That evening at dinner, Amy drank. It was enough for her to get tipsy but not so much to cause me real concern. I noticed, though, that her hands were shaking as she looked through the menu. 'Nah, there's nothing on that I want,' she announced, and turned to the children's menu. She ordered fish fingers and chips from it, and when her meal arrived the food sat on her plate going cold. Halfway through dinner she called to Neville, her bodyguard, 'Can you get me a KFC?' He drove the forty-minute round trip to nearby Rodney Bay and arrived back armed with a bucket of chicken and chips. She picked at it, just playing with it in her fingers and in her mouth, rarely swallowing any of it.

Over the past few years I had got used to seeing Amy do this. I say 'got used to' . . . it's more accurate to say that I learned to live with it. You don't ever 'get used to' your child having an eating disorder, but I couldn't force-feed Amy. Inside, I was always saying, 'Please, please eat something,' but I didn't ever vocalize that for fear of Amy digging her heels in. I suppose to a certain extent I'd normalized parts of Amy's behaviour, if that was at all possible. I'd certainly been exposed to it more than Richard, who found parts of our trip and being with Amy difficult.

Richard had not seen her much since she'd left home. Of course, he'd read the newspapers and we'd spoken a lot about her, but that was a very different story from actually being in her company. He was taken aback at how tiny she looked. He kept recalling a photo of Michael and Amy taken at a Bar Mitzvah when they were both seventeen. Amy was a good weight then. She looked healthy and fresh-faced. Now she was a size 6, able to fit into children's clothes, for God's sake. Richard had lost some weight himself in the intervening years, close to three stone, and it was fascinating that Amy picked up on that immediately. 'Uncle Richard, you're so skinny!' she had said to him on that first day. He looked back at her confusedly, thinking, 'Well if I'm skinny, you're a matchstick.'

In St Lucia, Richard saw hummingbirds in their natural habitat for the first time and he joked that Amy had turned into one of them. We didn't see her in the mornings, sometimes not even in the afternoons, and no sooner had she said hello than she was off again, hovering only for a minute or two. I noticed a deeper restlessness about her. She needed to be doing different things all the time, as if her brain was constantly on overload. She'd always been a nervous ball of energy, even at school, but now it was more pronounced. I had to hold on to the minutes I did spend with her, because within a flash I'd see her walking along the sand by herself, or messing around with the horses. 'Where's Amy now?' became a common expression.

I also suspected that, as well as what Amy was drinking in front of us, she was constantly disappearing to top up. Just as she'd done with hard drugs, she was covering it up, only letting me see what she wanted me to see. There was so much guilt and shame tied up with all of Amy's addictions that it was painful to witness. I just had to keep reminding myself that I'd chosen this when I decided I wanted

Amy in my life. It's the reality all loved ones are forced to confront if they decide to remain supportive of someone with addiction problems. I had to find a way to deal with it that I thought was right for me. Instead of constantly punishing Amy for what she was doing I wanted her to know that I believed she had the ability to recover. I always did believe that. I really did.

Amy's villa was a beautiful plantation-style building set out with teak dressers and rattan chairs, with a wooden staircase rising to a balcony above the living room. Next door had been rented for her and her entourage too. There, on the ground floor, a studio had been installed with every piece of equipment you could imagine flown in from London and Miami: guitars, amps, drums, speakers, microphones and monitors. It all looked very impressive, but I doubted she was doing any work there. It was as if everyone around her was on tenterhooks, waiting for Amy to create something. But I knew that she worked infrequently and spontaneously, if she wanted to work at all.

The St Lucia Jazz Festival had actually begun the day before Richard and I arrived in Cotton Bay, and the island was jumping. Amy was due to perform on the evening of Friday the 8th. Richard and I had spent our first few days on the island exploring, taking in impromptu jazz sessions and spending time with each other and Amy. According to Marjorie at the beach bar, Amy hadn't wanted to appear at the festival at all but the organizers had kept asking. I don't know the truth of that, but I suspect Amy would have played a part in convincing herself she was ready to perform again. By the time Friday rolled around, however, the tropical sunshine had disappeared and storm clouds had started gathering.

I hadn't seen Amy that day. Her band had arrived on the island and they were waiting to rehearse. Raye Cosbert had arrived too and was with her, and I was looking forward to seeing her on stage. Her headline slot had been billed as a comeback performance, which I winced at. The last thing Amy needed at that moment was the pressure of 'a comeback performance', but I kept my thoughts to myself – not that I ever had the chance to voice my opinion about Amy's career. In any case, it wouldn't have changed a thing.

At eight p.m., after Richard and I had eaten, showered and changed, a car came to pick us up. Amy's team had sorted us out with VIP passes and we were also due to attend the after-show party. As we neared Pigeon Island, a peninsula and nature reserve off the northern coast of St Lucia, I was filled with apprehension, and the weather didn't help my mood. You couldn't have got a more idyllic setting for a concert, but as we stepped from the car and into a waiting golf buggy I could feel in the air an oppressive humidity, as if the heavens were about to open. The wind was whipping up around us so loudly we could hardly hear each other.

The sound box was around 150 metres from the stage, and there two plastic garden chairs had been set up for us with the name 'Winehouse' taped to them. Someone had kindly organized a cool-box for the evening for us with a couple of bottles of wine and some soft drinks in it, and, thank God, we were under a canopy. KC and the Sunshine Band were just finishing their support set as we took our seats.

I was concentrating so hard on the stage that I was oblivious to the roar of the crowd around us. I certainly didn't notice that a large St Lucian man had edged his way up to the side of our box and was just standing there, staring and beaming.

'Are you Amy's mummy?' he called over as soon as he'd caught our attention.

With my face, it was hard to deny it.

'Are you *really* Amy's mummy?' he repeated.

I smiled and nodded my head.

He reached into his pocket and whipped out his mobile phone. I assumed he wanted a picture, which of course I would have gone along with, although not altogether comfortably. But no, he started dialling furiously.

'Mum?' he shouted down the phone. 'I'm talking to Amy

Winehouse's mummy . . . No, Mum, I can't put her on . . . just trust me, I'm here with Amy Winehouse's mummy!'

Richard and I were in fits of giggles. I knew there was a big place for Amy in St Lucia's heart but I had no idea meeting me would be this exciting. We ended up giving him the wine in our cool-box and he left grinning.

'I'm not going to open it,' he said as a parting shot. 'It's wine from Amy's mummy!'

Her set was about to start and from a distance, Amy looked like a doll walking onstage, so my eyes stayed fixed on the large screens to either side. I was watching her intently, with an instinct that I'd honed over many years with Amy. By now the heavens had truly opened and the rain was hammering down on the canopy roof – and when it rains on St Lucia, it really rains. The sound kept cutting in and out. Amy looked unsure, and unsteady on her feet. She kept taking her stiletto heels on and off and she was clutching on to the hem of her blue dress so tightly that I could see her knickers. It was hard to know what was going on but I knew she was drunk the minute I set eyes on her. I closed my eyes and breathed deeply, waiting for a comforting feeling of calm to wash over me: there were times when my yoga practice really helped.

The crowd started booing, and all I wanted to do was reach my arms out, pick Amy up and lift her out of it completely. But it was years since I'd been able to do that. However much I yearned to make things OK for her, I couldn't. At one point it looked as though she might pull things back together, but less than an hour into her set she finally walked off the stage. We waited anxiously, and then there was an announcement to say the gig had been cut short as a result of the torrential rain. But, to me, the reason was obvious.

Richard and I shrugged at each other. Not only did we feel uneasy, by now we were marooned in the sound tent. The ground where the crowd had been standing was swimming in mud and it was obvious a golf buggy wasn't going to get across to pick us up.

Amazingly, Amy's crew hadn't forgotten about me. Two strapping men appeared out of nowhere and I suddenly felt one on either side lifting me up, still glued to my garden chair. We collectively wobbled to the backstage area, with Richard holding an umbrella over my head. Anyone would have thought I was north London's answer to the Queen of Sheba!

All I wanted to do was see Amy. I looked around expectantly, but there was no sign of her or any of her team. Instead a car was waiting for us and we were taken back to the villa almost immediately. We didn't see her again until the next evening, when she surfaced for dinner.

'What happened last night, Amy?' I enquired gently.

'Don't, Mum,' she said. 'I'm too embarrassed.'

End of story.

As always, I left Amy with a complicated array of feelings. I felt better, though, knowing that Richard's son Michael was flying out a week after we left the island. He was halfway through teacher-training and she'd offered him a break to recharge. Like all of us, Michael had had to wrestle with a way to maintain contact with Amy and he too had chosen a gentler approach by accepting her as she was, however hard that could be. Accompanying Michael was Amy's school friend Lauren Gilbert and her brother.

Amy opened up with some of her friends in a way she didn't with the older generation, and over the years I've come to accept that there were facets to Amy's personality and her life that I did not see. During the week he was there, Michael spent time with her walking on the beach. They intuitively understood each other, even though Michael recognized that the effects of drugs and alcohol on Amy naturally meant that Amy never operated on a level playing field. We've only discussed this recently, but Amy did confide in Michael about her future. 'I'm determined to get clean and healthy, I really want it,' she'd said. She told him she desperately wanted children, even though physically that would have been impossible at that point. Amy had not now had a period for several years, but perhaps that was the dream that kept her focused on her recovery.

Amy loved being around children, but then I always saw her as a child stuck in time. It happened more around Mitchell than me, but she would often sit on a knee or suck her thumb and talk in a babyish voice. The child was another of her many characters. I couldn't always work it out, but it seemed to me that childlike interactions were uncomplicated for her and they fed her deep need for love. When I was in St Lucia I had watched her playing with an army of kids on the beach and I wondered then whether she would ever have children. What would she call them, what might they look like? I'd had to deal with a gamut of emotions most parents wouldn't experience in a whole lifetime but I still held on to those precious memories of when Alex and Amy were small. I remembered the happiness that giving birth to them brought me. I hoped that one day she would have the opportunity to feel the same happiness.

But for every minute Amy was looking ahead with Michael, the next minute she was hurtling backwards. Michael recalled one particular day midway through his holiday. It was lunchtime when Amy finally surfaced. Everyone was gathered at the beach bar sipping orange juice and eating when Amy strolled down the walkway. She looked a mess. She'd been horribly drunk the night before. She looked at everyone with an Amy look of contempt.

'One tequila,' she shouted to the barman.

'Come on, Amy, seriously, it's only one p.m.,' they tried to reason with her.

Amy scowled at them and turned back to the barman. 'Two tequilas!'

When they came, she drank them straight down and said, 'If you don't like it, fuck off.'

That was the last straw for Lauren, who launched into Amy about her 'recovery'. A few of Amy's school friends had mixed opinions about how Amy was handling her problems, and I think the least said about this argument the better. Let's just say Amy bit back. She regretted it, of course, but she refused to apologize to Lauren the next day, and Lauren found it hard to forgive her. Lauren should have known Amy well enough to know that confronting her head on was only going to be counterproductive. And Amy, well . . . there were a lot of things Amy should have realized, including the turmoil she caused for people around her. But addicts rarely do.

Amy returned home mid-summer. It was becoming expensive to keep her in St Lucia without any work being done and there was business back home she needed to deal with. My mother was very poorly and wasn't expected to live much longer. She was in a home in Willesden Green, and although my contact with her over the years had been minimal, I did see her regularly in her final weeks. When she died in July I went through the motions of helping arrange her funeral with Brian and Debra, but in reality I felt like I'd grieved for her many years before. Our relationship was never repaired, and she always remained distant. Nevertheless, we gave her a good send-off at Rainham Cemetery which the whole family turned out for.

Amy, of course, turned up late. She missed the ceremony, and not long after she pulled up with her security team the mourners due at the next funeral – a child's funeral – had started to make their way over on the hunt for an autograph. I didn't see it, but apparently Amy's contorted face did all the talking. She was so uncomfortable, especially as these people were due at a child's funeral. The final straw was when the ground warden himself strode over and presented his prayer book to Amy. She signed for him, but left shortly afterwards. Maybe she saw the funny side, I don't know, but defacing a Torah with a 'celebrity' autograph is unacceptable by anyone's standards!

Also that month – on Thursday, 16 July 2009, to be precise – Amy and Blake were granted a divorce by the Family Division of the High Court. Amy decided not to be present. Despite this official separation my suspicions remained: Blake and Amy were apart on paper but they were still in touch with each other. Nevertheless, the divorce was one step forward.

Amy was due to appear back in court to answer the charge of common assault against Sherene Flash – something she couldn't miss. Mitchell wanted to accompany her and get her there on time, which was always a palaver. Back in March, when she'd been charged, she was late appearing at Westminster Magistrates Court. Although she'd pleaded not guilty and been bailed without restrictions, her solicitor was angry with her. She came across as disrespectful to the court, and the fear was that she might do the same again. Amy was nervous about the upcoming trial. I spoke to her briefly the night before. 'Just keep calm and tell the truth,' I told her. Thankfully, justice prevailed. District Judge Timothy Workman concluded that he couldn't be sure the altercation with Sherene Flash was not an accident and the case was dismissed.

Of course, the trial attracted the usual media scrum. Mitchell had to get Amy through about a hundred photographers just to reach the door. I have Priscilla Coleman's artist's impression of Amy from that day up on my dining-room wall. Amy is sitting in her grey pin-striped suit with her head bowed taking notes. But there's another drawing of Amy by the same artist that I would have loved: Amy with her bare leg outstretched, pointing her toe under the nose of the district judge. He had asked if it was possible for her to have intimidated Ms Flash that evening. A 'yes' or 'no' was not enough for Amy. She marched out from behind the witness stand, lifted her leg up above her waist and gestured towards her ballet pumps. 'Could someone with feet this small be intimidating?' she asked him.

Apparently, he was lost for words.

14

Drinkin' Again

As soon as Amy's trial was over she began living full-time in the Hadley Wood house. While it was a good move for me because she was closer – that July I'd moved from my bungalow in Potters Bar to live with Richard in East Barnet – I was never so sure it was great for Amy. I was now a twenty-minute journey away which meant I could visit Amy more often when she was in London, and she was close to Alex and Riva and Mitchell's sister Melody too, so Amy was almost home, but she wasn't. Her life was so different now. She rattled around in that house. It was vast and ostentatious, all marble flooring and chandeliers. Amy tried to make it her home, though. Her figurine 'Elvis' phone sat on a table in the hallway – every time it rang it played 'Hound Dog' as Elvis jitterbugged. Her gym equipment occupied the back room. I've never seen plasma screen TVs so huge. A studio was installed for her in the loft room upstairs. But everything that fed Amy's creativity was shut off to her.

Her bodyguards continued to live in full-time, and she still, at first, had the problem of photographers camped outside. In March, when Amy had returned briefly from the Caribbean, she would climb over her neighbour's fence to get in or out of the house, mostly because it was easier than going the long way round, but all that resulted in were the most ridiculous photographs of Amy stuck on fences. At her request an injunction had now been granted to stop photographers pursuing her within a hundred metres of the property. The high court ruling was directed mainly at the paparazzi agency Big Pictures which had followed Amy relentlessly, but it also applied to anyone found chasing her.

Although the house was close by, I had to rely on Richard to drive me everywhere. I had been pretty much ordered to stop driving before I left my bungalow in Potters Bar since I'd had several accidents – nothing major, just reversing into a few bollards and the unfortunate remodelling of my garage door. My inability to get myself anywhere prompted my move to Richard's. I suspect it would have happened anyway, but I held out until the last minute: the thought of having to rely on anyone to take me places made me positively angry. I had also reduced my working hours to part-time and now relied on Richard to take me to work too. Before, I'd been such an independent person. But I've never seen the point in looking back. Us getting together and my moving in with Richard brought forward his plans to take early retirement, and it was reassuring to have him around.

Amy was afforded a degree of freedom in Hadley Wood that she hadn't ever had in Camden. Alex and Riva used to come to take her out without her bodyguards, which wouldn't have happened before. We also tried to make it over once a week. There were occasions when we'd call the house on a Sunday to say we were popping over only to be told by Andrew or Neville or whoever was on duty that Amy wasn't up to receiving guests. Monday lunchtime became a more regular slot – it was more likely she'd be around.

For me, that worked well. I always wanted to see Amy, but it was important to create a boundary around my time with her. That may sound selfish, but I saw it as self-care – making sure I was emotionally and physically strong enough to face her. I also had Richard to consider too: it was a lot to ask of someone to take my life on. I knew from experience that it was the throw of a dice as to which Amy I would find when I got there. Although I never stopped trying, pulling up in the car always gave me an uneasy feeling, and there were days when both of us approached the house worried about what situation we might have to step into.

'I'm not going back to drugs, Mum, I'm bored with it,' Amy had told me when she returned from St Lucia. She was still taking the Subutex, but according to Riva it was during that summer that she stopped, although no one knows exactly when. Amy's drinking had got progressively worse, however, so I was both proud of and disappointed with Amy. I know how much strength it was taking for her to beat the drugs, but I desperately wanted her to curb her alcohol intake too. She was by no means out of the woods, but if she could work towards being clean stage by stage, just like she'd done with heroin and cocaine, she'd be well again, I thought.

Whether she meant to or not, Amy continually offered up the promise of recovery. Whenever she said, 'I don't want to be an alcoholic,' the words I heard were, 'Mum, I'm ready to seek help.' Tragically, she never managed to overcome that hurdle. Since her passing, the sheer finality of Amy not being afforded one more chance has been one of the cruellest realities of all to come to terms with.

Although others in the family disagree, I got the impression that Amy was unhappy and bored in Hadley Wood, and that bothered me more than anything. Amy had a short attention span at the best of times, but boredom was another name for Amy's anxiety about her life. My God, Amy had never held back in presenting herself to the world superficially – taking her clothes off, being the life and soul of the party – but she could never sit with herself long enough to face herself. Being miles out of Camden only intensified that boredom. She had always propelled herself towards the action, and although she tried to fill the house with people, it seemed to me that she was in a lonely place. That might explain the explosion in the number of cats at the house – and when I say explosion, that's no understatement.

Amy had loved having Katie when she was younger and she'd

kept two cats at Jeffrey's Place, Monkey and Melina. Alex had rescued them one year when Amy went on tour, having left them with one defrosting piece of meat in a bowl. At Prowse Place she had many more. She even sent me a Mother's Day card one year signed from Amy, Alex, Riva and all the cats: Monkey, Melina, Chops, Kodger, Rita, Shirley, Gary, Moggy, Minty and Kola-Bottle. In Hadley Wood, though, the animals took over. There were four, then twelve, and in the end we counted sixteen living there. It wasn't long before the house, which was rented, became a health hazard. Despite there being a cleaner who came more than once a week, the cats had sprayed the carpets and the long curtains, and the stench was unbearable as soon as you opened the front door. I still have the two Burmese mix cats, Moggy and Minty, that Amy gave me in Potters Bar. Believe me, left to their own devices they'd spray on anything.

As I feared, our visits were a mixed bag – some good days, some bad. I had no idea who Amy had visiting her in Hadley Wood but there were times when that house looked as if every night was party night. Empty bottles, ashtrays and cigarette butts were strewn all over the back garden, which had its own barbecue hut and summer-house, and it was the same in Amy's lounge and kitchen. Amy had always been messy, but this was different. There was cat poop in places I didn't think possible. I watched as Amy surrounded herself with chaos and my heart cried out for her because, as I saw it, it was a reflection of what was going on in her mind.

In August there were two consecutive Mondays when Richard and I turned up, sat with Amy's bodyguards, drank tea and waited . . . and waited. Amy was upstairs but she didn't want to come down. Whether or not she was sleeping we do not know, but the message was clear. On days like that we never stayed longer than a couple of hours before saying, 'Come on, let's go.' But I always left feeling upset and disappointed that I hadn't been able to make contact with her, even if it was just to see her face.

On another week, a completely different story would unfold.

Around that time Salaam Remi flew over from Miami, and when we arrived he was with her working on new material. I'd never seen Amy work on her songs before, and I looked on fascinated. Amy's notebooks were strewn across the sofa and she was listening intently to what Salaam was saying, furiously scribbling into her pad. 'What do you really mean when you write this word?' he'd ask her, and she'd think about it and change the structure. 'Perhaps this word is better here,' he'd gently direct her. We left them to it, but I was struck by how Amy responded to Salaam's calm manner, and his ability to get her to think about her craft in a multitude of ways. She was visibly absorbed in the moment.

I'd not seen Amy look genuinely enthusiastic about writing for a while. Even Michael, who had sat with her in the studio in St Lucia in May, had commented that Amy hadn't appeared ready to create anything. Her band had stayed on following the St Lucia Jazz Festival to work out new songs with her, but nothing had come from these sessions. There was one occasion in particular when it looked as though a drunken Amy might contribute some ideas. Michael recalls a boiling-hot roomful of musicians and technicians, equip-ment humming, all eyes on Amy, waiting for her to open her mouth. 'Nah,' she said, 'can't do it,' and walked out.

To their credit, Island Records were still not pushing for a third album, but Amy knew that their patience wasn't infinite. Live performances were a way to keep the money rolling in, but touring did nothing for her state of mind. When she was at Guildown Avenue with me, writing music had been an anchoring force. It was the same when she went to New York to work with Mark Ronson. *Back To Black* became the means of relieving her depression. I wondered now whether she even wanted to carry on with music. On reflection, perhaps songwriting was too painful for Amy; maybe she resisted putting herself through it again.

As ever with Amy, life turned on a dime: one week she was absorbed with Salaam, the next she'd flip again. In early September, Amy was full of excitement. 'Mum, Mum, you've got to hear this!'

She was whirling around the kitchen like clock hands spinning on fast-forward. Busy, busy, busy, just like she'd been when she was a toddler. 'Come upstairs, Mum, I want you to hear something.' This struck me as unusual because ordinarily Amy didn't share her work with me.

She'd been learning a piano part to the Leon Russell track 'A Song For You', which she first sang all those years ago at Cynthia's husband Larry's fiftieth birthday. She loved that song, and she was drawn to the soul singer Donny Hathaway as a recording artist – she said he had an element to his creativity that felt uncontainable. That made me smile because, as I saw her, there were sides to Amy she'd never been able to suppress either – that never-ending unrest which had always been part of her personality.

It was a lovely moment actually. I sat beside her on the piano stool and she played down the scale – it was like the sound of rain tinkling down a window pane. Richard was bashing about on the drum-kit. 'I'm backing Amy Winehouse!' he was shouting. It was definitely better that way round, because whenever I'd heard Amy's drumming I knew there was a very good reason why she sang. We must have been there a good half hour, mucking around and talking.

Then, without uttering a single word, Amy stood up and walked out of the room. We sipped our tea and hung around for another fifteen minutes or so, then Richard poked his head out of the studio door to see where she'd got to – only to catch sight of Amy scampering across the landing and into her bedroom dressed in nothing but her bra and knickers and with a young man in tow whom Richard didn't recognize. The security guards must have let him in. When Amy's eyes caught Richard's she recoiled with embarrassment and closed her door behind her.

Richard was hesitant in breaking that one to me, but there was no way I was going to sit there indefinitely sipping tea while Amy entertained her 'companion' across the dividing wall. It would be an understatement to say that at times Amy made me feel so awkward and small that I questioned why I made the effort to see her at all.

The afternoon had been so much fun, and in an instant my gut felt completely knotted up. Only Amy managed to do that to me.

'There's no point in us hanging around,' said Richard, and he was right. We said goodbye to the guards and made a sharp exit.

Richard and I talked about what happened in the car on the way home. To be honest, both of us were stunned – as if anything could stun me any more. Amy's boundaries were always loose but now she'd lost all sense of respect. It was as if the life she was living wasn't real. It was a fantasy world where she just did what she wanted whenever she wanted to whoever she wanted, blind to who was around her. Unsurprisingly, Amy didn't bring it up the next time I saw her. But by then we'd stepped into another traumatic situation.

As I suspected, Amy and Blake were still in touch. In the months before her divorce was finalized she did say to me, 'I know I've got to divorce him, Mum, but I don't want to.' So even when the papers were signed I knew it wasn't the last she'd see of Blake. Riva had already told me that they were Skyping each other regularly.

One Monday afternoon, Andrew let us into the house and from the hallway I could hear Amy's raised voice in the living room. She was stamping around in her jogging bottoms and T-shirt. It was clear she was talking to someone on the phone, but I doubt it was a conversation we were meant to hear. For some unknown reason she'd left her mobile on speaker setting and I recognized the softly spoken voice on the other end of the line immediately. It was Blake.

'I can't talk to you when you're like this, Amy,' he was saying, which surprised me. 'You're drunk, I can't talk to you when you're drunk,' he kept repeating.

Amy was darting from one end of the room to the other. Bottles of Heineken beer were littered everywhere and she was swilling the lager in her mouth and then spitting it on to the floor and the wall. It was disgusting. This was my daughter, a girl who said, 'Sorry, Mummy,' if she even swore in front of me.

'We've got to meet, we've got to meet,' she said over and over to Blake.

'I can't meet you when you're like this.' Blake seemed very calm. 'You hit me and punch me when you're drunk, Amy. I can't see you until you get yourself clean.'

As far as I knew, Blake had been in and out of rehab in Sheffield, but I wasn't clear on whether he was still using drugs or not. It was the first time I'd ever heard him sound like an adult. Perhaps there was more to him than I'd given him credit for, but I was weary of thinking like that because I also knew how manipulative he could be. I was encouraged, though. If Blake was demanding that Amy sober up then he might be the one person she'd take notice of. The problem was, Blake could never stay clean long enough himself.

Richard and I sat at the far end of the room watching her. Once she'd hung up we said hello. She didn't refer to the conversation at all. She was far too plastered to have cared that we were there. She turned and walked upstairs. We hung around for a while, wondering whether she might reappear, but then Andrew came down to tell us she had gone to bed.

That September, Amy's drinking days seemed never-ending. Around the 14th, her birthday, I got word that she was 'out of it' most days, and Mitchell rang to say she'd checked herself into the London Clinic by herself to dry out. The fact that she was regularly checking herself in was positive, but as I said, it was not a detox facility, and there was no psychological dimension to her treatment there, which is why she favoured it – there was no one trying to unpick her mind and force her to face reality. Instead she said she felt comfortable there and she was very well looked after.

I visited her there a few times but her behaviour was so disconnected I often left feeling wretched. 'I'm watching *EastEnders*,' she announced during one visit, and that was it. She turned her head to the TV screen and didn't flinch. A couple of her friends turned up – I think Tyler and Violetta – and she welcomed them with, 'Go and have a meal downstairs and put it on my account.' The invitation wasn't extended to Richard and me. The atmosphere became so uncomfortable that in the end I signalled quietly to Richard that we should go.

If only she could have talked about how she was feeling. But she wouldn't, not to me or Mitchell or any of the medical staff. I wonder how much she even revealed to her friends. Her world seemed so closed and desolate at times. I had reports back from other family members that she feigned sleep when they visited. She was locked in this other world.

Amy was growing increasingly dissatisfied with her own body too. She'd told me she wanted breast implants. I'm not a huge fan of plastic surgery but I also wondered where the impulse was coming from. Since she'd lost all her weight she'd taken to wearing two padded bras, one on top of the other, to make her chest look bigger. She always looked at me since I'm quite well endowed in that department, and she'd say, 'Mum, can I have your chest? I want it!' I suspect she wanted to feel womanly again after she'd put her body through such abuse. She was always tinkering around the edges, and who knows, she may have thought a new body would squash whatever was going on inside, just like when she'd transformed herself with the beehive. Then again, I don't know if she thought too deeply about it. It was as if she was out shopping and had seen a pair of breasts she wanted.

On 8 October she made the split decision to have the procedure done while she was in the London Clinic. 'I got these done, Mum,' she said when I saw her in Hadley Wood shortly afterwards, sticking her chest out. I was at a loss for words. I can't say I was that impressed. Even with the implants, which were actually the right size for her body, she wore those gel-filled push-up bras so that her breasts were practically up near her chin. She *loved* her larger bust and couldn't stop showing it off. She even offered a very embarrassed Richard a squeeze. Thankfully, he declined.

I don't know whether these things are just something young girls say flippantly, but weeks later she also talked about getting her nose fixed too. It was overly small and she didn't like looking at it, she said. She didn't ever have that procedure done, thank God. I hated it when she said things like that because she was turning the perfectionist attitude with which she approached everything else in on herself. I willed her to accept who she was. Amy had the most beautiful nose. However, I did try to understand it from her point of view. It was impossible to imagine myself in her position, and it's only since her passing that I've come to realize that, in this country at least, she was possibly one of the most photographed women of her generation. Nobody but Amy had an inkling of the immense pressure that placed her under.

Amy's new figure changed nothing about her behaviour. On 25 October she hosted a party in Hadley Wood for Alex's birthday. None of the older generation were allowed to attend but the reports soon filtered back. It's now jokingly known as 'the disaster party'. Amy got exceptionally drunk and refused to let anyone near her jukebox, which Richard had filled for the occasion. As the evening wore on she tried to head-butt a friend of Riva's and then attempted to punch another, before successfully managing to head-butt one of Alex's friends. The climax was everyone being forced to leave and Alex and Amy having an almighty row.

The next evening she turned up late to the Q Awards in London's Grosvenor House Hotel and disgraced herself once again. Organizers had booked a suite for her so she would at least turn up on time – but that was wishful thinking. She was due to present the Most Inspirational Artist award with the reggae singer Don Letts, but she missed her cue and the ceremony carried on without her. Just as the winners, the Specials (a band Amy loved), arrived on stage, she charged through the crowd and interrupted their acceptance speech. As they turned to walk off, she grabbed a microphone and shouted to a hushed crowd, 'I know you've been to these awards a million times but give it up for the Specials!' Later on she heckled veteran Led Zeppelin lead singer Robert Plant during his acceptance speech. He paused, ignored her, and carried on, but by all accounts the guests were fed up with Amy and her interruptions.

The only consolation for me was that Amy was no longer being photographed lying in gutters or walking the streets half naked. She continued, too, to display moments of clarity. 'Mummy, I don't want to be drunk. I hate being an alcoholic. I don't want this any more,' she kept telling me. My reply was always the same, encouraging but realistic. 'I hate seeing you like this too, Amy, but only you can change your life. I'll always be here to support you in the decision you make.' Deep down, I wanted to say, 'I'll make everything all right for you,' but I knew that simply wasn't possible. Amy's addictions had taken on a life of their own.

In the lead-up to Christmas that year, Amy would have intense periods of drunkenness followed by intense periods of abstinence or frantic activity. Occasionally I'd find her in her back room furiously pedalling on her exercise bike; Michael, a PE teacher, went over a few times to Hadley Wood to work out with her. More often than not the session lasted for no more than five minutes before she gave up and wanted to do something else.

Mitchell told me that Amy was now disappearing for weekends to Sheffield to see Blake, and there were times when he came to London too. Amy always tried to cover it up but Andrew was driving her north and knew exactly what was going on. Although I was clear she had quit hard drugs, she was in a never-ending cycle of reliance on either Blake or one substance or another. When she got bored with one she moved on to the next, and so it went on.

One afternoon she announced she wanted to get back with Blake full-time. We were standing in the kitchen in Hadley Wood and she just came out with it. 'I want to remarry him, Mum,' she said.

Richard and I fell silent.

'You need to get yourself clean before you make that kind of decision,' I said.

But what Amy said changed week in, week out. It was exhausting keeping track of what was truthful and what wasn't.

That Christmas, Richard and I spent the day at home and Alex and Riva came to us for dinner. Amy had been invited but had refused to come over, saying she wanted to stay in Hadley Wood. I only learned about the aftermath of this later, because it was on Alex and Riva's way home that Amy phoned Riva. She was crying hysterically, and they changed direction straight away. She'd taken the cold remedy Night Nurse on top of a large amount of alcohol, and when they arrived at the house she was sitting on the top floor in the studio crumpled in a heap with the TV blaring. 'I hate Christmas,' she was sobbing. 'I hate Christmas since Nan died.'

Alex cuddled her until she drifted off to sleep.

She would never have let me in on thoughts like that; even others only ever got snippets of what was going on inside Amy's head. But Cynthia clearly played on her mind: she was the glue that had held both our families together. It was that nostalgia for the past that fuelled Amy's ability to write great stories and lyrics, and even fed into the characters she affected, but sadly it also fuelled much of her dissatisfaction. There was a constant yearning for stability in her life.

After several spells in and out of the London Clinic, doctors prescribed Librium for Amy, a drug used to calm anxiety and to help with alcohol withdrawal. At first she seemed to respond well to the treatment, telling me she hadn't had a drink at all over New Year. But it was her antics in the run-up to the new year that were haunting her in early 2010.

Amy had gone to the pantomime *Cinderella* in Milton Keynes Theatre on 19 December. After interrupting the entire performance by shouting throughout, she'd then pulled the front-of-house manager's hair and called him something I can't repeat. It was the day before Christmas Eve when she was arrested, and in January she was in court again, pleading guilty to common assault and disorder. She was given a two-year conditional discharge and ordered to pay

£85 in costs and £100 in compensation to Richard Pound, the manager. The fact that she was now beginning to address her drinking problems was the only mitigating factor.

Having only been in court three days before, I wasn't expecting Amy to remember my birthday on 23 January. Over the past few years it had been hit-and-miss as to whether she did remember. So I was thrilled that she'd picked out a book on Japanese art for me called *Japonisme*, which came with an inscription. In it, she referred to the book *Mommie Dearest*, the terrifying autobiographical account of growing up with the actress Joan Crawford by her adopted daughter Christina: 'To Mama, happy 55th and thanks for being such a wonderful mummy and never beating me with coat-hangers like Joan Crawford. I love you so much mama, always your little one, Amy x'. Although they were by now very hard to find, there were always glimpses of the old, warm, funny Amy to be had.

With the lease on the Hadley Wood house due to expire at the beginning of February, Amy needed another place to stay. She'd repeatedly complained about being so far out and said she wanted to return to Camden. I had assumed she would move back to Jeffrey's Place. I had not been made aware that Mitchell was already looking for an alternative house.

One afternoon in early February, Richard and I were driving back from town when my mobile rang. It was Amy. She sounded as if she was surrounded by busy traffic.

'Where are you?' I said.

'I'm in the hotel, Mum,' she told me.

'Which hotel? Since when?'

It turned out to be the Langham, bang in the middle of Oxford Circus.

'Dad arranged it,' she said. 'Come for dinner, Mummy, come now. Come tonight.'

I desperately wanted to see her. I had no idea she'd moved out from Hadley Wood or what the hell she was doing in the Langham. It was probably wrong of me to drop everything to be with her, but that's what ended up happening. If the contact was on her terms, perhaps the time we spent together would be quality, and I wanted to see for myself how she looked and sounded.

Richard and I arrived around 7.30 p.m. in the restaurant on the ground floor. She hadn't mentioned that Tyler was going to be there with his mum and stepfather, but that was fine. We sat together and waited for Amy, who seemed reasonably sober when she arrived, although it was clear she'd had a drink or two. We had a nice meal, but throughout it Amy was doing the same to Tyler's mother as she had done to Marjorie in St Lucia: she was draped around her neck calling her 'mummy'. 'I love you, Mummy,' she said to her at one point. 'You look after me like a mummy.' I found it very hard to take, but I sat there in silence.

Was it a test? Was she saying 'I can do what I want to hurt you, but if you really love me you'll still be there for me'? Was she even aware of what she was doing? It was so confusing because I'd always been there for Amy. Always. I'm sure Tyler's mum couldn't have felt too comfortable either, and Richard kept looking over at me. He knew how upset it made me. It was as if Amy was desperately searching for a person – a woman – to challenge her, as if she was begging for someone to grab her by the throat and tell her off the way Cynthia used to. But members of the family, including Mitchell's sister Melody, *had* spoken to her very directly about her drinking and she'd ignored all their pleas.

That was the first and the last time I saw Amy at the Langham. She spent much of February in Jamaica working with Salaam Remi, and at the beginning of March, Mitchell moved her into a penthouse flat in Bryanston Square near Marble Arch. Again, that was something I had to find out. Amy didn't tell me, nor did she tell me that Mitchell had bought and was doing up a house for her in Camden Square. It's hard for me to say this, but I felt completely out of the loop – another light switched to dark.

Amy lived in Bryanston Square for ten months in 2010 but I didn't visit her there once. We did speak on the phone, sometimes for a couple of hours. I'd fill her in on what Richard and I had been up to, or how the cats were getting on and how the family was, and she'd tell me where she'd been recently, or she'd ask about my health. But she didn't ever invite me down. In fact that year I saw my daughter most during her spells at the London Clinic. For whatever reason, the gulf was widening between us. I felt so sad about the way our lives were pulling apart. I know my condition played a part in it, but it was also Amy and everything that surrounded her. She seemed lost in it.

At the end of March, Amy started recording a track for Quincy Jones's seventy-fifth birthday celebration album *Q: Soul Bossa Nostra*. The pair had first met at the Nelson Mandela ninetieth birthday gig and he'd asked her to contribute to the album. Apparently during that first meeting she'd got down on her knees and kissed his hand, saying, 'I've known your music ever since you were my age, twenty-four years old, when you did *The Swingin' Miss "D"* with Dinah Washington,' and proceeded to reel off all the songs he recorded with her. Believe me, Amy knew her stuff. She had an almost encyclopaedic knowledge of the music she was interested in.

Quincy Jones had initially asked her to do 'You Don't Own Me', which was first performed by American artist Lesley Gore in 1963, but she insisted on doing 'It's My Party', which she recorded with Jones and Mark Ronson. It always amazed me that Amy wasn't the least bit intimidated in the presence of music legends. It didn't faze her one bit, and I don't think that was just Amy's professionalism. It was her humanity, too. She simply saw people as people with the same failings as herself, and she always wanted to work hard for those she admired.

It was just after she'd recorded that track that she rang me at home. She sounded excited about working with Quincy Jones and about the future. 'I've finished everything with Blake, Mum, and I've met this amazing guy.' I was all ears because when she'd first met Blake she'd kept it hidden. There was something surprisingly open about this confession, something reminiscent of the way she used to tell me about her life when she was a teenager, perhaps even something she was trying to regain.

She described coming out of her flat in Bryanston Square, turning the corner with Andrew by her side and catching the eye of Reg Traviss. He was sitting having a cigarette on a pub bench outside Inn 1888, on Devonshire Street near Marylebone. It was a pub his parents owned and one Amy had been in often. I don't know who asked who out but it wouldn't surprise me if Amy did the asking. She had no fear as far as romance was concerned. Richard's son Michael still laughs about her now because at school she'd insist on asking girls out for him. 'If you want to ask someone out, just ask them! What's the problem?' she'd say.

She and Reg had been on a first date and it had gone well. She said he was tall, handsome, softly spoken and gentlemanly. I didn't meet Reg until just before Amy's passing, but I understood why she had been attracted to him. He looks like a 1950s movie type with slicked-back hair and sharp suits. 'He's amazing, Mum, I really love him.' She was giggling. Amy saying she loved anyone rang alarm bells with me but I was quietly optimistic. Reg was a film director and he did seem to have a calming effect on Amy. In any case, I thought even the slightest move away from Blake would be good for her. I'd got the impression anyway that that relationship had run its course and she'd moved on.

By mid-May Amy was back in the London Clinic, where she stayed for a week. She returned in June. Every time she stopped drinking it was followed at some point by another bout of drunkenness. Naomi recalls her occasionally saying that she couldn't fathom her deep depressions because, to an outsider, her life was one most people would give their right arm for. 'I have everything I've ever wanted,' she'd told her. 'I shouldn't be feeling like this, but I am.'

My feeling is that Amy was at a loss about which direction to take. Both Naomi and Michael, and I believe Reg too, had repeatedly told her that the world was her oyster, that she could do anything she wanted with her life. But she knew that. She'd always known it. It's what I taught her. But somehow, somewhere on the journey, she lost her way.

15

Leader of the Pack

As the summer of 2010 drew to a close, Amy's drinking hadn't abated much, but because she was further away and I was seeing her less it didn't impact on me in quite the same way. 'How are you doing?' I'd ask her over the phone. 'I am trying, Mum, but it's really hard,' she would say to me. I'd try to be upbeat and encouraging but I didn't see that checking herself into the London Clinic, for what amounted to little more than a hotel stay, was ever going to get to the root of anything. Again, it had to be down to Amy. On reflection, perhaps we were more inclined to dismiss her drunken episodes because we were all so relieved she was free from hard drugs.

During that year, Alex and Riva had got engaged and had planned a party for the end of August. It was, for once, an event that brought our family together in a really positive way. I was so happy for Alex because, like Amy, he had lacked stability growing up; like all of us, he had also felt the ripple effect of Amy's addictions. That he wanted to put down foundations of his own could only be a good sign. Besides, Riva and he seemed so happy together.

I enjoyed the party but, sadly, it started with another drama. Amy turned up a little tipsy and the anxiety of the occasion got too much for Mitchell who tore into her soon after she walked through the door. Mitchell has a hot temper at the best of times, but this was the worst argument I'd seen them have and it ended with Riva comforting Amy, who was in floods of tears. The rest of the evening carried on without fuss. While I could understand Mitchell's frustration with Amy, in my view he sometimes went too far. He'd wanted her not to spoil the evening for everyone, but that's exactly what both of them threatened to do. Alex and Riva jokingly call it *The Mitchell and Amy Show*. On that occasion, I can't say I disagreed. But we all loved seeing them sing on stage together.

The rollercoaster of being drunk and being sober was a continuing pattern for Amy over the coming months. Riva now tells me that instead of drinking the Bloody Marys (with lashings more vodka than tomato juice) she'd been partial to in Hadley Wood, Amy had moved on to wine because someone had told her it was kinder to her system – that was Amy, still trying to kid herself. The problem was that she was now binge-drinking wine in phenomenal amounts. Amy was never a steady drinker. She would down a lot, then sleep, then down some more. If she was vacant on drugs, she was equally as vacant under the influence of alcohol, purely because she drank so much so quickly.

A worrying aspect for me was that Amy's doctor, Cristina Romete, had already expressed concerns about her thyroid, which was showing signs of abnormality. Amy had had several monitoring blood tests. Again, it's something I had to hear about second hand, but I knew the worsening of the problem was directly related to how much alcohol she'd been drinking. Alcohol suppresses the ability of the thyroid gland to produce hormones and can have disastrous knock-on effects, such as high blood pressure and long-term heart problems, tiredness and depression, and abnormal periods and potential infertility. I had enough medical knowledge to be able to understand Amy's physical symptoms, but that never allowed me to get inside her head, where the real problems lay.

Amy spent Christmas at Bryanston Square and in the new year prepared for her first tour since 2008, in Brazil. By all accounts it went better than everyone had expected, though, while I don't know exactly what went on, I'm sure there were some shaky moments. As soon as she returned from Brazil she moved straight into her home in Camden Square. The original Victorian terraced house had been divided into six flats, and Mitchell had converted them back to a three-storey house. Amy told me she was happy to be back in Camden. I hoped having a permanent home would make her feel more secure. But when I walked through the front door for the first time, it felt like less of a home and more of a place for Amy to lay her head.

Amy hadn't chosen the interior decoration, and the house struck me as having little of her spirit in it. Nevertheless, she was keen to show me around. The basement housed her music studio and gym equipment. The kitchen had been done out like a fifties diner with black and white chequered flooring, and the large living room at the back overlooked a small garden. There were two bedrooms on the middle floor, and her room was a huge space with a vaulted ceiling, dressing room and marble bathroom, occupying the whole of the top floor. She was worried that I wouldn't be able to get to the top of the house. By then I was losing the use of my right leg and was forced to walk with the aid of a stick. But I managed, although the stairs were steep. I loved her room, where she had all her family photos framed on bedside tables, and a painted picture of her and Alex on the wall, but the rest of the house felt lonely, like a hotel.

There were a few tell-tale signs of Amy dotted around. The restored 1950s American AMI Jukebox, which she had originally bought for Prowse Place, sat in the living room alongside the Spanish acoustic guitar she had used to write *Back To Black*. And there was one item that always made Richard laugh. Discarded on the radiator in the hall sat a commemorative gift from Island Records. In celebration of their fiftieth anniversary in 2009 she had been given a framed series of singles covers of all of Island's notable artists, from Bob Marley through to Amy. But she refused to hang it on any wall. One of the singles featured was by U2 and, for reasons unknown, she despised the band so much that it languished permanently on the radiator, tossed there in contempt.

It's hard to say, but in the long-term Camden Square could have been the place where Amy changed her life. For the moment, though, it was business as usual. Whenever Richard and I visited, it was a similar story to Hadley Wood: she'd be buzzing around one minute and nowhere to be seen the next. I couldn't put my finger on it, but for me, even the small spark she'd had in Hadley Wood was just not in evidence. She complained that her Camden friends had drifted away from her, and I know now that she told both Naomi and Riva that she thought the only people who loved her were those who were paid to love her – but that was so far from the truth that it hurts. Not everyone who came to see Amy at Camden Square was on her payroll. Then again, I could never keep up with the comings and goings of that house. Tyler was living there, as was Naomi for a period of time, sometimes Violetta, and a string of others. Everything was as transient as the rest of Amy's life. Perhaps I was too long in the tooth to understand, but to me it felt like a very expensive doss house.

Naomi, who was at least one of Amy's sensible friends, had moved in at the beginning of March, and Amy told me they had started working on dress designs for her upcoming European tour. According to Naomi, Amy was full of ideas. As it was a summer tour she wanted a calypso theme, and she thought it would be hilarious if her band were dressed in black frilly shirts and coral pink suits, which in the event were custom-made by the men's tailors Gresham Blake.

For Amy's dresses, Naomi sketched out patterns with her on the living-room floor. There were a total of twelve, printed with Miami kitsch designs. There were palm trees and pineapples, flamingos and butterflies, and there was one dress I've seen since that made me smile. The print is a series of ocean waves identical to those in *The Great Wave*, the painting by Katsushika Hokusai that Amy replicated on her wall in Guildown Avenue all those years ago.

Amy and her life might have changed but some things about our years together had stayed with her.

In the end, the dresses took around two months to produce and Naomi resorted to being very sneaky. Amy refused point blank to wear a thong underneath and instead insisted on French knickers bought from her favourite lingerie shop Agent Provocateur. As the panty line would be visible, Naomi secretly had Lycra petticoats stitched in beneath the silk so the material appeared smooth around her body. How Naomi was going to get her in and out of those outfits I had no idea. As it turned out, she didn't have to. Amy only ever wore one of them because the tour was cancelled following her first, disastrous appearance.

That spring of 2011 Amy may have been looking ahead to the tour but it was becoming more and more obvious that she was burying her head in the sand over her health. Riva, who visited Amy often during that time, describes Amy as being either sober or completely comatose – there was rarely a halfway house. Whereas before she was drinking and dressing it up as fun, now she was blotting out her life completely. She would never have said it, but the pressure on her to tour Europe that year was greater than ever. Perhaps, too, she wanted to prove to herself that she could do it. But as the weeks rolled on, she just got worse.

I can't imagine what it must have been like to live with Amy twenty-four hours a day, but I've heard enough stories from others to know that it wasn't pleasant. Soon after she moved in at Camden Square, Alex and Riva visited Amy only to find her in a chair passed out so that her head was lolling back into the kitchen sink. They rushed towards her thinking she'd died and carried her to the living-room sofa, but she was catatonic and they ended up staying with her until she'd slept it off.

There was another occasion when Amy hadn't washed for more than a week. When Riva managed to get her upstairs and into the bath her hair was matted on her head and her body and fingernails encrusted with dirt – like an urchin from a Charles Dickens novel. Any psychiatrist who saw her could not have failed to identify her as high risk, but Amy could still not be sectioned under the Mental Health Act: she would have to voluntarily put herself forward for treatment.

I continued to visit her when I could, but my mobility was becoming increasingly impaired and a trip to see my daughter was often easier said than done. Amy always tried to maintain some semblance of dignity in front of me. Even so, I never met the same Amy more than once. On some days she behaved like a small child, sucking her thumb, talking in a baby voice and sitting on my knee; at other times she'd adopt the aggressive, butch act, the Rizzo character – the girl who had 'out-Jaggered Jagger'. The more vulnerable she felt, the more pronounced that persona would become. I think she brought her characters out as coping mechanisms, to get her through anxious moments or stressful situations.

In all honesty there was rarely a time at Camden Square when Amy was a whole person. Rather, she continued to be this fragmented girl, a series of creations I suppose I'd become accustomed to. Riva recalls only one day she spent with Amy in 2011 when she seemed stable. She hadn't been drinking for a few days, and she came downstairs with her hair scraped back off her face and her skin glowing. She sat with Riva and Naomi and they talked. Amy wasn't trying to be funny or aggressive; she wasn't throwing things around or being any of the people who inhabited her mind. It was a glimpse of the real Amy – my Amy. I occasionally saw her like that in the London Clinic too, when she was dry, but those memories are few and far between.

It was well into April before I was made aware of this development, but on 30 March Amy's doctor, Cristina Romete, had written to her. The letter had apparently sat in the kitchen at Camden Square and it wasn't until Richard and I visited that one of Amy's security team waved it in front of us and begged us to read it. It was utterly devastating. Dr Romete had set out Amy's medical problems very starkly. She was concerned that her thyroid was now severely underactive, which meant her body was now not producing enough hormones. Not only would that contribute to Amy's depression, it could affect her fertility and her heart function in the long run. She could not be sure if Amy would now need lifelong medication.

Added to that, however much Amy was kidding herself and others that she had curbed her drinking, she had not. Tests conducted during February showed that she was consuming around thirty times more than the safe limit each week. The letter warned her that while she might stubbornly go down the path of alcoholism to make herself feel as though she was in control, the only person she was harming was herself. Amy's bulimia wasn't mentioned, but I understand now that she was constantly making herself sick. Her diet consisted of softer foods like scrambled eggs that she could bring up more easily. The constant pressure that purging must have put on her internal organs would have been immense.

Dr Romete did acknowledge that Amy had made substantial improvements over the past two years and that she couldn't force her to undergo treatment – a scenario I knew only too well. However, she had the impression that Amy believed she was 'getting away with it'. Unbelievably, Amy hadn't yet sustained liver damage; in fact I was astounded when Amy's post-mortem results confirmed that her vital organs remained intact. In the spring of 2011, though, the facts could not have been clearer: if she carried on like this, she could die.

I took a deep breath and handed the letter back. I was very shaken and so tired I ached. Over the last five years I'd seen or heard about Amy in the most extreme physical states, and at desperate times I'd convinced myself she was going to die. I'd learned to suppress every reactive feeling of panic. I wouldn't have been able to function otherwise. I suppose that's my pragmatism, the only way I've got through this. I certainly feared at that moment that if I thought too hard I would unravel completely.

I did not raise the subject of the letter with Amy that day. I'd been told that she'd read it, and, as far as I could see, she had thrown it aside. She was furious when its contents were eventually discussed. I understand there were a few more letters from Cristina, and they prompted a meeting at Camden Square which I was not present at. By then Riva had suggested contacting the Priory to see whether Amy might be admitted, but it would be a while yet before Amy would agree.

Amy had built such a thick wall around herself, and I'm sure she'd convinced herself that if she asked for help she was a failure. I was exactly like that at her age too. Still, I prayed she would take that brave step before the damage became irreversible. Whether or not Amy was 'out of control' in terms of her behaviour is another matter. By the time Amy got to Camden Square her life had ceased to be her own. The more I think about it, the more I am convinced that everything she did had to do with attempts to maintain control – but she was controlling all the wrong things. She was diligent in taking care of everything that was habitual to her, but ate and made herself sick and drank to excess, then stopped drinking, then repeated the cycle. Amy was fiercely intelligent and I desperately wanted to shake her into admitting that she had serious problems. But I always held off doing that as I knew it would have fallen on deaf ears.

April turned out to be a mixed month. On the 6th she went back into the London Clinic, but four days later she discharged herself, and was soon drinking heavily again. On one occasion, one of the bodyguards told Mitchell, she had woken up at four a.m., drunk a bottle of wine, gone back to sleep and woken again at eight a.m. to drink another. The next day Mitchell found her so drunk that she was collapsed on the kitchen floor. I've learned since Amy's passing that that was not an uncommon sight. It's likely that Amy was suffering alcohol-induced seizures far more frequently than anyone ever realized.

In a way it would have been safer for Amy to drink continuously: abstaining for days then downing whole bottles of wine was so harmful. I saw it as Amy's way of trying to take charge of her health without having to face doctor's orders, but this new cycle terrified me. She was walking on the same knife edge she had always done. The cold turkey approach she had used to quit drugs had been less threatening to her body; alcohol was such a deep-rooted habit for her that sudden withdrawal put her body under extreme stress. Having spent a lifetime dispensing drugs to recovering alcoholics, I was acutely aware that seizures could become a greater problem for her, but I simply never realized just how little time Amy had left to turn things around.

'You need to stop drinking bit by bit, Amy,' I said to her over the phone when she announced she had been dry for a few days. 'What you're doing is dangerous. It needs to be supervised.' Her reply was always the same: 'I'll be fine, Mum. Don't worry about me. How are you, anyway?'

Amy drank openly in front of certain people while she was living in Camden Square. I was not one of them, and Richard's son Michael wasn't either. He visited Amy soon after she moved in there and he told me she was clearly embarrassed because she'd stashed the wine in another room and kept sloping off to have a drink.

'Why are you doing this?' he remembers asking her.

'Don't bug me about this,' she'd replied. 'I'll sort it when I want. I said I'd deal with the drugs. I did, and I'll do it with drink. Look at my life. I can't live a normal life. I can't walk to the shops. I can't do stuff. I hate it.'

Amy lifted her T-shirt to show him the skin around her liver. It was yellow, jaundiced, and Michael has since admitted to finding hugging her uncomfortable because he could almost feel her body disintegrating in his embrace. I know how painful that felt too. I try now not to think too much about it.

Despite her sickness, Amy did display moments of promise. She had mentioned taking up yoga again and she did have three lessons with a teacher who visited her. I felt incredibly buoyed by that. Amy used to come to yoga classes with me in the Methodist hall in

Barnet when she was sixteen and I'd always talked to her about its benefits. 'You should start a yoga class, Mum,' she'd say, but I was never that good. Any positive step she took to replace her destructive habits encouraged me, and there were moments too when she seemed genuinely on top of things – like on 23 March, when she recorded the duet 'Body And Soul' with Tony Bennett in Abbey Road's studio three. 'I'm singing with Tony Bennett!' she shouted down the phone to me, and she said afterwards that although she was nervous she loved every minute of it. 'I'm going to go home and put all of my Tony Bennett records on,' she said, laughing.

Richard and I visited her again in late April. For as long as I cared to remember I'd learned to pick up clues about what state I might find Amy in: whether there were empty bottles in the garden or in the house; whether her blinds were closed in her room upstairs; the expression on the face of whoever was on duty as the door opened. This time, Amy was upstairs getting ready, and she was completely sober when she came down. Reg was taking her out, and he was due to pick her up at two p.m. She appeared – on time, remarkably – in full beehive and make-up, and I can honestly say that I hadn't seen her that upbeat for a while. She looked healthy and clean, and she sat with us in the kitchen, though she was clearly on edge. Every time a car pulled up outside she leaped out of her chair and peered out of the window.

'Is that Reg now?' I asked.

'Nah, not yet,' she replied, slumping back down.

I watched her intently. It reminded me of when Amy was little, when she used to rush to the window to see if Mitchell's car was pulling up. She was always disappointed when she realized it wasn't him. By the time we left, two hours later, she was still on tenter-hooks. Reg hadn't shown up. I don't know if he ever did.

Amy did say Reg had a positive effect on her. I understand their relationship had its ups and downs, but not, thank God, like the high drama of Amy and Blake. Whenever Amy talked about what they'd been doing she'd say they'd been to the West End or to the cinema or they'd been relaxing at home. She would never have phoned me and told me where she'd been with Blake – which I can only assume was because it always involved drugs.

Whether or not Amy and Reg would have stayed together, I do not know. From what I know of Reg he is a nice guy, but Amy complained he'd get wrapped up in his work and would often be away for days, filming on location. Amy had wanted Reg to move into Camden Square soon after they met but for the moment he said he preferred to keep his flat in Marylebone. I was always prepared to keep an open mind about someone until I'd met them, but I quietly wondered whether Amy had fallen for someone who again, for different reasons, was unavailable to her.

That April something else happened which has never left my mind, because it was so bizarre. For several months Richard and I had been talking about getting married. We'd now been living with each other for a while and marriage seemed the obvious next step.

I believe Richard is the best thing that has happened to me. I would have been able to cope with Amy with the support of my family, but having someone there I could share the day-to-day stresses with certainly eased the burden. There were times when just being able to hold on to a sense of normality really mattered – going home and putting dinner on, talking about everyday things. Perhaps for someone who didn't know me or my family beforehand it would have been too daunting, but, thankfully, we'd been friends for so long that we were able to discuss and decide everything together from the outset.

Just like we had done when we started going out, we wanted to tell Amy properly that we'd got engaged. In fact, I think she was the first person we told. We'd arranged to go over one Sunday, and I remember it so clearly. We were sitting at the kitchen table and she was buzzing around us.

'Richard and I are planning on getting married,' I announced very matter-of-factly.

She stopped and spun round. 'When?' she asked.

We hadn't yet set an exact date, but were hopeful it would be later that year.

'You know I'm not going to be there, don't you?' she replied without hesitation.

We both stared at her, but by the time Richard had the chance to ask why, she was already making her way out of the door and upstairs.

Like many moments of my life with Amy, I have replayed that incident over and over in my mind. What did she mean by it? Undoubtedly she and Alex thought Richard and I getting together was as unlikely as a meteorite hitting Earth, but I couldn't imagine a reason why she wouldn't have wanted to be there. I accepted it, because with Amy I knew I had no choice, but I felt both bewildered and disappointed. I wanted Amy to be there – I'd never stopped wanting her to be part of my life – and neither myself nor Richard could work out what had prompted the comment. She had no touring schedule booked for later that year. Was she being overly dramatic, referring to the fact that she couldn't go anywhere without her entourage? Somewhere, deep down, did she acknowledge how little time she had left? It was, and remains, a complete mystery to me.

It wasn't until May that Amy was finally persuaded to enter the Priory for psychiatric treatment. Riva had already initiated a crisis meeting there with a consultant psychiatrist and me, Richard, Mitchell, Jane, Melody and Alex to discuss how we might persuade Amy to go. She would be able to enter the drug and alcohol programme, but only if she put herself forward. She was still not deemed a danger to herself or others.

As it happened, Dr Brenner came to Camden Square, and it was Amy's friends, including Tyler, Naomi and Riva, who persuaded her to change her mind. I was not present, but I did hear later that Amy had tried to punch Dr Brenner and had told him to shut up, which doesn't surprise me, but I guess he'd seen it all before. In the end it was Reg who told her that he thought she should put her fears aside and go, and she reluctantly agreed. Sadly, I think neither Mitchell nor I nor any doctor could have propelled her towards that decision, only her own peer group.

Having said that, on 24 May when she was eventually driven to the Priory, she was hell-bent on turning round. She insisted on stopping off en route to buy a bottle of vodka from an off-licence in Bounds Green and she drank it down in the car. When she got there it took her a good two hours to calm down. Sitting on the bed in her room, she told Riva, 'I love you, but I fucking hate you right now.' Amy stayed in the Priory until the 31st, when she checked herself out. As far as I know, her stint there changed very little. Amy simply rejected professional help. She wanted to be in control of her own treatment and she continued to delude herself that she could do it alone. We didn't know it then, but that was her last chance to help herself.

The next time I saw Amy was on 12 June, at a warm-up gig for her European tour at the 100 Club in the centre of town. Friends and family were invited, and although I wasn't convinced that Amy wanted to tour she seemed on better form than I'd expected her to be. She did her usual calling out to aunts and uncles and friends in the crowd, she even managed to poke fun at Mitchell's wife Jane by calling her 'the Wicked Witch of the West', but she didn't once call out 'Mum' to me. I look back on that evening with mixed feelings. Others have assured me that Amy barely knew what she had said to anyone during that year, but I also wonder whether it was because she never had to chase my affection. I had always been there for her.

As I remember it, the gig went well. Dionne Bromfield came over to say hello, the young singer whom Amy had taken under her wing – not her 'goddaughter' as was widely reported. Amy had first met Dionne when she was thirteen. She was the first person Amy signed to her Lioness record label, which was set up in 2009, and Amy nurtured her talent. Dionne was always quick to point out to me how much Amy talked about me and her family to her. Amy appeared reasonably sober on stage and she had fun with her band. At one point her throat was hurting and she asked someone to pop out and get her some honey. I wouldn't have said Amy was back to her best, but it was nice to see her enjoying herself.

We left soon after the gig finished and I didn't speak to Amy again before she flew to Serbia on 18 June to start her European tour. Richard and I hadn't booked flights yet but we had made a tentative plan to go out and support Amy; we'd discussed flying out to Italy and Spain in July and we wanted to combine seeing her with a short holiday. We'd not told Amy yet that it was a possibility but, as things turned out, we didn't get the opportunity to go.

According to Mitchell, nerves got the better of Amy in the run-up to her tour and she'd wanted to cancel, but then changed her mind at the last minute and boarded the plane with Raye Cosbert. Her first night in Belgrade was shambolic. Amy was drunk before she'd even got on stage. She forgot the words to her songs. She fell over and shuffled around, turned her back on the crowd, but insisted on doing a full set. I've seen some footage of that concert since Amy's passing but I find it too difficult to watch. It confirms to me what I already knew: that something was very wrong with her. It's also a devastating reminder of how powerless to help my daughter I continued to be.

Amy's next stop was Turkey, but Raye made the decision to cancel the remaining eleven dates. Reg had already arranged to fly out and meet Amy in Istanbul, and they stayed there for a few days before flying home. I spoke to her a couple of times on the phone, but she mentioned nothing of the aborted tour.

While she was away we had a drama of a different sort at home. Richard's mum, Doreen, who lived nearby, was found in her garage having collapsed there three days earlier. When Richard had made his regular trip to see her he couldn't raise her at all. He ended up having to smash the chain off the door before calling an ambulance. She was alive, but it was obvious that her health was deteriorating rapidly. She stayed for a couple of weeks in hospital. By July she'd been discharged but we were constantly popping in and out to make sure she was OK.

With all this going on I didn't get a chance to catch up properly with Amy after her return. Richard and I decided to go over to Camden on 22 July. We phoned ahead to speak to Andrew, who had told us to come over but warned us that Amy had been drinking. Apparently she had had a few weeks of sobriety after flying back but something had caused her to fall off the wagon earlier that week. I suspect it was more likely that Amy had days on and days off drinking, but without being on hand every day it was impossible to know.

That afternoon, Richard and I pulled up at around two. As we made our way up the stairs I noticed some broken bottles of white wine on the front patio. I breathed deeply. The expression on Andrew's face as he opened the door said it all – pained and worried. Amy was upstairs, he told us. She was sleeping but she wasn't in a good state. I wanted to stay. I hadn't seen her for several weeks and I was keen to hang around until she woke.

As we made our way into the kitchen I saw that my old brown suitcase was upright by the fridge. Strewn across the table was a mountain of old pictures. I got a cup of tea on the go while Richard started to look through them. There was Amy with a pair of comic sunglasses on that looked far too big for her two-year-old head; Alex and Amy dancing together in the back garden at Osidge Lane; Katie, our cat, sitting by the front door in Greenside Close; Cynthia and Larry; me on my wedding day; Debra and Brian and all of Amy's American cousins. I held each one in my fingers. They were all the family photos I'd passed to her. Some of them I even remembered taking.

This was the life I knew the best. Those stories were as familiar to me as breathing. I looked around the room. It felt cold, yet I believed one day it would be filled with the warmth and laughter of the girl I'd raised.

Richard and I stayed there, absorbed in memories, until Andrew popped his head round the door.

'Do you want me to see if I can wake her?' he asked.

'Please, yes, have a go,' I replied.

Half an hour passed and there was still no Amy. But soon we could hear footsteps coming down the stairs. As Andrew turned the corner, I saw Amy was slung over his shoulder in a fireman's lift. It was obvious he'd washed her and dressed her and tried to put her beehive on to make her look respectable. He placed her in the empty black Keeler chair beside us but her head slumped forward on to the table. She reeked of alcohol. It was coming out of every pore.

I closed my eyes for a long moment. There was an uncomfortable silence until Amy half came round.

'You're looking at the photos, Mum,' she slurred. Her head was upright now and she was trying to focus on them. She picked one up of Alex as a baby and held it close to her face. 'Wasn't Alex a beautiful baby,' she remarked before her head collapsed back on to the table and the photo slipped from her hand.

It was another ten minutes before she looked at another, and about half an hour after that I signalled to Richard that we should go. The best place for Amy was in bed. I just couldn't sit there and watch her like that.

'We're going to go now, Amy,' I said.

'OK Mummy,' I could just about make out.

As I moved around the table, Amy struggled to get out of her seat. I grabbed on to her arms and pulled her up until her hands wrapped around my neck.

'This is so wrong, Amy,' I said to her quietly. 'You know what you are doing to yourself. I hate to see you like this.'

'I sorry Mummy, I love you Mummy,' she mumbled, hanging off me.

'I love you too,' I replied.

I don't remember there being much conversation in the car on the way back to East Barnet. The photographs and Amy were churning around in my head. I'd never seen Andrew having to carry her downstairs like that before. 'Tomorrow will be a better day,' I kept saying to myself, and I was sure it would be. I was convinced of it.

That evening we ate and went to bed. I'd check in with Andrew the following day, I thought.

I woke the next morning around nine. I'd had a restless night because it was hot and the windows were wide open to let in some fresh air. I went to my regular Alexander Technique appointment at eleven, and when Richard and I returned home I went upstairs to wash and change, then pottered around a bit.

I heard the phone go just as I started to put some washing away, but either Richard or his daughter Jess must have answered.

Richard came up to see me shortly after. He looked ashen when he entered the room. I knew immediately from his eyes that something was horribly wrong. He walked over to me, took my hand and sat me down on the corner of the bed.

It's Doreen, I reckoned immediately. She's gone. Expected, but a shock none the less.

'Jan, she's gone,' he said, squeezing both my hands now, his voice breaking uncontrollably. 'Your baby's gone, Jan. Amy's gone.'

Amy.

My whole body started to shut down. I was staring at Richard, who was talking, but I couldn't make sense of anything he was saying. I sat suspended in time, the life draining from me.

'It's Amy. Your baby's gone, Jan. Amy's gone.'

She was twenty-seven. Exactly the same age I was on the night I gave birth to her.

16

Time Out for Tears

For several minutes before Richard came upstairs he'd been pacing around the living room trying to think of the best way to break the news of Amy's death. The call had come from my cousin Martin, but Richard hadn't believed the message at first: Martin is a bit of a joker, and not always a good one.

'Are you having a laugh?' Richard had said to him.

'Richard, I'm serious,' Martin had replied in a slow, clear voice. 'Alex is on his way over to you. Please believe me. Amy is dead.'

Once Richard had helped me into the living room, we sat in silence together. I felt bewildered. It felt as if on the way down I'd put one foot in front of the other without being conscious of it. I don't recall who spoke first, but once the silence had been broken the room echoed with question after question. What happened? Where is Amy now? Who found her? What happened after we left yesterday? Was Amy alone? Please God, she didn't die alone, did she? All these words flying around as the adrenalin surged through my body.

I could hear the sound of someone knocking at the door – a sound that would be repeated throughout the day – and Alex and Riva came in. Alex and I clasped each other. I could hardly bear to let go of him. 'Thank God you're still here,' I kept thinking. He was bereft, and when I saw that, another feeling of powerlessness welled up

258

inside me. I wanted so desperately to tell him that it wasn't true, that there had been some mistake, but I couldn't. All that was left for us to do was comfort each other. There were no tears. All of my energy went into holding myself up in the face of the shock. In spite of everything Amy had been through, I couldn't have been less prepared for this day.

Martin was next to arrive, followed by Richard's son Michael. Alex desperately wanted to go to Camden Square. He needed to be near Amy, which I understood. Michael, Martin, Jess and Riva stayed with me while Richard drove Alex into town. We'd been told that it wouldn't be long before the press started to gather in the square and the decision was made to go sooner rather than later. I chose to stay put where I felt safe. I only wanted people I knew around me. Besides, I'd never felt comfortable at Camden Square.

The last thing I wanted was those close to Amy hearing about her death through a news broadcast, and as it turned out, telling friends and relatives became a race against time: news of Amy's death broke less than half an hour after Richard took the call from Martin. Richard had immediately rung round as many people as possible, including members of my family, and Martin helped when he arrived, but it was impossible to reach everyone. Later that day my brother Brian had the unenviable task of driving to my dad's flat in Cheshunt, Hertfordshire, and breaking the news to him. He was completely devastated.

By mid-afternoon Richard and Alex were weaving their way through the streets to Camden, past the places where Amy played as a child, past the corner of Jeffrey's Place to the edge of the square. Richard made a point of not switching on the radio and trying to keep the conversation light in an attempt to distract them from what might lie ahead. But Alex was in another world. Every part of that journey held a memory for him that triggered a new wave of grief.

They parked. Sky News had already set up shop, and a police cordon had been erected. At first, Alex sat in the car while Richard – who, thankfully, the photographers didn't recognize – approached the officer at the barrier. 'I have Amy Winehouse's brother in the car,' he whispered. 'Can we enter the house?' But he was told to step back. Under the circumstances it was frustrating for Richard to be held there, but we are grateful to all the officers on the scene. Richard could have been anyone, a fan or a journalist, and the appropriate checks were made before he and Alex were allowed to duck under the cordon.

They were immediately met by Superintendent Raj Kohli and directed towards a waiting police car. Such was the media presence that they were instructed to keep schtum until they were inside the car. There were microphones everywhere and journalists desperate to eavesdrop on any developments. In fact a whole host of precautions had already been taken, half of which Richard hadn't even considered. Because of Amy's history no access would be allowed to number 30. It had been declared a crime scene and a forensics team would be combing the property. Although foul play was not at this stage suspected, all investigations had to be carried out, and in the end this took all of four days.

Back at home, our kitchen had been commandeered by anyone and everyone. People with far clearer heads than mine were in a better position to take charge. We spilled out into the garden with the sun beating down. How many cups of tea were consumed that day, I dread to think. 'I'm so sorry, Janis' echoed around me. I did more hugging that afternoon than I've done in a lifetime. It helped. It really helped. But, on reflection, until the point when I saw Amy's body, less than forty-eight hours later, I could not accept her death. Just like most of the last seven years, it felt like someone else's story.

By around five I'd had word that Mitchell, who was in New York, was flying back, and Richard had texted me to say that Mitchell's sister Melody and her husband Elliott had joined them at Camden Square. Apparently Melody was overcome with grief and had demanded to be let into the house. Like everyone else she had been told it was a no-go area, and like everyone else she'd been ushered towards the same police car in which Alex and Richard were waiting. Melody sat on the back seat sobbing with Elliott beside her, unable to calm her down.

Although none of us were thinking logically that day, there was one thing we were clear on: as a family, we were keen that no details of Amy's passing should leak out until a formal cause of death had been established. Until we knew the facts, everything else was speculation. Not that I watched any of the news reports, but I've come to learn that speculation was rife. Despite an initial statement at 9.30 that evening saying that Amy's death remained unexplained, stories very quickly appeared that she had died of a drug overdose.

Given the course of Amy's life, many may ask what difference that made. To me and the rest of the family, the answer is a huge difference. I knew how far Amy had come. I knew in my heart that she was clean of hard drugs, and it was important for us that that was recognized. Whatever the circumstances, I also knew that she died attempting to free herself from her addictions. I cannot continuously torture myself by thinking about what could have been, but it gives me some comfort to know in my own mind that Amy did not want to die. She wanted to live.

Back at Camden Square late that afternoon, Richard caught sight of Reg. They'd only met once before, briefly at Amy's 100 Club gig. He recalls watching Reg standing there alone and lost. One of the forensics officers emerged down Amy's front steps, carrying one of her cats wrapped in a blue sheet. Kitty had been caught trying to get in through the cat-flap, desperate to be fed. To prevent the cat from contaminating any evidence she'd been bundled up, and she was thrust into Reg's arms, before eventually being passed to one of his friends whose car was parked nearby.

With no news coming through, by early evening Richard and Alex had returned home. I, for one, was pleased that they were not present when Amy's body was removed from the house and placed in a private ambulance. I don't think Alex or Richard could have coped with that, and Richard, I know, does not regret missing that particular horror. Although I needed to see Amy, I wanted to be alone with her, away from the world's attention and the click-click-click of the cameras, which had become such an unwelcome part of my life.

That evening we talked. Reliving the day's events and trying to make sense of it all became the best form of therapy. We still do it now: sit together and talk about Amy and about that afternoon. Sometimes we figure her out; at other times she is the ball of confusion she always was. Our laughter acts as a barometer of how far we've come in our grieving, but for me these times are also about never forgetting her. However, that evening the conversation was as far from reflection and laughter as it could be. My mind was so void of feeling that I was struggling to process even the tiniest piece of information.

Some details had emerged about her death. We knew by now that Amy was alone when she was found. I can only imagine how terrifying it must have been for Andrew, her bodyguard, who was the person who raised the alarm. There's nothing that comforts me about Amy's death, other than that she was in her room, her safe place, her sanctuary, and she would not have known anything about what was happening to her. Amy's death could so easily have been played out as publicly as her life, and I do not know how I or the rest of the family could have stomached a final indignity like that. We've had to cope with a lot of things, but thank God, not that.

It must have been past midnight when I finally called it a day. I was exhausted, but my body still felt like a tightly coiled spring. Richard helped me upstairs, and as he closed the bedroom door my legs suddenly felt as though they might give way beneath me. Without warning, the tears welled up from somewhere deep inside. Little by little I let go of some of the tension. I sat on the bed with Richard's arm around me and, in the stillness of the dark, I cried and cried until I had no tears left.

Eventually I must have drifted off, but I only caught snatches of sleep before waking, gripped with anxiety. Every time I opened or closed my eyes I saw Amy. I trawled through the events of Friday,

22 July – the last time I'd seen her alive. She was drunk, yes, but did that mean by the next morning she'd be dead? I kept going over our goodbye, how she'd draped her arms around me and how, as we left, I had told her that I loved her. I desperately held on to that. I told her that I loved her. She died knowing that.

It was mid-morning on Sunday the 24th when Mitchell and Jane made it to East Barnet. Mitchell looked awful. Not only had he been on an overnight flight, but landing back in London he'd been faced with the full force of Amy's death without having had the evening we'd had to process everything. Strangely, I needed to see Mitchell, and he needed to see me. Although our lives were separate, Alex and Amy remained our bond throughout. We'd each experienced Amy from a unique perspective but, at that moment, each of us understood what it was to be her parent. Fortunately, everyone was kind enough to give us the space to mourn together. We stood in the living room and cried and hugged. The tears flowed again that afternoon when one of Amy's backing singers, Zalon, turned up. Just looking at him crumpled in the chair opposite set me off, and we wept together.

Soon, though, it was time to put our anguish aside in order to deal with practical matters. Later that afternoon a family meeting was called to discuss the next few days. Richard and I, Mitchell and Jane, Melody and Elliott, Alex and Riva and old friends Val and Haydon Harrod were all there, but even thinking about, let alone organizing, a funeral felt like a mammoth obstacle to overcome. Neither I nor Mitchell was in a fit state to pick up phones and do any arranging, and ultimately it was Richard and Mitchell's friend Howard Grossman who stepped in and took the brunt of the work.

Because it was the weekend a post-mortem could not be completed until Monday, and only after that would Amy's body be released. In accordance with Jewish tradition, her funeral would take place within the next day, but the finer details were still up in the air. I've since read several articles claiming that while Amy was alive I'd discussed with her what cemetery she wanted to be buried in, but that is not true. Again it may have been my gallows humour, misunderstood by the press, because I probably did once say to her in jest, 'What cemetery am I putting you in?' never thinking it would actually happen. In fact Amy died without making a will. Unbelievable as it may sound, neither she, we, nor her management prepared for her death. Perhaps it was denial, I don't know, but for me it was sheer optimism. I always expected her to pull through.

Amy had always said that, just like Cynthia, she would never want to be buried, so a cremation was unanimously agreed upon. Other than that, we had no inkling of what Amy might have wished for. In an inspired moment during that meeting it was Richard who first mooted the idea of eventually placing Amy's ashes with Cynthia's, and once he'd said it, it sounded like the most obvious and fitting plan.

The more urgent headache, however, was how to contain the press that we anticipated would be present at Amy's funeral. Our phones had not stopped ringing, so we'd already had some indication of what lay ahead. Amy's life had been so chewed over and spat out, as far as we were concerned there was no question about it: the ceremony would remain private. In order to throw journalists off the scent, it was decided that one funeral would be booked at Edgwarebury Cemetery in north London under the name 'Winehouse' but that Amy's committal would take place at Golders Green Crematorium under the name 'Emma Shaffer'. Shaffer was Richard's mother's maiden name, but even now he has no idea of how or why the name 'Emma' came into his head.

First thing on the morning of Monday the 25th, a couple of hours before we were due at St Pancras Court to identify Amy's body, Richard made the initial phone-calls to work out what was possible, but as it turned out the details of both funerals were leaked anyway, and all the plotting we did to keep journalists at bay was futile. We still don't know how the information was released, but I think we realized early on that there wouldn't be much we could control.

Despite the activity going on around us, I could not help dwelling on the enormity of the day ahead. It was a day I hoped I would never see. Alex and Riva did not attend the coroner's court with us. Alex couldn't face seeing his sister and no one tried to persuade him otherwise; today, Riva says she is not sorry that the last picture she had of Amy was when she was alive. It's a personal choice. I knew seeing Amy would be harrowing, but I can now reflect on that morning as an important part in my grieving process. I needed to be with her.

We drove into Camden with Mitchell and Jane and met Raye and Reg there. Disturbingly, photographers had already crowded the narrow walkway to the court entrance, and while I remember the atmosphere as being solemn and respectful, it was also overwhelming. Thank God, the whole experience was made easier by the coroner's officer, Sher Duff, who was waiting for us and who guided us through the mayhem with her no-nonsense attitude and welcomed us into the waiting room with amazing warmth. Sher is a tough cookie with cropped red hair and a Scottish lilt, and we all agreed we couldn't have been in a safer pair of hands. She ran through the stages of what we could expect with an enviable calm. Like many of our dealings with officials in recent days the information was cold and clinical, and I listened to it as if it was someone else's child being discussed.

We were not to be alarmed, Sher told us. The left side of Amy's face would be reddened because, before she was found, she had lain face down in one position for several hours – how many was still unclear. As a post-mortem had not been carried out yet, Amy would be behind a glass screen; of course, we could spend as much time with her as we wished.

It was only as we were led out across the courtyard to a corner door that I became unsteady. This wasn't someone else's child. This was my girl, and the thought of her lying cold in a mortuary coursed through every muscle in my body. I prayed that she'd been taken care of gently, with respect. I tried to concentrate on the task in hand, but a chilling fear kept circling in my mind.

Sher punched in a security code and Richard and I and Mitchell and Jane were ushered into a tiny room, no bigger than a box room. Built into the wall on the left-hand side was a single pane of glass. My eyes scanned the stark white walls and lino floor and then slowly moved up to rest on Amy. Laid out on a gurney, she was draped in a white sheet up to her petite neck with her eyes softly closed. She was within touching distance but, agonizingly, I could not reach her. She looked peaceful, free from the torment with which she had lived the last few years of her life.

My body burned with pain, an indescribable pain, but I couldn't take my eyes off her. She was thirteen again, lying in bed in Greenside Close, having slept in on a school day. I was standing over her, calling her name, her eyes flickering into life. I found myself placing my hand up against the glass and I couldn't stop myself calling out to her one last time. 'Get up, Amy. It's time to get up. Come on now, lady, no messing around,' I repeated over and over. The salt tears stung my face, but she just lay there, sleeping on. She was beautiful, but I yearned to see those dark brown eyes one last time – the windows to everything Amy was, and everything we'd lost.

Had the glass not separated us from her, Mitchell would undoubtedly have thrown himself on to the gurney, and I suspect I would not have been far behind. The others filed out while he and I stayed with Amy for another fifteen minutes before letting Reg and Raye have their moment with her.

'Can you believe that's our baby?' Mitchell said to me, barely able to speak.

'No,' I replied quietly.

Something felt so wrong about us being there. It should have been Amy looking at us, not this – definitely not this. We told her that we loved her very much. We'd always loved her and we always would. We left slowly, glancing back for one last long look. I didn't see Amy's body again.

*

While we struggled to come to terms with Amy's death privately, the news soon reached us that well-wishers had been leaving flowers, candles and letters in Camden Square. After that morning, the last place I wanted to be was among throngs of people, but we felt it was important to go. With hindsight, it's a trip all of us are glad we made.

I hadn't expected to see such an enormous shrine opposite Amy's house. There were messages of love and support in their thousands, and while they were very humbling and touching to read, they were unsettling too. It was Amy the star the fans were grieving for, the person they'd seen on album covers and in newspapers, whereas for us, that was never Amy. We didn't really know their version – for us, that Amy was a fantasy. The fact that I'd seen Amy's body a few hours before only intensified that feeling: she'd looked almost as naked as the minute she was born.

Looking back at photographs from that afternoon, my face says it all: wave upon wave of anguish. As I walked along the inside of the police cordon, something tore deep inside me. I'm not sure my heart has ever pieced itself back together. I vaguely remember strangers hugging me and in particular one woman tapping me on the shoulder. 'Thank you for giving birth to Amy,' she said. I looked into her eyes, slightly confused. What woman is ever thanked for doing what is the most natural in life? It was lovely but, I have to confess, also completely bewildering.

Of the hundreds of cards I received in the immediate aftermath of Amy's death it was the messages from people who had known Amy that undoubtedly affected me the most. One, from a school friend called Gemma, still makes me smile:

I'm not sure if you remember this Janis, but one day me and Amy were going to Brent Cross and you told her to buy shoes for a Bar Mitzvah. You made it very clear that she wasn't allowed shoes with big heels. Well, Amy being Amy, came back with black PVC stilettos with a huge platform and heel. It was those things Amy did which were priceless. I loved her originality and confidence. She was one of the most amazing people I ever knew . . . I'm so glad and honoured to have known such a wonderful person before the fame took over.

Another, from my friend Morag, a fellow parent whose daughter Lauren went to school with Amy, read as follows:

Superstar, world renowned etc, but still my best memory of Amy is the cheeky picture of her in her Osidge uniform. They both looked like that when they used to skip back to Ashmole and the labs to help tidy up. More often than not they ended up using the lab as a stage with the Bunsen burners (unlit) as microphones. If the dark days ever start to ease, look back fondly to happier days when your precious daughter gave you so much joy.

I can safely say I have now reached a point where I can look back to those happier days. I can even look at the letter handed to me that Monday morning in London by ABC News with a nod of tired resignation. We had only just identified Amy's body when it was shoved in my hand. 'As you know, Amy Winehouse was much-loved in the US and "Good Morning America" would love to welcome you on to our programme when you are ready to share the story of your special daughter . . .' Talk about a gannet swooping down on dinner. Mitchell tore his up immediately and I pushed mine into Richard's hand, but it was hard to ignore the insensitivity of such a request only two days after Amy's death. I did know she was much-loved in the US, thanks. I was her mum!

But if Monday the 25th seemed like a daze of events, Tuesday the 26th was just as confused. Thankfully, Amy's funeral arrangements had been taken care of by an army of people and I was not burdened with worry about what might or might not go wrong. I'm glad I wasn't asked if I wanted to say something during the service. I couldn't have got up in front of all those people and spoken.

Mitchell gave a wonderful eulogy and said all that needed and should have been said.

Edgwarebury Cemetery held three hundred people but Golders Green Crematorium seated only a hundred, so the previous evening a list had been drawn up of who could be fitted in. We had no idea who was flying in from around the world, so it had been a stab in the dark as to who might be there. We just hoped no one would be too offended if their name had mistakenly dropped off the list. Just like the last three days, our home continued to be a gathering place, and from early on Tuesday morning, mourners started to flock there. There was the expected assortment of family and friends, but how everyone else got wind of the address we have no idea. There were friends of Amy's we'd never met, but they were welcomed in just the same.

Though I was still numb, I seemed to take it in my stride, but Richard still finds the experience difficult to comprehend. Not only was he unable to get into his own kitchen for four days, but people like Mark Ronson were chatting away with Amy's Auntie Rene, my cousin Martin and my dad in the back garden – two worlds suddenly colliding. At one point Richard went to the front door to check whether the entourage of cars had turned up, when he was accosted by our next-door neighbour, Marian. 'Is that Kelly Osbourne?' she whispered, and pointed. Sure enough, propping up the tree opposite Richard's drive and dragging on a newly lit cigarette was Amy's friend and Ozzy Osbourne's daughter. 'I have no idea,' replied Richard, and hurried back inside to ask. I wasn't sure what she looked like either. My dad, who was in his nineties, looked even more confused. 'Who's she?' he kept saying. I think it was Alex who eventually settled that one for us.

I can laugh about this now, but the atmosphere was very different as we piled into the waiting cars before the cortege rolled towards Edgwarebury Cemetery. There was no sign of any reporters or cameras on that initial part of the route, but word had got to us that neighbours had been offered payment by several newspapers to use their gardens as a base. All had refused, and thankfully it wasn't something I was aware of at the time. All morning the police had been checking up and down the street clearing any unwanted visitors loitering around. What we couldn't avoid, however, was the bank of cameras directly outside the cemetery. Turning into the lane and moving towards a front line of press was nothing less than intimidating.

In our car, Richard sat with me and my dad, and I don't remember a word being spoken. Other than the journey to identify Amy's body, it was probably the most distressing trip I've ever had to make, but I did it. We all did it, but how we did it I still do not know. For my dad, it must have seemed otherworldly. He had barely any concept of Amy as a star and was suffering from the early stages of dementia. 'What's all this?' he kept saying to me as the long lenses pointed into the front windscreen and hundreds of flashbulbs blinded us. I took his hand and held it – I knew how much it must have terrified him.

Inside, Amy's coffin was already raised in the prayer hall. I felt surprisingly composed as Richard helped me through the doors. Through the bare and unfussy chapel we walked and took our seats at the front, and for a moment the hum around me faded. I couldn't feel Amy in the room. For me, her coffin was there and I knew her body was too, but I couldn't feel her. She was somewhere else. I still have that feeling when I visit her headstone – I can't explain it. I'm not an overly religious person but a spiritual calm did fill me. 'If this is what will be, then this is it, Janis.' None the less, losing a child must surely be the cruellest of all fates.

In keeping with Jewish tradition we had a closed coffin – a simple black box with a black drape drawn over it. But, in keeping with Amy's unconventional spirit, the family had raised no objection to a few of Amy's friends washing her, applying her make-up and attaching her beehive to her hair one last time. They dressed her in the iconic yellow dress she wore at the BRITs in 2007, and I can only imagine how bittersweet that experience must have been for them. Amy, on the other hand, would have absolutely loved it.

I can honestly say that Amy's funeral came and went. It sounds strange, but I felt little connection with it. The tears rolled down my cheeks but it still didn't feel real. It was a simple service – traditional prayers for the dead and Mitchell's eulogy – but I think back on that day as another of Amy's performances. Fortunately I wasn't aware that there had been a scene earlier when it was discovered that a journalist had found his way into the grounds and was openly taking notes. He was removed quickly by the bodyguards, but I had to ask – how low can a person go?

When we finished at Edgwarebury we then had to make our way to Golders Green to stand through exactly the same ceremony – Amy's last show take two. I don't mean for this to sound cold, but the sheer number of press and people there made it feel like an event rather than my daughter's final journey. What other family would have to go through such a torturous farce? The number of cameras welcoming us at Golders Green was even greater than an hour or so before, even though the second service had been designed to foil the press. You couldn't have made it up.

The day was a sombre one, but I've since heard tales that I can't help but smile at. The singer Bryan Adams scrounged a lift with Michael and Jessica for the short distance between ceremonies – their childhood hero squashed next to them on the back seat of a taxi. Apparently, by the end of it Jess had him singing her favourite hit 'Love A Woman' while she sang alongside. Again, it's a moment Amy would have absolutely loved.

I went through the motions in Golders Green. At the end of the chapel her coffin again rested, now without the black drape, and I filed past at the ceremony's close, leading the other mourners out into the bright sunshine. Locked in my own private world, I placed my hand gently on the head of the box. 'Bye, Amy, I love you,' I whispered quietly, and stood there for a moment with my fingers flush against her coffin. I needed to make contact with my daughter one final time, and I will never be able to describe how that felt. It brings me both comfort and unbearable sadness to think about it. The reality was I'd lost her so many times before.

For the rest of that day and for the next three days there were happiness and tears in equal measure. By the end of the Shiva – the time in the Jewish faith set aside to mourn and ease the family through tragedy – I felt a little calmer, although, if I'm honest, the shock didn't leave me for months. To the world, I suspect Amy's funeral was an ending, but for me it was just a beginning. Each month since that day has brought me more closure on Amy's life, but even so I can never say goodbye.

The amount of tea Mitchell's Auntie Rene and cousin Shelley made in those three days was unbelievable. Mitchell, Alex and I were so well looked after by everybody during that time. Our house was too small to accommodate all those people who wanted to sit Shiva with us so, kindly, the Southgate Progressive Synagogue opened their doors every day that week and we sat and chatted and remembered Amy in the good times and bad. There was some business to attend to as well: on Thursday, 28 July, Amy's home in Camden Square was returned to us by police and it was time to set foot in it for the first time since Amy's passing. We were all still so stunned that for me, anyway, it felt like sleepwalking over the threshold.

Amy's kitchen was just how we'd left it, untouched. I glanced at the photographs still on the table and made my way into the living room. Jane and Mitchell were already there, and Jane was sat there staring at the sofa. There were five outfits laid out on it, placed there by Naomi alongside a handwritten note. Amy had been due at Nick Shymansky's wedding the day after she died and Naomi had gone off to a festival the day before. 'Have fun, see you Monday' the note read. I just stood there staring at the dresses, yearning for Amy's body to fill them.

Richard had wandered downstairs to the studio, and he confessed later that he'd stopped at the only photograph of Amy in the house, positioned on the wall by the staircase, and called her every name under the sun. That turmoil of emotions was normal. I've often told Amy off in my head for dying. 'Why did you have to do this to me?' was one of my many questions. But as time passed I focused more on the pain Amy must have been going through for her life to get to that stage, and in some ways that is harder to bear. The kitchen cupboards were completely bare of food. Just hundreds of bags of Haribo sweets stuffed into the drawers remained.

Upstairs, Amy's room remained exactly as it was when she was taken from it – even her pillow still had her head mark fixed in its creases. She'd been sick in the bathroom and nobody had thought to clean it before we entered the house. Another heart-sinking moment. Richard found her Spanish guitar behind her bed. I opened her wardrobe door and took a few items that for me were all about Amy: a bag of her worn ballet pumps, a couple of the shirts she'd designed for Fred Perry, and two of her pink bowling jackets embroidered with her signature 'Amywoo'. Everything else was meaningless. And I couldn't stay up there for long.

As we made our way through the rooms we could hear the fans crowded around the gate singing 'Back To Black'. I stood there on the staircase listening to them. It was truly amazing, and gut-wrenching too. Later that afternoon I was pleased to be back home. It's taken me a long time to grasp the enormity of that week, and even now I recall fragments of it that have been buried in my mind.

On the last night of Shiva we all decided to throw off our funeral garb and celebrate Amy's life at Jazz After Dark in Soho, a club Amy loved and frequented. I was all for having fun among the tears and I adored that evening. What better therapy for the soul than to watch Mark Ronson onstage with my sister Debra's son Gabriel on drums, all of us drowning our sorrows in Amy's music. Apparently there were commentaries in some of the papers saying how inappropriate it was for us to do this. In honour of Amy, I stick two fingers up to anyone who tells a family how they should grieve.

It's Amy's music that I now regard as my most lasting reminder of her. I love it. I love her, and my life is incomplete without her, but

I know that she died having achieved more than most people do, and certainly most women do, in a lifetime. There's one interview of Amy I've seen since her passing that always sticks in my mind. 'I'll be singing until I drop dead,' she giggles. She always did want to be true to herself. Bless you, Amy. You were.

Epilogue

Life After Amy

It's nine a.m. on a fresh April morning in 2014 and I am perched in the open hatch of a purple-coloured plane more than 13,000 feet above the Cambridge countryside. My face and body are being buffeted by the wind and I am wondering why I ever agreed to take part in this mass parachute jump. When I was first asked, back in 2013, I didn't hesitate to say yes. Why not? Life is for living, and I reckoned that having MS shouldn't stop me from taking part in such an exciting challenge. But that was on paper. Now I'm actually doing it, it's a very different feeling.

It's too late to turn back now, though. My jump has already been delayed twice due to bad weather so this is 'take three'. Only minutes before, when the plane had started to climb and the airfield near the village of March became a pin dot below, I tried to put out of my mind the magnitude of the drop. Now my legs are dangling helplessly over the edge. I can't look down, so I grit my teeth and fix my eyes ahead, on the blue sky. My stomach is turning over and over, but before I have time even to contemplate chickening out, the experienced instructor I am tightly strapped to has pulled my head back into his body and launched us from the aircraft.

My eyes shut tight in panic and my arms clutch my chest. The wind is now screaming around me and I am falling, falling, falling, veering between sheer terror and total exhilaration. I can barely catch my breath as I hurtle 120mph through the air, the hard ground getting closer and closer to me. Finally, when the parachute is deployed, we start to gently glide down and I know we are on the home straight. I may even live to tell the tale.

My parachute jump was the final event in a string of celebrations to mark what would have been Amy's thirtieth birthday. Even if I'd wanted to, I couldn't have said no to raising money and awareness for the Amy Winehouse Foundation, the charity Mitch and I set up in the aftermath of Amy's death. Three years now AWF has been up and running, and we've gone from an idea that was formed in the months after Amy's passing to a fully fledged organization that makes a real impact on the lives of vulnerable young people – but more of that later.

To get to this stage has been both a painful and positive journey. In the years since Amy's passing I have come to accept what I already knew: that I lost Amy long before that became a reality. The trauma of losing her is still with us, of course – I don't think any individual or any family comes out of something like this unscathed. Mitchell and I are dealing with the loss of our daughter; Alex is trying to cope without his sister; not to mention the other relatives who have lost a niece, a cousin, a granddaughter; and, of course, the friends who lost a friend. I'm told repeatedly that the world lost a great talent too, but I think that's for others to say. Amy was simply my little girl with big dreams and a lot of determination.

In 2011, following the funeral and after we'd cleared Amy's belongings from Camden Square, Richard and I travelled to Florida. We'd booked the holiday way before that awful week and decided not to cancel. I'm a firm believer that life goes on, however hard it is to bear, and Amy certainly would not have wanted me to sit around in mourning indefinitely. That summer there was no better place to go than Miami and Florida – my place of solace in good times and bad, the place I found my independence, the place Amy and I discovered together, and the place of her ill-fated marriage to Blake. Travelling there that August knowing that Amy was no longer with me took on an even greater significance, and the grief was never far below the surface. In every place there were memories of her, Joan's pool in Boca Raton and Collins Avenue in downtown Miami to name just two. We talked about Amy and we wept. There's one thing I can say about my daughter, she never left us without a story to tell.

Just as we had begun to wind down, our trip was cut short by another death in the family. Richard's mum Doreen passed away while we were abroad and, sadly, we had to fly back to help with funeral arrangements and steel ourselves to mourn one more time. With everything that had been happening I hadn't been in regular contact with Doreen, but I knew she had a soft spot for me, just as I had for her.

We returned to the US in September 2011, this time to New York to appear on the Anderson Cooper chat show to discuss addiction and the Amy Winehouse Foundation, which at the time we were in the process of setting up. Everybody has different ways of dealing with grief, and Mitchell ploughed himself into the project from the start. Nor did his need to act stop when we lost Amy: in fact it intensified. Today, the Foundation is not only a force for good in terms of the work it is pioneering, it has become a unifying force for our family, a positive channel along which to focus our energies, and I dare say the one part of Amy's life where we come together as one.

It was on our return from New York, when Richard and I were sat in JFK airport, that something unusual happened. We ordered burgers and ate and chatted until our flight was called. Suddenly, faintly audible through the Tannoy system, we heard the intro-duction to 'Back To Black' and my heart jumped with pride and pain. Just as I looked up, a white feather was drifting down through the air and it landed gently on Richard's burger. I smiled. Maybe I believed it was Amy's spirit because that's what I wanted to believe. I don't know, and it doesn't bother me what other people might make of that. When you lose a child you are always looking for a sign that they are still with you. Anything to get you through is my motto.

It transpired in the days after Amy's funeral that during Mitchell's eulogy a black butterfly had landed on Kelly Osbourne's shoulder then fluttered around the prayer hall at Edgwarebury Cemetery. Two days after that we were with Mitchell, Jane and Reg at Melody's house when a blackbird flew in through the open window and landed on Jane's foot. When we took it out into the back garden it circled again and again and kept coming back and landing next to us. Mitchell says that sometimes he can still feel Amy on his shoulder, whispering in his ear. For me, she is in my thoughts and dreams constantly. I feel better knowing she is there.

Richard and I also decided not to cancel our wedding, which had by then been planned for 17 September. It was debatable whether it would go ahead because Richard felt that outsiders might think it disrespectful to marry so soon after Amy's passing. We spent a long time discussing it and came to the conclusion that we couldn't live our lives being worried about the opinions of others or be made to feel guilty for wanting to feel fulfilled. It was not an easy conversation to have, not least because it forced me to confront the difficult questions that remained after Amy's death. That nagging doubt about what I could have done differently has been a hard one to overcome, but it is very slowly being replaced with a calmer feeling of acceptance.

Our wedding, while very happy, was a private affair, which was just as we wanted it. Alex and Riva, Michael and his girlfriend Lauren, Jessica and my dad Eddie came to the short ceremony at Enfield Register Office. Afterwards we had a quiet dinner and toasted Amy. Only months before she had predicted that she wouldn't be there, but reassuringly, I felt her by my side throughout.

Amy's birthday a few days earlier had been one of the most difficult days to face. Fortunately I'd spent it with family and friends – the support network that has been vital to me throughout. The last image I ever had of Amy was lying in the mortuary in St Pancras

Coroner's Court and it took months for that vision to recede and to be replaced with lighter, happier memories. I'm not even sure I'm all the way there yet. Unlike for other families who lose a loved one there are constant reminders of Amy everywhere: music playing; an artwork on a London wall; a documentary on TV. All those things used to make me feel panicky and uncomfortable, because they happened without warning. Riva told me recently that, at first, she felt the same; she'd even made a waiter switch off *Back To Black* in a restaurant a month or so after Amy's passing. I think for all of us, though, that pain has gradually metamorphosed into a feeling of sheer amazement. 'That's my daughter,' I think now. 'Wasn't she incredible!'

One of the battles I have had to continue to fight has been to keep some kind of control over information about Amy. Because her life was lived so publicly I feel that there is often an assumption that we don't care what enters the public domain. Nothing could be further from the truth. The fact was that Amy did not want parts of her life to be lived publicly either, despite how it may have appeared to the outside world.

It should have come as no surprise to me, but a few days after Amy's passing Mitchell rang me to see if I'd received the coroner's report of the post-mortem into Amy's death. Despite our being told that the letters would be sent out simultaneously, mine had not dropped through the letterbox as anticipated. As it turned out, in the chaos of that week I'd given an incorrect address to the coroner's assistant and the letter ended up at a house further down our street. It was only when I was contacted by the coroner's officer, Sher Duff, to say that an unscrupulous neighbour had tried to sell the report to a newspaper that I realized what had happened. Apparently, the newspaper – I don't know which one – did not want to publish the report and handed it in to the police. Suddenly, after Amy's passing the tabloid press finally had a heart.

The letter (once it finally arrived) and the subsequent inquest into Amy's death in October 2011 confirmed what we all knew in our hearts: Amy did not have hard drugs in her system on the night of her death. There were traces of Librium, the drug she had been prescribed for alcohol withdrawal, and, of course, there was alcohol. The police had recovered two large and one small vodka bottles from Amy's room and she was found to have had 416mg of alcohol per 100ml of blood in her system – five times higher than the legal drink-drive limit. The most likely explanation is that she suffered an alcohol-induced seizure, but we will never truly know. Amy's weight at the time of her death was perhaps for me the most shocking aspect: she was a mere six and a half stone, and there is no doubt in my mind that that was also a major contributing factor.

More details emerged too, some of which I had not been aware of earlier. On the evening of Amy's death, Dr Cristina Romete had visited her at home at around 8.30 p.m. It was a routine visit, and in court Dr Romete described her as 'tipsy'. It would have been a good few hours after Richard and I saw Amy, so we can only assume that by the evening Amy had slept off some of her drunkenness, then had started to drink again later. Dr Romete had asked Amy if she was going to stop drinking. Her answer was that she didn't know but that she specifically 'did not want to die'. I believe that that was Amy being honest. In the months leading up to her death I had already sensed that she wanted to change her life, not end it. In order to do so, though, she would have had to confront the very habits she mis-takenly believed were holding her together. In the long-term, perhaps, age and experience might have helped her over that barrier, and I'm sure that she thought, just as we did, that she had time on her hands to decide. It is a terrible irony that she died still thinking she was in control.

Andrew, who had seemed a shell of his former self when he appeared at the inquest, said that he last spoke to her at two a.m., when she had been in her room playing drums. He checked on her again in the morning at around ten a.m. and assumed she was asleep. It was only when he realized Amy was lying in the same position when he looked in on her again at 2.30 p.m. that he raised the alarm.

She had been dead for several hours. I don't blame Andrew, nor was I angry with him at the time. I know he is still tortured by the fact that Amy died on his watch. Like many others, he could not have prevented her death.

The coroner, Suzanne Greenway, recorded a verdict of misadventure. For me, there is no better word. Amy's life was an adventure, but it was such a wild adventure that it finally destroyed her.

The verdict gave me some closure, but by November all of it was thrown into doubt. Honestly, I couldn't have made it up if I'd tried. A month after Amy's inquest Suzanne Greenway resigned amid allegations that she was unqualified to do her job. In order to fulfil her role as an assistant deputy coroner she needed to have been registered in England as a solicitor for five years, but she had only been registered for two and a half. She had been appointed by her husband Dr Andrew Scott Reid and had carried out thirty inquests in total, twelve of them at St Pancras Coroner's Court, Amy's being one of them. As an inquiry into her appointment was launched, a second inquest into Amy's death was scheduled, for 8 January 2013, which we did not attend. Thankfully, its findings confirmed the original verdict: Amy had died of alcohol poisoning and her death was accidental.

I, for one, could not have gone through the process of challenging a coroner's verdict at that time. The year 2012 had taken its toll on me in more ways than one. In January, my dad, who had been steadily declining over the previous year, also died, and the hole that already existed in my life grew bigger. Eddie kept a picture of Amy on his bedside table right up to the time of his death; he even told me that she had visited him – a comment that surprised me because my dad was not a superstitious man. I took it as a good omen. Unlike my mother's death, my dad's passing hit me very hard. He had been the one stabilizing force in my life, and I miss him every day. On the day of his funeral, Alex turned to me through floods of tears and said, 'Please don't be next, Mum. Please don't die.' I tried to comfort him as best I could, but this was the first time I'd seen him scared about my own medical condition. Believe me, if I could change all that happened I would, because what my children have had to experience, no mother would have wished on them. For me, though, the best example I can give to Alex is to remain positive and continue to live life to the full in spite of my disability.

Fortunately there were some happy occasions that year too. In February we attended the Grammys in LA and ended up receiving a posthumous award on Amy's behalf for her recording of 'Body And Soul' with Tony Bennett – the last recording she ever made. Other than the sheer spectacle of the Grammys, that occasion certainly got filed in the 'surreal box' for a whole set of unforeseen circumstances.

When we arrived in LA, on 11 February, news had just started coming through that the soul singer Whitney Houston had died of a suspected drug overdose, and that she had been found in her bathtub in the Beverly Hilton Hotel. It was the same hotel we were due to go to that evening to attend a party hosted by music producer Clive Davis, the man who famously discovered Whitney Houston.

Although Amy had no connection to Whitney Houston, on a very personal note I understood what it must have been like for her family to hear that news. We had just gone through months of anguish ourselves and the feelings were still raw inside me. We weren't sure whether the pre-Grammy party would now go ahead, or even whether it was appropriate for us to go. The whole city was in such shock and the streets were littered with the familiar sight of TV crews and cameras.

The party did go ahead and we decided there were far more important people than us to decide what was right and what was wrong. Personally, I didn't really understand the critics who claimed it should have been cancelled. When Amy passed, I loved our night at Jazz After Dark because we paid the most fitting tribute to her there; but I have to confess, the party in LA that night was a whole different ball-game compared to a jazz club in Soho. Never have I seen so many diamonds and ball gowns and tuxedos in my life. The suite was bursting with famous faces, and Richard ended up in an unexpected tight spot, too. The compère for the evening, rapper P Diddy, tried to get through a narrow doorway at the same time as Richard, whereupon they found themselves face to face with their stomachs wedged against each other, both jostling to get free. P Diddy was exactly as his name would have you believe, small; it was Richard who'd put on a few extra pounds around the middle. Soon after, Richard also realized that the bushy-haired stranger stood next to him outside having a cigarette was Slash from Guns N' Roses. We ended up doing so many double-takes that night that my head was spinning.

The Grammy ceremony the next day was just as mindboggling. When Amy's name was called alongside Tony Bennett's, Mitchell and I made our way to the stage to the deafening applause of the audience and, of all things, a standing ovation. By the time I'd finally made it up the stairs, this time without the aid of my stick, I was truly overwhelmed by the sheer noise of the crowd, and desperately trying to remain calm and collected inside. 'This is Amy's mum,' Tony Bennett announced, and the room erupted again. For the first time, blinded by the lights and peering out over all those thousands of faces, I caught a glimpse of how Amy must have felt and how intimidating all that attention can be.

Fortunately I had the very kind Tony Bennett welcoming me to the microphone. He is such a sweet gentleman; he told me later he had cried when he heard about Amy. Like all of us, he'd had his fingers crossed that she would pull through (he later generously donated more than £80,000 to the Amy Winehouse Foundation). Such a warm feeling came over me whenever anyone recognized Amy's achievements, but, as ever, it was always tempered by a searing sense of loss. Amy had been so thrilled to work with Tony Bennett. She should have been there to enjoy it.

Later that month the BRIT Awards also paid tribute to Amy with a filmed sequence about her life which included our family photos. And in 2013 I was reduced to tears again when Amy was nominated in the category Best British Female Solo Act for the album *Lioness: Hidden Treasures*, a compilation of unheard tracks her record company released five months after her passing. Three larger-than-life-sized pictures of her flashed up on the screen as the nominations were called and I couldn't control my emotions. Whereas before I'd have been sat there wondering when or if Amy was going to show up, now I felt the crushing weight of her absence, made obvious by the empty space at our table, and I welled up. She'd received the first ever posthumous nomination in BRITs history, and although the award went to the singer Emeli Sandé, she paid tribute to the other women she shared a platform with. No disrespect to Emeli, but I thought Amy should have won. Even after she's gone I still root for her to come out on top. But I guess that's just a mother's pride talking.

Happily, Amy lives on in the work of the Foundation. From its launch on her birthday in 2011 we have made great strides. In March 2012 we began piloting the first ever drugs resilience programme for schools in St Clement Danes secondary in Hertfordshire. To date, the programme has been rolled out to two other secondary schools in England, and with £4.3 million lottery funding granted to us at the end of 2013, our five-year goal is to be present in fifty schools around the country reaching a potential 250,000 children. In fact the resilience programmes have highlighted a growing need for quality drugs education and our aim is to encourage everybody to talk more openly about drug and alcohol abuse and the underlying causes. As a parent, I wish I'd had the same information available to me when I was raising Amy. We are learning more every day about the causes of addiction and how better to help other young people in difficulty.

It is an alarming truth, but the resilience programmes were born from the simple fact that drug and alcohol education does not form a compulsory part of the national curriculum. Although the subject is often taught as part of Personal, Social and Health Education

(PSHE) classes, it is at the discretion of schools and individual teachers as to how much time is allotted. In fact, around 60 per cent of state schools offer an hour or less per year of drugs education to secondary school children, and 70 per cent of former state school pupils cannot recall any drugs education at all.

From early on we teamed with the drug and alcohol treatment charity Addaction to deliver structured sessions which for the first time are tailored not only towards children but parents and teachers too. Rather than a 'no drugs' message, we believe in educating children to make an informed choice and encouraging them to think about why they might be attracted to drugs or alcohol. Incorporated into the discussions are thirty-minute talks by former addicts who share their often moving life stories of addiction and recovery. For the first time ever, a team from Harvard University in the US will survey the children before and after they have taken part in the resilience programme so that we can learn from, and build on, the approach.

In listening to other young people share their stories, I have come to realize how tied up issues of self-esteem are with addiction, and that strikes a deep chord within me when I reflect on Amy. While Amy was a bright and gifted child, her behaviour growing up was not dissimilar to many of the young people I have come into contact with through the Foundation. Several have described how their high-risk behaviour was evident way before a drop of alcohol ever touched their lips or before they ever tried their first drug. Our own resilience programme manager, Dominic Ruffy, is one such addict in recovery, and his story is both harrowing and filled with hope.

Amy was lucky enough to have had the opportunity for her creativity to flourish, and she always possessed the determination to achieve success, but the ordinary nature of her childhood story exists everywhere, in every school and youth club and college up and down the country. And, while I always understood her battle with addiction from a medical perspective, I am still wrestling with the emotional triggers that may have exacerbated Amy's condition and the devastating knock-on effect felt by us as a family in dealing with her problems.

It is important to remember that many young people don't take drugs, but the resilience programme offers everyone an opportunity to discuss the underlying causes of addiction. Alongside educating teachers and parents in how to identify children most at risk and to understand the pressures young people face, many brave teenagers have also spoken for the first time about their vulnerabilities and why they think they are tempted to turn to coping mechanisms that can have terrible effects on their mental and physical health. Some have talked about feeling different, others about having a desperate desire to fit in; some have poor body confidence and low self-esteem, and perhaps they already have an eating disorder or are prone to self-harming; some may come from homes where parents place undue academic pressure on them; and some may live chaotic lives already – perhaps even with an addicted family member. Whatever the reason, the routes into substance misuse are varied and cannot be stereotyped into a typical case. If the signs are picked up early enough, however, there is a chance to reverse the process before habits become ingrained. Alcohol was a far harder habit for Amy to kick because she'd been drinking for a lot longer than she'd ever been taking hard drugs.

We've discovered that there is a real need for all those who are involved in addiction, or at risk of addiction, to talk. In partnership with other organizations, like the Angelus Foundation founded by author and broadcaster Maryon Stewart following the death of her daughter Hester in 2009 as a result of taking the 'legal' drug GBL, the Foundation is working to try to achieve this. In 2012, a petition with close to three thousand signatures was lodged with Parliament asking for effective drugs education to be a compulsory part of the national curriculum. It's a small start, but it's a lobby that's growing. Nobody wants to believe that what happened to Amy could ever happen to their child, but I was that parent once too, and the bottom line is, it can.

Just as Amy did, there are many children who will at some point turn to drugs or alcohol as a way of dealing with problems in their lives. Although the number is relatively small, a few will go on to develop full-blown addictions. Between 2011 and 2012 some twenty thousand young people were involved in specialist drug and alcohol treatment programmes in England, but many others who are high-risk and vulnerable to substance abuse remain unidentified. Current figures show too that while 77 per cent of under-eighteens complete rehabilitation programmes successfully, this simply means that they are no longer addicted to the specific substances for which they sought treatment. So, just like Amy, a young person could be free of heroin or cocaine but they might then move on to cannabis or alcohol and still be categorized as a 'success' within the system.

But we don't want the only memory of Amy to be her battle with addiction. She was so much more than that. Amy's musical legacy lives on through the Foundation too. Our Amy's Yard Music Programme gives talented young people the chance to use Amy's own studio in north London and to work with professional producers and engineers who will nurture their talent, confidence, skills and self-esteem. Every young person who takes part in the programme has been referred by one of our partner organizations, including the Roundhouse music venue and the New Horizon Youth Centre in Camden, and the Pilion Trust in Islington. All three work with young people who face unemployment or homelessness, suffer from mental health issues, or have a history of offending. Last year, at our annual fundraising gala, all the young people who accessed studio time through the Foundation performed for guests, and it was very moving for me to watch.

At the beginning of 2013, I travelled to New York to present a cheque for £15,000 to the prestigious Brooklyn Conservatory of Music to help fund scholarships through their Teen Jazz Scholarship Program. Earlier this year I went back to enjoy their annual gala and present a further £30,000 to the program, through which students receive private lessons and jazz theory classes, and get a chance to rehearse and play sessions with a big band for thirty weeks of the year. In the UK we fund several music and performing arts projects including a scholarship to the Sylvia Young School.

Without community projects, Amy would not have had the start she had. We recognize how important they are in allowing young talent to thrive. Recently, we prevented the Weekend Arts College in Hampstead, north London, from closing. The college, which specializes in jazz as a basis for music tuition, gives lessons to around six hundred pupils every weekend, but until we stepped in, its funding was teetering on the edge and organizers were struggling to keep it going.

There are a number of other projects towards which we direct our funds that would have been close to Amy's heart, for example the LauraLynn Hospice in Dublin which cares for children with life-limiting illnesses. We also support mentoring projects for children such as that at the London Irish Centre. In the past we have donated to the Chestnut Tree House hospice in Arundel, the Hopes and Dreams charity and the Little Haven's Children's Hospice in Essex. We have recently funded a £42,000 music therapy room at the Haven House Children's Hospice in Woodford Green, Essex, which will provide children with a safe, familiar environment where they can enjoy and explore music under the watchful eye of a qualified therapist.

For me, though, Amy's thirtieth-birthday celebrations marked the biggest turning point for us as a family and for the Foundation. In September 2013, Alex, who ordinarily keeps his feelings tightly under wraps, helped curate a most poignant exhibition of Amy's life, *Amy Winehouse: A Family Portrait*, at the Jewish Museum in Camden. It was an idea that came to Alex and Riva after they visited the Jewish Museum in San Francisco while on honeymoon in 2012. Putting the exhibition together became part of their grieving process – that and their visit to the Charles M. Schulz Museum (the creator of Charlie Brown and Snoopy) in Santa Rosa. Both confess that they spent ten minutes in the car park overcome with tears before they could even make it to the entrance. It was the Charlie Brown theme tune being piped through the outdoor speakers that set them both off. In the end, Amy's own cuddly Snoopy, alongside her *Cat in the Hat* and *Postman Pat* books, her records and some of her clothing formed part of their very personal and incredibly moving tribute to Amy which, I have to admit, astonished me too.

For a week during those celebrations Amy's adopted borough of Camden played host to many other events in support of the Foundation and we cannot thank the former Mayor of Camden, Councillor Jonathan Simpson, enough for letting us and Amy take over. We sold merchandise through Amy's pop-up shop while Camden's Proud Galleries hosted the photographic exhibition *For You I Was a Flame*, which included some previously unseen photographs of Amy.

We celebrated the tenth anniversary of the release of Amy's album *Frank* with another event at the Proud Galleries. The evening, organized by Classic Album Sundays, included a Q&A session with Darcus Beese from Island Records and Nick Shymansky, part of Amy's first management team. The occasion culminated with a full play of *Frank* which now, more so than ever, leaves me lost for words. I was also overwhelmed, although in a slightly different way, by the comedy night organized by the Black Cap pub in Camden which saw a selection of drag queen divas shimmy their way through most of Amy's back catalogue. I haven't laughed so much in ages, and with names like Baga Chipz and Le Gateau Chocolat as well as another act I have come to know well – Amy's tribute act Laura Jane Butler – it would have been an evening Amy herself would have giggled her way through.

At the end of Amy's birthday month, a first group took part in the mass parachute jump, followed by another group, which included me, this April. I think I can speak for everyone when I say I am still recovering from that experience.

I've learned since Amy's passing to hold on to positive things wherever possible, but I've had to take the rough with the smooth. To say I've seen the worst and the best in human behaviour would be an understatement. There will always be people who try to take advantage of Amy's death. Indeed, shortly after her passing several of her dresses, including her wedding dress, went missing from Camden Square and they have never been returned – something which upset the family very much. I've also received the odd letter from opportunists asking for personal items of Amy's such as a pair of her ballet pumps or a souvenir from Camden Square, no doubt to sell on for profit. At first that kind of unscrupulousness weighed on my mind, but now I dismiss it as par for the course. I don't really feel as though I have any other option.

By the same token, Amy's most loyal fans have followed her from the beginning and supported us throughout. Believe it or not, I speak to a lot of them over Twitter, and a few have come to visit us from places as far afield as Brazil and the US. We always make them feel welcome. Last year I even received a self-published book of art-work inspired by Amy's image called *An Album for Amy*. I was absolutely gobsmacked at some of the paintings, drawings, graffiti and poems. Street artists such as Bambi and Pegasus have also paid tribute to her by decorating several walls in Camden with her image – one Amy in the form of an angel is on a wall outside Starbucks where I'm told she used to appear regularly to chat to staff.

There have been some happy coincidences too. Richard and I were invited to an awards ceremony last year and a young girl approached me to say hello. She was with her mother whom Richard recognized immediately, but he couldn't remember where they had met. The woman didn't know either, so we all stood there racking our brains until suddenly it came to Richard: her name was Angela, and it was the same woman, the nurse, who was at Richard and Stephanie's party when I collapsed just before my MS was officially diagnosed; Angela was the person who checked my pulse and waited with me upstairs until a taxi arrived. How my life has changed since then. Her daughter was a big fan of Amy's and she had followed her music and her career. I'd like to think that those rare moments are more than just chance happenings, that perhaps they are even meant to be.

My relationship with the tabloid press remains as interesting as it has always been. Just before Amy's thirtieth celebrations I agreed to an interview to talk about the anniversary of her death and to promote the work of the Foundation. Infuriatingly, the *Sun* ran the story alongside the picture of Amy wandering in her red bra outside her flat in Bow. How they could shoehorn an article about the positive strides we were making into an excuse to print lurid pictures of Amy I have no idea. Did they have no inkling how much that would hurt me? I would never have agreed to the interview had I known that. But you'd think I would have learned by now. However, my desire to use Amy's story and our story for the benefit of other families coping with addiction overrides the desire of the tabloids to sensationalize Amy's life purely to sell newspapers.

As a family, we gather every year on the anniversary of Amy's death. I also regularly make the journey to Edgwarebury Cemetery to Amy's headstone which we placed there a year after her passing. Just like Amy, it stands out from the crowd with black marble and pink writing. Whenever I go, it comforts me that she is never alone. Pebbles are always scattered across it, placed there by every single visitor who comes to her grave. For me, though, it's a marker of her passing – a place where I remember Amy but not the place where she remains. Amy was a free spirit in life and I believe so too in death, and I can only hope that our lives will touch each other again.

It was last year when we were unveiling an artwork of Amy in Camden that a little girl called Isabelle came up to me with her own handmade card. On the front was a picture of me and Amy, and it reminded me of the little cards Amy used to draw. Written inside was the most moving message: 'Dear Amy's Mum, I am sorry that Amy died. I love her songs. You are a very brave lady and we are still very sad.'

The truth is, I don't feel brave. I feel like an ordinary mum who, despite life's challenges, educated myself and raised an extraordinary daughter. It's a life I could never have predicted, but it's the life I've been given and I try to see it as a blessing. Of course, Amy's death feels unbearable at times. I miss her laughter and her cuddles, her enthusiasm and her fearlessness. But, through the Foundation, it brings me great comfort to know that she will be a guiding light and a powerful force in many young futures well after I am gone.

Some Information about the Amy Winehouse Foundation
www.amywinehouse.com

The Amy Winehouse Foundation works to prevent the effects of drug and alcohol misuse on young people. We also aim to support, inform and inspire vulnerable and disadvantaged young people to help them reach their full potential.

We work in three core areas:

- To inform and educate young people about the effects of drug and alcohol misuse, as well as to support those seeking help for their problems and those needing ongoing support in their recovery.
- To provide support for those most vulnerable, including those who are disadvantaged through circumstance or at high risk of substance misuse.
- To support the personal development of disadvantaged young people through music.

Today – and with your support – the Foundation is helping tens of thousands of vulnerable young people throughout the UK and abroad. Each and every donation allows us to help these young people to overcome drug and alcohol addiction and many other difficult issues such as eating disorders and self-harming.

How To Support Us

If you would like to organize your own fundraising event for the Amy Winehouse Foundation, we would like to make this as easy as possible for you. Whether you want to jump out of a plane, hold a big party for all your friends or put on your own gig to showcase your talent . . . anything is possible!

To make the whole process easier you can now set up your own Amy Winehouse Foundation fundraising page in minutes by following the link below, which means your friends and family can sponsor you at the click of a button, and you can easily keep track of your progress without all the paperwork. With just a few clicks, you can set up a Just Giving page and start raising funds for the Foundation!

www.justgiving.com/amywinehousefoundation/Raisemoney

Other Useful Contacts

Addaction
A UK charity working with individuals to help them recover from dependency, and also the families and loved ones of people in recovery.
www.addaction.org.uk   tel. 0207 251 5860

Alcoholics Anonymous
An organization concerned solely with the personal recovery and continued sobriety of individual alcoholics.
www.alcoholics-anonymous.org.uk   helpline: 0845 769 7555

Angelus Foundation
A UK charity formed to help society understand the dangers of 'legal highs' (unclassified substances), to reduce the harm they cause to young people and their families, and to save lives.
www.angelusfoundation.com   tel. 020 37007 185

Beat
Beat is a national charity devoted to research into and prevention of eating disorders.
www.b-eat.co.uk   adult helpline: 0845 634 1414   youth helpline: 0845 634 7650

Frank
Frank is the national drugs information service set up by

government to offer friendly and confidential advice on drugs.
www.talktofrank.com   helpline: 0800 77 66 00

The MS Society
A UK charity investing in research and help through information,
support and campaigning on multiple sclerosis.
www.mssociety.org.uk

Narcotics Anonymous
An organization that works with men and women for whom drug
addiction has become a major problem.
www.ukna.org   helpline: 0300 999 1212

The National Self-harm Network
A UK charity offering support, advice and advocacy services to
people affected by self-harm directly or in a caring role.
www.nshn.co.uk   helpline: 0800 622 6000

Acknowledgements

The last few years of my life have been both uplifting and un-bearably sad, but there are people without whom the journey would have been much harder. Without them, too, I would not have been able to write this book.

My husband Richard has been my anchor, and his love and support have guided me throughout. Thanks must also go to my darling son Alex. My love for him has kept me going more than he'll ever know. My daughter-in-law Riva, my sister Debra, brother Brian and sister-in-law Jann have all been part of my support net-work, as well as my friends Stephanie, Penny and Jill, my cousins Joan, Martin and Barry, Mitchell and Jane, Richard's children Michael and Jessica, Melody and Elliott, and Rene and Shelley. Thanks too to everybody at the MS Action Therapy Centre in Walthamstow.

There are people in Amy's life I would also like to thank: Naomi Parry, Henry Hate, Tony Bennett, Tyler James, Nick Shymansky, Darcus Beese, Mark Ronson, Salaam Remi, Reg Traviss, Catriona Gourlay, Monty Lipman, Lucian Grainge, and Amy's bodyguards Andrew, Neville, Anthony, Biggs, Grandad and Chris.

At the Amy Winehouse Foundation there is a dedicated team

who work tirelessly in Amy's name. They include Rowan Carnihan, Natalie Webb and Dominic Ruffy, and at Metropolis, Raye Cosbert, Trenton Harrison Lewis and Petra Smith. I'd also like to thank the former Mayor of Camden, Jonathan Simpson, for his help and generosity.

This book would not have been possible without my agent Maggie Hanbury. Helena Drakakis worked patiently with me to help tell my story, and I'd also like to thank my editor Michelle Signore and everybody at Transworld.

Last but not least, a big thank you must go to Amy's fans. They keep Amy alive in my head and in my heart, and for that I am eternally grateful.

Picture Acknowledgements

Second section

Page 4: Amy appearing on *Later With Jools Holland*: © Rex Features

Page 5: Amy with her Ivor Novello award: © Rex Features; Amy with trademark beehive: © Rex Features

Page 6: Amy and Janis at the Riverside Studios: © Rex Features

Page 7: Both photos: © Richard Collins

Page 8: Both photos reproduced courtesy of North London Skydiving Centre

ABOUT THE AUTHOR

Janis Winehouse was born in New York but grew up mainly in London. While bringing up her son Alex and daughter Amy she completed two degrees – an Open University degree in science followed by a Bachelor of Pharmacy at the University of London. Janis raised Amy on the music of Carole King and James Taylor and supported her throughout her musical career. In 2003, Janis was diagnosed with multiple sclerosis and was forced to take early retirement in 2009. She now devotes her time to raising money for the Amy Winehouse Foundation and the MS Society. She lives in north London with her husband Richard and three cats, Gizzy, Moggy and Minty.